Saving America's School Infrastructure

A Volume in
Research in Education Fiscal Policy and Practice:
Local, National, and Global Perspectives

Series Editors: Christopher Roellke and Jennifer King Rice

Saving America's School Infrastructure

Faith E. Crampton
University of Wisconsin Milwaukee

David C. Thompson
Kansas State University

Editors

INFORMATION AGE
PUBLISHING

80 Mason Street • Greenwich, Connecticut 06830 • www.infoagepub.com

Library of Congress Cataloging-in-Publication Data

Saving America's school infrastructure / edited by Faith E. Crampton,
David C. Thompson.
    p. cm. – (Research in education fiscal policy and practice)
Includes bibliographical references and index.
  ISBN 1-931576-17-3 – ISBN 1-931576-16-5 (pbk.)
  1. School facilities–United States–Finance. 2. School
facilities–United States–Planning. 3. School plant management–United
States. I. Crampton, Faith E. II. Thompson, David C. III. Series.
  LB3218.A1S34 2003
  371.6'0973–dc21

                                                          2003000499

Printed in the United States of America

CONTENTS

III. The Future of School Infrastructure Funding

EDWARD M. KENNEDY
MASSACHUSETTS

United States Senate

WASHINGTON, DC 20510-2101

Senator Edward M. Kennedy
Foreword
Saving America's School Infrastructure

One of the greatest challenges to modern-day public education is to bring our school facilities up to 21st century standards so our school children enjoy safe and healthy learning environments. In fact, no one can read Professor Crampton's and Professor Thompson's book without realizing the crisis that children and families face every day in crumbling public schools. They have brought together in one volume the best minds in the country to address the crisis in funding for school facilities. This is a crisis that affects virtually every community across the nation. Such a book, combining scholarly research with insightful policy analysis, is long overdue.

This crisis is real. America's schools need over $268 billion in new investments to meet today's needs. The research in this volume portrays this national tragedy in its many forms—from overcrowded and unsafe urban schools to aging and crumbling rural facilities. In every community, school districts struggle to finance appropriate adaptations so that children with disabilities can learn to their full potential. At the same time, new research reinforces what every educator across the land already knows—the condition of our schools determines how well our students learn.

The American Society of Civil Engineers recently released their 2001 Report Card on America's infrastructure, and gave America's schools a D minus. They report that fully 75% of the nation's school buildings are inadequate to meet the needs of today's school children. In 1995, the U.S. General Accounting Office estimated that it would cost communities $112 billion to repair and modernize the nation's schools. Since that report, just seven years ago, the needs have more than doubled with more children than ever attending schools that are unsafe and out-of-date.

Saving America's School Infrastructure, pages vii–viii
Copyright © 2003 by Information Age Publishing

Our crumbling public schools come on top of other education challenges that demand immediate attention and resources. Ninety percent of all American children attend public schools. Enrollment is at an all-time high of 53 million children. Of these students, 13 million are from poor families. Two million more teachers will need to be hired just to keep up with rising enrollments. Nearly one third of all public schools are more than half a century old. Fourteen million children in a third of the nation's schools attend classes in substandard buildings. And these problems exist in almost every community in America—urban, rural, or suburban.

Over the past year, I was proud to work with President Bush and my colleagues of both parties to pass the No Child Left Behind Act—the reauthorization of the Elementary and Secondary Education Act. And I was honored to join the President in January when he signed this important school reform legislation into law. Unfortunately, we do not provide adequate resources to carry them out, including the improvements to school facilities called for in this book.

Sending children to dilapidated, overcrowded facilities sends the wrong message to these children. It tells them they don't matter. Students know that their facilities are crumbling around them, but unfortunately their voices go unheeded. We need to do all we can to ensure that children are learning in safe, modern buildings.

We have heard a cry for help from our communities to provide the funding needed to rebuild and modernize America's school infrastructure before it is too late. Working together, every community, every state, and the federal government can do more to create conditions for improvement—not in a few schools, but in all schools; not for a few students, but for all students. We have an obligation to give all children a quality education in safe and modern schools—and a future of fulfilled dreams and realized hopes.

PART I

OVERVIEW AND SCOPE OF THE PROBLEM

UNMET SCHOOL INFRASTRUCTURE FUNDING NEED AS A CRITICAL EDUCATIONAL CAPACITY ISSUE

Setting the Context

Faith E. Crampton
University of Wisconsin Milwaukee

ABSTRACT

The relationship of the physical environment of schools to student achievement has remained an enduring research issue in education with broad policy implications for the adequate and equitable funding of education for over 70 years. This chapter utilizes the backdrop of earlier research to explore the crisis in school infrastructure funding that emerged in the 1990s, given the confluence of years of deferred maintenance and increased enrollments, linking it theoretically to notions of human capital and social capital. School infrastructure and its funding represent physical capital that works in tandem with human capital and social capital to build capacity for education reform and enhanced student achievement.

Saving America's School Infrastructure, pages 3–26

INTRODUCTION

One purpose of an opening chapter is to set the context for those that follow, and, by doing so, give readers a deeper appreciation of the particular policy and research issues around school infrastructure which will be addressed in subsequent chapters. Because the study of school infrastructure, its funding, and its relationship to student success has a rich history and research tradition, it is necessary to provide context from a number of perspectives. To that end, this chapter is divided into four sections. In the first section, the historical, theoretical, and conceptual underpinnings of research into the relationship of school infrastructure and student success are addressed. This section begins with a brief historical overview of the enduring research interest in the field of school infrastructure, an interest that dates from the 1930s. In turn, the historical overview serves as a backdrop for development of a deeper theoretical understanding of school infrastructure as an education capacity issue grounded in human capital and social capital development. The first section closes with a consideration of the conceptual issues facing scholars as they study the relationship of school infrastructure to student success; that is, given the breadth of the field of study, how can infrastructure be defined effectively for the purposes of research while remaining understandable to a broader audience of policymakers, educators, taxpayers, parents, and community members? In the second section, a cross-section of recent studies is reviewed, noting that, over the last decade, this body of research has matured substantially. The third section presents the results of a comprehensive 50-state study on the magnitude of unmet school infrastructure funding need. While individual state needs, ranging from \$220.1 million to \$47.6 billion, are stunning, the total funding need of \$266.1 billion is staggering.[1] The final section summarizes the chapter and sets forth recommendations for future research.

HISTORICAL, THEORETICAL, AND CONCEPTUAL PERSPECTIVES

The role of school infrastructure as a factor in student success has been a subject of study by researchers, within and outside education, for nearly 70 years. As early as 1935, in the *Review of Educational Research,* Holy noted that those areas in which research on school infrastructure was critical included, "....[The] effect of good school buildings and equipment on educational achievement."[2] However, while interest in this field of study has endured, scholars have acknowledged the inherent challenges in reaching definitive conclusions about the magnitude of the role of infrastructure in light of issues with the quantity and quality of research in a complex field of study that spans several disciplines. For example, three years later, Holy reaffirmed the need for research in the introduction to a special issue of the *Review of Educational Research* dedicated to school infrastructure, and he reflected upon the paucity of basic research,[3] expressing concern with the uneven quality and generalizability of existing published research because "...a majority of these publications are either based upon opinion or deal with small, isolated areas of study."[4] Forty years later, Weinstein would observe that research on the impact of the physical environment of the school on student behavior, attitudes, and achievement had grown considerably, particularly in the preceding decade, but, like Holy, still lamented its eclectic nature and quality.[5] According to Weinstein, school infrastructure remained, "a field that almost defies categorization and integration,"[6] in large part because researchers come from a range of disciplines, such as "architecture, sociology, psychology, and education."[7] In addition, Weinstein addressed the challenges of interpreting research across the domains of the "practical," or practitioner-oriented, literature and the scholarly, or more traditional academic, literature.[8] A few years later, in 1982, McGuffey expressed more confidence in the evolution of the research on the impact of at least some infrastructure variables, such as building age and maintenance, but issued a general caution: "The available research is a mixed bag of study types and methodologies presenting diverse problems of sampling, measurement, and statistical analysis."[9] In the most recent synthesis of this body of research literature in 1997, Lemasters reinforced findings of earlier studies, particularly those around building condition and maintenance,[10] but found it necessary to set parameters in her synthesis to address issues of rigor.[11]

At first glance, one might conclude from this brief historical overview that, in spite of high levels of interest and a growing body of research over the course of the 20th century, a conclusive link between school infrastructure and student achievement remains elusive. However, a more nuanced conclusion recognizes the complexity of the field and resulting heterogeneity of the body of research. Further, it should be pointed out that quality in terms of sophistication of research methods in this field, like others in education, has evolved over the course of many decades and will continue to do so in the future.[12] Given these multiple challenges, it is notable that significant results have emerged from a number of studies, such as those that address the impact of school building condition on student success.

To that end, the focus of this chapter lies with the results of recent research, while still honoring the contributions of earlier studies. Recent studies are most relevant to the assessment of current infrastructure needs and demonstrate greater analytic sophistication and more robust results. As such, they provide a solid foundation for advocating parity in funding for school infrastructure.[13] The most recent scholarship has taken advantage of multivariate statistical analysis and modeling, including the specification of a production function. Production-function analysis is grounded in classical and neoclassical economics and, when used to model the relationship of school infrastructure and student achievement, variables relevant to school infrastructure serve as inputs or independent variables with student achievement serving as the desired outcome or dependent variable. Implicit in this approach are theories of human and social capital development, with a recognition of the supporting role of school infrastructure and its funding as sources of physical capital.

Recent research in the development of education capacity for reform and greater student success dovetails theoretically with the importance of human, social, and physical capital. The construct of educational capacity, while dating back to the 1970s, emerged in the 1990s as a strategy to undergird education reform, not only as a response to earlier "failed" reforms, but also as a means to address the growing emphasis on reforms that targeted student achievement through the establishment of statewide standards, school and district accountability measures, and high stakes testing.[14] After nearly a decade of education reform activity following the release of *A Nation at Risk*,[15] scholars, practitioners, and policymakers recognized that building education capacity was a necessary precondition for most, if not all, sustained educational change. Typically, research and policy literature in this area has focused on the provision of greater professional development opportunities for classroom teachers as a means of enhancing their capacity to improve student performance. Over time, the concept of educational capacity has broadened so that, at present, it is inclusive of students' readiness to learn as well as the human, physical, and fiscal resources needed by schools to achieve educational goals. Like their counterparts in school infrastructure research, scholars in education capacity have engaged in theory building only recently. For example, in 1997, Spillane and Thompson grounded their research on development of education capacity for instructional reform in theories of human capital and social capital development and took initial steps toward the inclusion of physical capital in the paradigm.[16] Although their research focused much of its attention on human capital and social capital development, limiting discussion of physical capital to fiscal resources, it is important to note that physical capital generally is defined more broadly in the economics of education literature as physical inputs, of which infrastructure is one.[17]

Drawing from Coleman's earlier work, Spillane and Thompson defined human capital development as follows: "...[H]uman capital is created by changes in persons that bring about skills and capabilities that make them able to act in new ways."[18] In building education capacity for reform, this definition was operationalized to refer to teachers' and administrators' individual commitment to reform and their disposition to learn new instructional strategies to improve student achievement.[19] Social capital referred to the creation and maintenance of professional networks, both formal and informal, as well as collegial relations that supported local school districts' ability to effect ambitious instructional reform.[20] Examples of professional networks included relationships established by teachers and administrators with local universities, state departments of education, professional associations, and philanthropic foundations. Effective collegial relationships that supported reform and therefore enhanced education capacity were characterized by trust and collaboration.[21] In grounding education capacity in human capital and social capital development, the authors were careful to note their interactive nature; that is, they developed in tandem.[22]

In turn, physical capital supports development of human and social capital. Although Spillane and Thompson did not explore the role of physical capital as fully as that of human and social capital, it is possible to extend their argument. While building education capacity encompasses the interactive development of human, social, and physical capital, the latter makes a unique contribution as a foundation, as well as a facilitator of human and social capital development. Without sufficient fiscal resources, development of human and social capital in schools and districts will be stunted. For example, without adequate fiscal resources, opportunities to learn new instructional strategies through release time and professional development activities might be limited; or opportunities to build professional networks through attendance of relevant conferences and workshops could not be supported. School infrastructure, as a component of physical capital, also supports development of human and social capital. School- and district-based professional development activities need sufficient and appropriate spaces in order to be conducted effectively. In the same manner, establishing and maintaining collegial relationships within and across schools and districts requires the quantity and quality of physical space that fosters such interaction.

As noted previously, school infrastructure is a complex field. To fully appreciate results of a range of studies and the extent of unmet funding need, it is helpful to define school infrastructure, first on a more general conceptual level, and then with greater specificity to operationalize that definition. Thompson and Wood distinguish infrastructure from older, more traditional terms, as follows:

> Different language has been used over the years to describe the physical environment of education. School plant and facilities have been the common terms of describing school buildings, and capital outlay usually has referred to all aspects of paying for the permanent facility and equipment needs of

schools. In a broader and more recent context, the term "infrastructure" has been used more frequently as it captures the whole range of capital needs in a single word.[23]

Their overarching definition of school infrastructure serves as a backdrop for discussion of the multiple components of school infrastructure that must be considered in creating the physical environment of schools. At the same time, it is desirable to operationalize these in a manner understandable to a broad audience of policymakers, educators, taxpayers, parents, and community members, particularly as these are the stakeholders who grapple with the fiscal ramifications of creating and maintaining a physical environment conducive to student learning. Based upon a synthesis of the research literature,[24] Crampton, Thompson, and Hagey developed the following comprehensive definition of school infrastructure, consisting of six components: (1) Deferred maintenance; (2) new construction; (3) renovation; (4) retrofitting; (5) additions to existing buildings; and (6) major improvements.[25]

More specifically, deferred maintenance refers to maintenance necessary to bring a school facility up to good condition; that is, a condition where only routine maintenance is required. If a facility is in such poor condition that it cannot be brought up to good condition, or if it would cost more to do so than to construct a new facility, deferred maintenance can refer to replacement of an existing facility. New construction may be a response to current overcrowding; to federal, state, or local mandates that require additional facilities, such as class size reduction measures; or to projected enrollment growth. The construction of a new facility includes the building(s); grounds (purchase, landscaping, and paving); and fixtures; major equipment; and furniture necessary to furnish it. Renovation of an existing facility includes renovations for health, safety, and accessibility for the physically challenged. Renovation may also include renovations necessary to accommodate mandated educational programs. Retrofitting of an existing facility applies to areas such as energy conservation (e.g., installation of insulation or energy-efficient windows) and technology readiness (e.g., electrical wiring, phone lines, and fiber optic cables). Additions to existing facilities may be necessary to relieve overcrowding; to meet federal, state, or local mandates, such as class size reduction measures; or to accommodate projected enrollment growth. The cost of additions usually includes the fixtures, major equipment, and furniture necessary to furnish them. Finally, major improvements refer to improvements to grounds, such as landscaping and paving.

Taken together, the definition of the physical environment of education as school infrastructure can be operationalized through these six major components. These, in turn, provide a framework accessible to a broad range of audiences, from scholars to laypersons, seeking a greater understanding of the impact of variables such as building condition and funding levels on student achievement.

RESULTS OF RECENT RESEARCH

This section of the chapter explores a cross-section of recent research on the relationship between the physical environment of schools and student achievement. Greater attention is paid to studies that attempt to quantify the impact or effect of school infrastructure, as compared to qualitative or descriptive research. While qualitative studies often provide graphic and moving portraits of the unacceptable conditions under which some students try to learn, they are limited in their generalizability because they are usually based upon a small number of case studies.[26]

The five studies described in this section were selected as representative of research trends over the last decade in analyzing the relationship between the physical environment of schools and student success. They exhibit a maturation of research design and analysis over previous decades; more specifically, they utilize a production-function approach that calls for multivariate statistical analysis. For ease of comparison, the studies are summarized and analyzed using a four-part framework for analysis, consisting of: (1) variables studied; (2) classification of the study as scholarly, practical, or technical;[27] (3) description and analysis of research methods; and (4) description and analysis of results. For all studies, the outcome variables were measures of student learning expressed as test scores, and all studies used the school as the unit of analysis. In addition, these studies reflect important themes captured later in this chapter and volume, for example, on the role of the physical environment in student success in urban versus rural school settings,[28] as well as results from a statewide study of elementary schools in Texas, a state with one of the highest unmet school infrastructure funding needs in the country.[29]

Over the last decade, dissertation research has come to represent an important source of new scholarship linking the physical environment of schools to student success.[30] In this section, the results of studies based in two dissertations on schools in Virginia are presented as representative of this research. One focused upon small, rural high schools, while the other studied urban high schools. The benefit of studying these two groups of schools, while using a similar methodology, lies with the ability to compare and contrast the relationship of student achievement and school facilities at opposite ends of the geographic spectrum, which is particularly important as rural schools are sometimes less prominent in policy discussions and media coverage of unmet funding need. Cash's doctoral research examined the relationship of building condition and student achievement in small, rural high schools in Virginia for the 1991–1992 academic year.[31,32] To be considered for the study, selected high schools were located outside Standard Metropolitan Statistical Areas in Virginia with a senior class of fewer than 100 students.[33] This yielded an admittedly small population of 47 schools, of which 43 participated in the study, a response rate of 91%.[34] In order to assess school building condition, Cash designed and administered a comprehensive survey, the "Commonwealth Assessment of Physical Environment,"[35] while student achievement was measured via scores on the Test of Academic Proficiency, a state-developed test for 11th graders.[36] The conceptual model used to ground the research was reflective of production-function modeling, and data were analyzed using analysis of covariance (ANCOVA) and simple linear regression.

Buildings were rated either "substandard," "standard," or "above standard," based upon the results of the survey. Of the sample, ten schools were rated "substandard"; 21 "standard"; and ten "above standard."[37,38] These ratings were then compared to mean student achievement scores which had been adjusted for socioeconomic status.[39] The comparison revealed that scores for all subtests, as well as those for the composite, rose with improvement of overall building condition. Based upon composite achievement test scores, students in a school whose physical environment was rated "substandard" scored, on average, at the 47th percentile on the statewide test, whereas students in schools rated "above standard" scored at the 52nd percentile, a 5% increase.[40] Simple linear regression was used to determine the role building age played in building condition. Results indicated that approximately 18% (R^2 = .1835) of the variation in school building condition was due to age, a small, but statistically significant ($p<.003$), finding.[41] Cash concluded: "Building condition is more than a static condition. It is a physical representation of a public message about the value of education. To encourage academic excellence… schools must represent a better way of life—a promise of the future. Schools should reflect the environment of success."[42]

Hines, in large part, replicated the Cash study, utilizing a sample of urban high schools in Virginia, where urban high schools were defined as those within Standard Metropolitan Statistical Areas with a population greater than 100,000, and a student enrollment greater than 25,000.[43] Of the 88 high schools that met the criteria, 66 participated in the study, a response rate of 75%.[44] To assess school building condition, Hines administered the Commonwealth Assessment of Physical Environment, developed by Cash, with minor modifications to make it more applicable to urban settings.[45] Student achievement also was measured in the same manner using the Virginia Test of Academic Proficiency scores for the 1992–1993 academic year. Hines replicated Cash's use of analysis of covariance to adjust student achievement scores for socioeconomic status.[46] Of the sample, eight high schools were rated "substandard"; 35 "standard"; and 22 "above standard."[47] It is interesting to note that in comparison with Cash's sample of small, rural high schools, Virginia's urban high school facilities were in relatively better condition. Whereas 24% of the rural high schools were classified as "substandard", only 12.3% of urban high schools fell into this category. Hines found also that the condition of the physical environment of the school affected student achievement. Scores for every subtest, as well as the composite, rose with improvement of overall building condition. Students in "substandard" school buildings scored, on average, at the 52nd percentile while their counterparts in "above standard" facilities scored dramatically higher, at the 66th percentile.[48] Hines' conclusions echoed those of Cash; that is, the condition of the physical environment of the schools children attend has a significant impact on their academic success.

In contrast, the next two studies, one published in *Urban Education*, a peer-reviewed journal, and the second, a technical study commissioned by the Council of Educational Facilities Planners International, examined the relationship between school infrastructure and student success in two urban school districts, Washington, D.C., and Milwaukee. In a study of the Washington, D.C. schools, Berner hypothesized: "(a) that the condition of public school buildings in the D.C. public school system is affected by parental involvement and (b) that the condition of the school building in turn affects student achievement."[49] The rationale for the first hypothesis lies with a body of research that indicates parental involvement has a beneficial effect on student achievement. As such, Berner took this body of research a step further by hypothesizing parental involvement in the form of the size of a school's Parent Teacher Association (PTA) budget per student would result in better overall building condition. The second hypothesis reflected a production-function approach whereby the dependent variable was 1990 student scores on the Comprehensive Test of Basic Skills (CTBS). Statistical analysis included multiple regression (Ordinary Least Squares [OLS] and logistic). The sample included 52 schools at the elementary, middle, and high school levels. Independent variables included: building condition; school age; school size (enrollment); PTA membership per student; and PTA budget per student. Socioeconomic variables, defined as mean personal income in the census tract where the school was located and racial composition of the student body, were added as control variables.

Berner found support for the first hypothesis in that the PTA budget per student was statistically significant at the .10 level.[50] In addition, school age and size impacted building condition. Using OLS multiple regression analysis, these variables accounted for 28% of the variation in school building condition (Adj. R^2 = .28) which is somewhat low, but may have been an artifact of the sample size. With regard to results, the analysis found that for every \$10 increase in PTA resources per pupil within a school, the building condition improved by .029 on the scale of building condition.[51] Berner concluded that this relationship existed because the school-based PTA would likely invest resources in maintaining and improving the physical environment of the school. Logistic regression results reinforced the result of the OLS analysis.[52]

The second hypothesis, regarding the relationship between building condition and student achievement was also supported, with the condition of the school having a strong impact on CTBS scores.[53] Here too the explanatory power of the equation as modeled was fairly modest at .28 (Adjusted R^2 = .28), but the coefficient for building condition, −10.845, was large and statistically significant ($p < .05$). In other words, if a school were to improve its condition from "poor" to "excellent", one would predict an increase of 10.9 points in the school's average achievement test scores.[54] An alternative model, using dummy variables for schools in "poor" and "fair" condition, supported the strong influence of building condition on student achievement.[55]

This study was particularly interesting as it couples more traditional production-function analysis of the relationship of building condition and student achievement with the potential of parental involvement to play a role in improving the physical environment of schools in the same manner that previous research has demonstrated how parental involvement enhances student success in other arenas. Berner concluded that with regard to the first hypothesis, "...in Washington, parents can play an active role in improving the condition of children's schools."[56] For the second hypothesis, she concluded that building condition did affect student achievement, while acknowledging the importance of controlling for income and racial composition of the community surrounding the school.

In a technical study commissioned by the Council of Educational Facility Planners International, Lewis sought to establish a relationship between the condition of school facilities and student achievement in a sample taken from the Milwaukee Public Schools system that was inclusive of elementary, middle, and high schools.[57] School condition was determined by a survey of facilities conducted by a private firm, Construction Control Corporation, who trained school system staff to assess the "general health" of selected facilities via a proprietary evaluation form.[58] A five point rating scale was employed for survey items: Poor; marginal; average; good; and excellent. Weighting factors were added so that a final score could range from 1,000 points for a school in poor condition to a maximum of 5,000 points for a school in excellent condition. Student achievement scores came from the 1996 Wisconsin Student Assessment System (WSAS), a statewide battery of tests. For analysis of the data, Lewis used multiple regression based upon development of a production-function equation that specified as independent variables building condition and a number of student characteristics, such as attendance, mobility, truancy, suspensions, poverty, and race, added as controls. The results indicated that indeed it was important to control for these variables, as they yielded statistically significant coefficients.[59] At the same time, the coefficient for building condition was also statistically significant, accounting for 16% of the variation in student scores on the mathematics component and 14% of the science component of the WSAS.[60,61] As a whole, the independent variables accounted for 44% of the variation in mathematics scores (Adjusted R^2 = .44).[62] In the social sciences, the ability to explain this magnitude of variation with the specified equation is considered meaningful because of the difficulty of controlling for all of the possible variables that enter into the education process. Lewis concluded that building condition contributed significantly to student achievement in the Milwaukee Public Schools.

The final study to be reviewed in this section, a statewide study of 2,860 Texas elementary schools, provided a larger context for consideration of the relationship of school infrastructure and student success.[63] Instead of utilizing building condition as a key independent variable, Harter analyzed the amount spent on "school upkeep", or maintenance, in relationship to student achievement for the 1992–1993 academic year and discovered evidence of the importance of maintaining school facilities. Student achievement data were taken from the Texas Assessment of Academic Skills (TAAS) in fourth grade mathematics and reading. Harter employed descriptive statistics as well as multiple regression, based in a production-function approach, to analyze the impact of a range of variables on student achievement. Independent variables included student characteristics such as academic potential and socioeconomic status (both used as control variables); geographic variables relating to school location; school size; and expenditure variables, broken out by spending categories, of which one was school upkeep or maintenance.[64]

Descriptive statistics included mean per-pupil expenditures by spending categories for low-achieving versus high-achieving elementary schools. For the purposes of the analysis, schools scoring in the first and second quartiles were classified as low-achieving, while those scoring in the third and fourth quartiles were classified as high-achieving. On average low-achieving schools spent substantially less on maintenance per pupil than high achieving schools. Low-achieving schools in the first quartile spent $13.10 per pupil, and $16.24 at the second quartile. High-achieving schools spent $17.48 and $17.90 per pupil at the third and fourth quartiles respectively.[65] In other words, the highest-achieving schools spent 36.6% more on maintenance than the lowest-achieving schools.

Results of the multiple regression supported the overall importance of maintenance expenditures, as well as reinforcing the divide between high-achieving and low-achieving schools in resources allocated to school upkeep. Regression results for the full sample indicated that school upkeep was statistically significant and accounted for 9.8% of the variation in mathematics scores and 6.4% of the variation in reading scores.[66] Taken together, the independent variables accounted for 39.1% (Adj. R^2 = .391) of the variation in mathematics scores and 50.6% (Adj. R^2 = .506) of the variation in reading scores. As expected, independent variables added to control for student characteristics were statistically significant, but, of all expenditure categories, only school upkeep and teacher salary "supplements," a type of career ladder or incentive pay, were statistically significant. Harter concluded, "Spending for regular school upkeep... relates positively to student outcomes."[67]

All in all, this cross-section of recent studies points to the critical importance of the physical environment of schools—be they rural, urban, elementary, middle, or high schools—in relationship to student learning. For example, in rural Virginia high schools, state test scores for students in school buildings that were given the top rating of "above standard" condition scored five percentile points higher than those in schools whose condition were rated at the lowest level, "substandard". For students in urban Virginia high schools, the improvement was even more dramatic—14 percentile points. Research on other urban schools, such as those in the Washington, D.C. system and the Milwaukee Public Schools, yielded similar results. In both of these studies, building condition accounted for an important, and statistically significant, portion of the variation in student test scores. In Washington, D.C., building condition accounted for 28% of the variation in student test scores,[68] and it was estimated that student test scores would rise, on average, 10.9 points, on a districtwide test if the condition of schools rated as "poor" were improved to "excellent" condition. In Milwaukee, the research focused specifically on mathematics and science scores on Wisconsin's state tests. Here, building condition accounted for 16% of the variation in mathematics scores and 14% of the variation in science scores. Finally, a study of Texas schools reinforced the importance of sufficient funding of regular maintenance in elementary schools given its relationship to student achievement on state tests. On average, the highest achieving schools, those in the highest quartile in the state, spent 36.6% more per pupil on "school upkeep" than those in the lowest achieving, or bottom quartile of schools. These studies provide dramatic and concrete evidence that failure to fund school infrastructure adequately and equitably carries a real price tag in terms of lost opportunities for students to achieve to their highest potential.

QUANTIFYING UNMET SCHOOL INFRASTRUCTURE FUNDING NEED[69]

Earlier sections of this chapter have provided the backdrop for discussion and quantification of the staggering extent of unmet funding need for school infrastructure in this country. The previous section has established that a body of research exists with significant findings on the relationship between the physical environment of schools and student success. Further, it has been posited that school infrastructure is a critical education capacity factor that contributes to development of human capital and social capital, essential to the success of education reform. Not only do education reforms and growing enrollments place new demands on school infrastructure, so also does deferred maintenance. Documented as early as the 1980s,[70] the backlog in deferred maintenance was estimated in at $112 billion in 1995.[71] Because few states fund school infrastructure in any meaningful manner,[72] and little federal assistance is available, the condition of schools has continued to worsen over a 20 year period, creating serious health and safety issues. The burden for financing repairs and upkeep has fallen upon local school districts with disparate wealth and ability to address them, creating grave inequities in facilities that have been cited in a growing number of court cases.[73]

Undoubtedly, the best policy decisions on adequate and equitable funding of school infrastructure must be based upon up-to-date and comprehensive state-by-state estimates of unmet funding need. Previous estimates, while helpful in gauging total need in areas such as deferred maintenance, have been based on national samples to provide national totals.[74] By providing state estimates, the research results presented in this section of chapter can serve to break the gridlock in current policy debate, be it at the federal or state level, as to the magnitude of unmet funding need. For the purposes of this study, data were collected from multiple sources, permitting development of a comprehensive database and crossvalidation of data.[75,76] Several variables played a key role in the determination of a state's unmet funding needs in school infrastructure. These variables included current enrollment, enrollment growth trends, age and condition of school facilities, and regional cost factors. It was also hypothesized that urban school districts generally would have higher total unmet funding needs because of their high concentrations of poor students and aging facilities, and the hypothesis was supported by the data.[77]

The results of this research eclipsed that of earlier studies.[78] In 1995, a study conducted by the U.S. General Accounting Office estimated school infrastructure funding needs at $112 billion, utilizing a national sample.[79] At the request of the U.S. Congress, estimates were limited to deferred maintenance and health, safety, and accessibility issues.[80,81] Unlike previous

research, this study included not only funding needs for deferred maintenance but also needs for new construction to accommodate enrollment
growth and existing class size reduction efforts. Taken together, a total of
$266.1 billion unmet funding need was estimated, more than twice the
1995 estimate of the U.S. General Accounting Office (See Table 1.1).

Table 1.1.   Total Unmet Funding Need for School Infrastructure by State

State	Total Need ($)	Per Pupil($)/5 yrs.	Per Pupil($)/10 yrs.
Alabama	1,519,210,061	398	221
Alaska	727,014,291	1,074	588
Arizona	4,748,568,494	983	536
Arkansas	1,761,701,495	758	422
California	22,000,000,000	704	386
Colorado	3,805,239,627	1,045	574
Connecticut	5,000,000,000	1,828	1,033
Delaware	1,046,354,648	1,836	1,022
Florida	3,300,000,000	271	151
Georgia	7,061,967,931	942	517
Hawaii	752,533,936	713	386
Idaho	699,469,537	517	278
Illinois	9,213,000,000	824	458
Indiana	2,477,797,613	486	269
Iowa	3,359,129,953	1,386	776
Kansas	1,793,241,845	774	430
Kentucky	2,441,607,196	749	418
Louisiana	3,104,098,619	812	454
Maine	452,064,540	448	253
Maryland	3,891,926,876	905	504
Massachusetts	8,919,014,500	1,822	1,025
Michigan	8,071,127,040	963	541
Minnesota	4,517,232,516	1,068	597
Mississippi	1,038,890,864	406	226
Missouri	3,475,160,989	759	423
Montana	901,492,663	1,101	607
Nebraska	1,608,849,896	1,119	622
Nevada	5,256,000,000	2,888	1,568
New Hampshire	409,511,478	403	226

Table 1.1.   (cont.)

State	Total Need ($)	Per Pupil($)/5 yrs.	Per Pupil($)/10 yrs.
New Jersey	20,709,650,065	3,247	1,810
New Mexico	1,410,624,747	778	422
New York	47,640,000,000	3,214	1,802
North Carolina	6,210,938,727	902	502
North Dakota	420,000,000	749	420
Ohio	20,900,000,000	2,302	1,291
Oklahoma	2,204,070,041	732	410
Oregon	2,407,425,974	859	475
Pennsylvania	8,465,134,387	927	521
Rhode Island	1,420,952,603	1,882	1,060
South Carolina	2,574,018,400	803	451
South Dakota	498,604,766	706	390
Tennessee	2,273,702,904	466	257
Texas	9,467,620,774	453	248
Utah	8,490,336,757	3,385	1,841
Vermont	220,090,007	425	239
Virginia	5,701,313,528	986	548
Washington	5,478,902,777	1,067	589
West Virginia	1,000,000,000	686	384
Wisconsin	4,762,337,059	1,087	608
Wyoming	530,888,665	1,125	614
Total	266,138,818,788		

Funding estimates varied dramatically across states, from $220.1 million in Vermont to $47.6 billion in New York . Descriptive statistics revealed that there was substantial skew in the data, with the median state need at $2.8 billion but the mean at $5.3 billion, pointing to a cluster of states with extraordinarily high total funding needs. (See Tables 1.2 and 1.3.) In fact, five states—New York, California, Ohio, New Jersey, and Texas—accounted for almost 50% of the total. State totals are affected by a number of variables, such as the size of current enrollment, projected enrollment growth, age and condition of school facilities, as well as regional cost factors. To place state totals in perspective, Table 1.1 also lists estimates of unmet funding in per-pupil terms based on amortizing the total state funding need over five and ten years, taking into account changes in enrollment over time. Because school infrastructure projects are usually financed over multiple years, amortization gives a more realistic sense of funding need. In addition, most of the state assessments utilized in this research projected needs over this time span. Over a five year period, unmet funding need ranged from $271 per pupil in Florida to $3,385 per pupil in Utah.[82] Median per-pupil funding need was $880 while the average was somewhat higher, at $1,095. Over a ten year period, Florida and Utah also emerged at the extremes, with $141 per pupil needed in Florida, and $1,841 in Utah. Median per-pupil funding need was $489, and the ten year average, $608.

Table 1.2. Descriptive Statistics for Total School Infrastructure Funding Need

Minimum	$220,090,007
Maximum	$47,640,000,000
Mean	$5,322,776,376
Median	$2,839,058,509
Range	$47,419,909,993
Standard Deviation	$7,908,712,728
Sum	$266,138,818,788
Kurtosis	17
Skewness	4
N	50

Table 1.3. Descriptive Statistics for Per Pupil Funding Need Over Five and Ten Years

	Per Pupil Funding ($)/Five Years	*Per Pupil Funding Need ($)/Ten Years*
Minimum	271	151
Maximum	3,385	1,841
Mean	1,095	608
Median	880	489
Range	3,114	1,689
Standard Deviation	752	417
Kurtosis	3	3
Skewness	2	2
N	50	50

Although per-pupil amounts may appear more manageable than state and national totals, they represent a substantial new investment over time. For example, over the 1999–2000 school year, states and local school districts spent \$30.7 billion for capital outlay,[83] or \$711 per student, on average. Estimated interest on school debt, which is usually associated with capital outlay or school infrastructure, was estimated at an additional \$8.7 billion, or \$202 per student, on average.[84] Together, states and local school districts spent, on average, \$913 per pupil for school infrastructure and associated debt service in the 1999–2000 school year. Adding \$1,095 per pupil, using a five year amortization, would represent. an increase in per-pupil funding of over 100%; while, under a ten year amortization schedule, adding \$608 per pupil, would result in a 67% increase over current funding levels.

Regardless of how the funding needs are disaggregated or amortized, the data presented in this section speak for themselves. There is a national crisis in funding school infrastructure that numbers in the hundreds of billions of dollars. Even when broken apart by state, those states with the lowest total need require additional funding in the hundreds of millions of dollars; and those states most at-risk need billions of new dollars to address the repair and renewal of current facilities as well as the construction of new schools to address growing and shifting enrollments as well as education reforms, like reduced class size.

CONCLUSION

This chapter has sought to establish school infrastructure and its funding as a critical education capacity issue that can support or suppress the success of education reforms, and, in doing so, to set the context for the chapters which follow so that the reader has a fuller appreciation of the range of policy and research issues embedded in the relationship between school infrastructure and student achievement. The relationship of the physical environment to student achievement has remained an enduring research issue in education with broad policy implications for the adequate and equitable funding of schools for over 70 years. Utilizing the backdrop of earlier research, the chapter explored the crisis in school infrastructure funding that emerged in the 1990s, given the confluence of years of deferred maintenance and increased enrollments, linking it theoretically to notions of human capital and social capital development. School infrastructure and its funding represent physical capital that works in tandem with human capital and social capital to build capacity for education reform and enhanced student achievement.

Through production-function modeling, recent research has operationalized the conceptualization of school infrastructure and its funding as physical capital. Although production-function approaches in educational research are not without controversy as conceptual and methodological weaknesses are inherent in this analytic approach, the use of such modeling represents a maturation in this particular body of research and has yielded significant results. Nonetheless, scholars must not rest upon their laurels; rather they must look to methods by which future studies on the relationship between the physical environment of schools and student achievement can be further strengthened. As such, the field is at a crossroads in terms of next steps. While current approaches based in production-function research reflect advances in modeling and statistical analysis, alone they will likely prove insufficient, as they have in other areas of education research, to fully explain the factors that affect student achievement. Future research in this area will benefit, from both a research and policy perspective, by being grounded in a larger theoretical and educational context. The evolution of research in this often-overlooked area of education is promising, but it is inevitably limited due to the lack of strong theoretical underpinnings that serve to consistently guide research design and ground findings. Therefore, the next generation of research on the relationship of school infrastructure and student success must undertake the arduous task of theory building begun in this chapter, treating school infrastructure as a critical educational capacity issue to ensure that it receives the attention it deserves in the education policy arena. Finally, in order to broaden the educational context, the chapters which follow explore issues heretofore undeveloped in the research. As such, they will play a pivotal role in setting the agenda for the next generation of scholarship in the relationship of the physical environment of schools and student success.

NOTES

1. Faith E. Crampton, David C. Thompson, and Janis M. Hagey, "Creating and Sustaining School Capacity in the Twenty-First Century: Funding a Physical Environment Conducive to Student Learning," *Journal of Education Finance* 27 (Fall 2001): 633–652.

2. Thomas C. Holy, "Needed Research in the Field of School Buildings and Equipment." *Review of Educational Research* 5 (October 1935): 510.

3. Thomas C. Holy, "Status of Research in the School Plant Field," *Review of Educational Research* 8 (October 1938): 367.

4. Ibid.

5. Carol S. Weinstein, "The Physical Environment of the School: A Review of Research." *Review of Educational Research* 49 (Fall 1979): 577–610.

6. Ibid., 602.

7. Ibid., 578.

8. Ibid., 599.

9. Carroll McGuffey, "Facilities," in *Improving Educational Standards and Productivity: The Research Basis for Policy*, ed. Herbert J. Walberg (Berkeley, California: McCutchan Publishing Corporation, 1982), 273–274.

10.   Linda Kay Lemasters, "A Synthesis of Studies Pertaining to Facilities, Student Achievement, and Student Behavior" (Ph.D. diss., Virginia Polytechnic Institute and State University, 1997), 196–197.

11.   Ibid., 8.

12.   Note that quality may refer to other factors, such as the quality of data available, selection of appropriate research method, and execution of the chosen research method.

13.   For a fuller discussion of the rationale for parity in funding of school infrastructure with funding of school district operating costs, see the final chapter of this volume: Chapter 11, "Striking a Balance in School Infrastructure Funding," by David C. Thompson.

14.   See, for example, Jerry W. Gilley, "Understanding and Building Capacity for Change: A Key to School Transformation," *International Journal of Educational Reform* 9 (April 2000):109–119; Diane Massell, "State Strategies for Building Local Capacity: Addressing the Needs of Standards-Based Reform," *CPRE Policy Briefs* RB–25-July 1998; William A. Firestone and James R. Pennell, "Designing State-Sponsored Teacher Networks: A Comparison of Two Cases," *American Educational Research Journal* 34 (Summer 1997): 237–266.

15.   National Commission on Excellence in Education, *A Nation at Risk: The Imperative for Educational Reform* (Washington, D.C.: 1983).

16.   James P. Spillane and Charles L. Thompson, "Reconstructing Conceptions of Local Capacity: The Local Education Agency's Capacity for Ambitious Instructional Reform," *Educational Evaluation and Policy Analysis* 19 (Summer 1997): 185–203.

17.   Elchanan Cohen and Terry G. Geske, *The Economics of Education,* 3d ed. (New York: Pergamon Press, 1990), 161.

18.   James S. Coleman, "Social Capital in the Creation of Human Capital," *American Journal of Sociology* 94 (Supplement 1988): 101–102, quoted in Spillane and Thompson, 190.

19.   Spillane and Thompson, 190.

20.   Ibid.

21.   Ibid., 193.

22.   Ibid., 196.

23.   David C. Thompson and R. Craig Wood, *Money & Schools,* 2d ed. (Larchmont, New York: Eye on Education, 2001), 254–255.

24.   See R. Craig Wood, David C. Thompson, Lawrence O. Picus, and Don I. Tharpe, *Principles of School Business Management,* 2d ed. (Reston, Virginia: Association of School Business Officials International, 1995); William T. Hartman, *School District Budgeting* (Reston, Virginia: Association of School Business Officials International, 1999); and John R. Ray, Walter G. Hack, and I. Carl Candoli, *School Business Administration: A Planning Approach,* 7th ed. (Boston, Massachusetts: Allyn & Bacon, 2001).

25.   Crampton et al., 647.

26.   See, for example, Jerry M. Lowe, "The Interface Between Educational Facilities and Learning Climate" (Ph.D. diss., Texas A&M University, 1990). Jonathan Kozol, *Savage Inequalities: Children in America's Schools* (New York: Harper Perennial, 1992); and Jeffery A. Lackney, "Quality in School Envi-

ronments: A Multiple Case Study of the Diagnosis, Design, and Management of Environmental Quality in Five Elementary Schools in the Baltimore City Schools from an Action Research Perspective" (Ph.D. diss., University of Wisconsin Milwaukee, 1996).

27. Because quality and rigor have been issues in the field of school infrastructure research, studies are here defined as scholarly, practical, or technical to assist lay readers in drawing conclusions regarding the applicability of findings. Scholarly studies are usually representative of more traditional academic works, such as articles published in peer-reviewed journals, such as the *Journal of Education Finance,* books published by companies that target academic and research audiences, and dissertation research that, while conducted by new scholars, is supervised and approved by academic faculty with expertise in the area of study. Practical research is that research geared primarily towards practitioners and often is not peer-reviewed, such as articles published in *Phi Delta Kappan* and *School Business Affairs.* See, for example, Daniel L. Duke, "Challenges of Designing the Next Generation of America's Schools," *Phi Delta Kappan* 79 (May 1998): 688–693; and Glenn I. Earthman, "The Best Possible Environment for the Most Productive Learning," *School Business Affairs* 63 (July 1997): 21–24. Such research also includes papers presented at professional organizations whose membership is predominantly practitioners. See, for example, Glenn I. Earthman, and Linda Lemasters "Where Children Learn: A Discussion of How a Facility Affects Learning," A paper presented to the Annual Meeting of the Virginia Educational Facilities Planners, Blacksburg, Virginia, February, 1998. The third category, technical literature, refers to studies published by for-profit and non-profit organizations with a strong interest in the field of study. These would include nonprofit, professional organizations such as the Council of Facilities Planners International and advocacy groups, like the Environmental Working Group. See, for example, Zachary Ross and Betsy Walker, *Reading, Writing, and Risk: Air Pollution Inside California's Portable Classrooms* (Washington, D.C.: Environmental Working Group, 1999). Examples of for-profit organizations include consultants and consulting groups, such as the Heschong Mahone Group. See, *Daylighting in Schools: An Investigation Into the Relationship Between Daylighting and Human Performance* (Fair Oaks, California: Heschong Mahone Group, August 1999). Like the practical research, these studies are usually not peer-reviewed. It is important to note that some studies blur the lines between these three categories, as they are published in more than one venue.

28. For a fuller discussion of the school infrastructure funding needs of urban school districts, see Chapter 5 of this volume, "Capital Needs and Spending in Urban Public School Systems: Policies, Problems, and Promises," by James G. Cibulka and Bruce S. Cooper; and for school infrastructure funding needs for rural school districts, see Chapter 6 of this volume, "Funding School Infrastructure in Rural America," by Jeffrey Maiden.

29. At $9.5 billion, Texas ranks fifth in the nation, behind New York, Ohio, California, and New Jersey in unmet school infrastructure funding need. See the next section of this chapter, "Quantifying Unmet School Infrastructure Funding Need," for greater detail.

30. See, for example, Davison Duane Lowe, "School Facilities in California: An Empirical Study" (Ph.D. diss., University of Southern California, 1996); Scott Andersen, "The Relationship Between School Design Variables and

Scores on the Iowa Test of Basic Skills" (Ph.D. diss., University of Georgia, 1999); Patti D. Ayers, "Exploring the Relationship Between High School Facilities and Achievement of High School Students in Georgia" (Ph.D. diss., University of Georgia, 1999); Kathy J. Gentry, "The Relationship Between School Size and Academic Achievement in Georgia's Public High Schools" (Ph.D. diss., University of Georgia, 2000); and Diane O'Rourke Swift, "Effects of Student Population Density on Academic Achievement in Georgia Elementary Schools" (Ph.D. diss., University of Georgia, 2000).

31. Carolyn S. Cash, "Building Conditions and Student Achievement and Behavior" (Ph.D. diss., Virginia Polytechnic Institute and State University, 1993).

32. It is important to note that Cash's research also addressed the impact of building conditions on student behavior, evidenced by suspensions, expulsions, violence, and substance abuse. Although it is beyond the scope of this chapter to discuss the results of this portion of her research, it is noteworthy that the relationship between these student behavior variables and building condition were not as robust as those for student achievement.

33. Ibid., 30–31.

34. Ibid., 38.

35. The survey included a total of 27 items, of which 26 were directed toward specific structural and cosmetic building elements of the physical environment. Items were selected for inclusion based upon a review of research. Sixteen were structural: building age; windows; flooring; heating; air conditioning; roof leaks; adjacent facilities; locker condition; ceiling covering; science lab equipment; science lab age; lighting; wall color; exterior noise; student density; and site acreage. Ten items were cosmetic: interior wall paint; interior paint cycle; exterior wall paint; exterior paint cycle; floors swept; floors mopped; graffiti; graffiti removal; classroom furniture; and grounds (Cash, 37).

36. The Virginia Test of Academic Proficiency is comprised of a composite score based upon scores from subtests on mathematics, reading comprehension, written expression, sources of information, social studies, and science (Cash, 33).

37. Ibid., 45.

38. Note that although 43 schools responded, two of the surveys were not usable (Cash, 38).

39. Socioeconomic status was the covariate of the percent of students in a school who were not eligible for free or reduced-price lunch (Cash, 44).

40. Cash, 46.

41. Ibid., 74.

42. Ibid., 83.

43. Eric Hines, "Building Condition and Student Achievement and Behavior" (Ph.D. diss., Virginia Polythechnic Institute and State University, 1996).

44. Ibid., 44.

45. Ibid., 40.

46. Hines did not, however, replicate the second part of the Cash study, where she used simple linear regression to determine the relationship between school building condition and age.

47.   Ibid., 54.

48.   Ibid., 54.

49.   Maureen M. Berner, "Building Conditions, Parental Involvement, and Student Achievement in the District of Columbia Public School System," *Urban Education* 28 (April 1993): 11:6–29.

50.   Ibid., 18

51.   Ibid., 19.

52.   Ibid., 21.

53.   Ibid., 24.

54.   Ibid., 23.

55.   Ibid., 24.

56.   Ibid., 27.

57.   Morgan Lewis, *Facility Conditions and Student Test Performance in the Milwaukee Schools* (Scottsdale, Arizona: Council of Educational Facilities Planners International, 2001).

58.   Ibid., 4.

59.   Results were statistically significant at the .05 probability level, with a one-tailed test. Lewis maintained that the use of a one-tailed test was appropriate to a directional hypothesis, based upon a body of research that has established a positive relationship between building condition and student achievement.

60.   Ibid., 8.

61.   Results were not statistically significant for the language and social studies components of the WSAS, but the coefficients were positive.

62.   Lewis did not report the R^2 for the equation containing science scores as an independent variable.

63.   Elizabeth A. Harter, "How Educational Expenditures Relate to Student Achievement: Insights from Texas Elementary Schools," *Journal of Education Finance* 24 (Winter 1999): 281–302.

64.   Spending categories were limited to some, but not all, operating expenditures. Excluded were expenditures for district administration, student transportation, food services, data processing, and community services. Also excluded were capital expenditures for facilities acquisition and construction.

65.   Harter, 292.

66.   Ibid., 295.

67.   Ibid., 295.

68.   The R^2 of .28 reflects the inclusion of socioeconomic variables as independent variables added as controls.

69.   This section draws significantly from Crampton et al., 633–652.

70.   See American Association of School Administrators, Council of Great City Schools, and National School Boards Association, *The Maintenance Gap: Deferred Repair and Renovation in the Nation's Elementary and Secondary Schools* (Arlington, Virginia: January 1983); Ann Lewis, *Wolves at the Schoolhouse Door: An Investigation of the Condition of Public School Buildings* (Washington, D.C.: Education Writers Association, 1989); and Sharon J. Hansen, *Schoolhouse in the Red: A Guidebook for Cutting Our Losses* (Arlington, Virginia: Amer-

ican Association of School Administrators, 1992). See also, two special issues of the *Journal of Education Finance* on the status of state and local funding of capital outlay, David S. Honeyman, R. Craig Wood, and David C. Thompson, editors, 13 (Winter 1988) and 13 (Spring 1988), with reports from 24 states and one Canadian province; and a special issue of the *Journal of Education Finance* on the crisis in school infrastructure funding, Faith E. Crampton and David C. Thompson, editors, 27 (Fall 2001).

71.   U.S. General Accounting Office, *School Facilities: The Condition of America's Schools* (Washington, D.C., February 1995).

72.   For a fuller discussion of state funding mechanisms for school infrastructure, see Chapter 2 of this volume, "Financing School Infrastructure Needs: An Overview Across the 50 States," by Catherine C. Sielke.

73.   For a fuller discussion of the history of school finance litigation and school infrastructure funding issues, see Chapter 8 of this volume, "School Finance Litigation: A Strategy to Address Inequities in School Infrastructure Funding," by David C. Thompson and Faith E. Crampton.

74.   U.S. General Accounting Office, *School Facilities*; and Laurie Lewis, Kyle Snow, Elizabeth Faris, Becky Smerdon, Stephanie Cronen, and Jessica Kaplan, *Condition of America's Public School Facilities: 1999* (Washington, DC: U.S. Department of Education, National Center for Education Statistics, June 2000).

75.   Sources included policy and research literature; proprietary policy and research databases; a fifty-state questionnaire; and a five year analysis of state legislative trends in funding school infrastructure. Proprietary policy and research databases included Lexis-Nexis; NCSLnet, an online electronic database of the National Conference of State Legislatures; and State Policy Archives, an online electronic database of the Council of State Governments. The latter two proved to be a rich source of fugitive literature, such as state reports and assessments that often had little or no circulation outside state government agency circles. The questionnaire, distributed to state affiliates of the National Education Association, was completed in collaboration with the appropriate state agencies, such as state departments of education. The questionnaire had a 100% response rate. See also, Faith E. Crampton, *Survey of State School Finance Legislation 1998: Overview, Abstracts, and Trend Analysis*, NEA Research Working Paper (Washington, D.C.: National Education Association, October 1999). This publication offered insight into which states had recently conducted statewide school infrastructure assessments, based upon legislation requiring such an assessment or creation of a statewide commission to study school infrastructure funding issues.

76.   For a complete description of data collection and methods, see Crampton et al., 636–639.

77.   Although states with larger concentrations of urban school districts did have larger state totals for unmet funding need, this information is not a basis for drawing the conclusion that rural states are "low need." For these types of comparisons, per-pupil funding needs found in columns 3 and 4 of Table 1.1 are instructive.

78.   The release of the preliminary results of the study precipitated a flurry of requests for briefings by both Republican and Democratic Congressional members and staff; and by senior staff of the U.S. Department of Education and White House Council of Economic Advisors. Requests for briefings and

invitations to present findings also came from national constiuency groups, such as the National Conference of State Legislatures (NCSL) and Organizations Concerned About Rural Education (OCRA). The release of the preliminary draft of the study in sparked national media attention, with articles in newspapers, such as the *Washington Post* and the *Los Angeles Times*. See Doug Smith, "Catch-Up Costs Billions," *Los Angeles Times*, 3 May 2000, B2; and Kenneth J. Cooper, "School Building Needs Tallied," *Washington Post*, 3 May 2000, A10.

79.   U.S. General Accounting Office, *School Facilities*.

80.   A recent update of the previously cited U.S. General Accounting Office (GAO) study was conducted by the U.S. Department of Education (DOE) which placed the total at $127 billion. See, Lewis et al., *Condition of America's Public School Facilities: 1999*. The DOE study is referred to as an update rather than a replication for a number of reasons explained in some depth in the DOE study. Hence, the results of the GAO and DOE studies are not comparable, according to the DOE. For example, the GAO study included cost estimates for schools to meet federal law on access for the disabled while the DOE study did not. On the other hand, the DOE asked respondents to estimate new construction costs two years into the future while the GAO study did not. In addition, there are a number of methodological differences and issues between the studies. For example, the DOE study utilized a much smaller sample of schools. Both studies used the school as the unit of analysis although district officials were the initial point of contact. However, the DOE study notes that in an unspecified number of cases school principals estimated costs, raising concerns about the accuracy of the estimates.

81.   For a fuller discussion of accessibility issues for students with disabilities and school infrastructure, see Chapter 7 of this volume, "Infrastructure Funding Considerations and Students with Disabilities," by William T. Hartman.

82.   Both Florida and Utah have rapidly growing enrollments. Therefore, the lower per-pupil funding need for Florida may appear puzzling. It is important to note that Florida has been more proactive with regard to state funding of school infrastructure than many other states, for example, passing the "Smart Schools Act" (House Bill 17) in 1997.

83.   National Education Association (NEA), *Rankings & Estimates: Rankings of the States 1999 and Estimates of School Statistics 2000* (Washington, D.C.: 1999), 94. Note that the definition for "capital outlay" while similar to that of school infrastructure in this study is not identical. See, NEA, *Rankings & Estimates*, 9, where "capital outlay" is defined as: "An expenditure that results in the acquisition of fixed assets or additions to fixed assets, which are presumed to have benefits for more than one year. It is an expenditure for land or existing buildings, improvements of grounds, construction of buildings, additions to buildings, remodeling of buildings or initial, additional, and replacement equipment."

84.   Ibid., 94.

CHAPTER 2

FINANCING SCHOOL INFRASTRUCTURE NEEDS

An Overview Across the 50 States

Catherine C. Sielke
University of Georgia

ABSTRACT

Funding school infrastructure needs has not been a priority of the states; however, state support for funding has grown over the years. Still, the local voter-approved bond issue is the major source of revenue for school district infrastructure needs, but, in many cases, lack of voter support means school infrastructure needs continue to go unmet. In states that provide no support, there are few options left to provide the fiscal means for meeting school infrastructure requirements. In those states that require local effort to qualify for state aid, lack of support for the bond issue may render the local district unable to participate in the state funding program. Even with all of the funding mechanisms available, the question of equity still arises, and it is a particularly complex issue when discussing school infrastructure needs.

Saving America's School Infrastructure, pages 27–51

INTRODUCTION

The funding of school infrastructure may well be one of today's most complex school finance topics. State funding mechanisms often mirror those used to fund basic educational programs, but these mechanisms are frequently combined with other funding as states attempt to equalize funding while at the same time they seek to address pressing facility needs, such as health and safety issues. Although different approaches, such as special local option sales taxes, lease-purchase agreements, and developer or impact fees have emerged, the voter-approved local bond issue is still the backbone of funding school infrastructure needs.

This chapter is divided into six sections. It first describes the methodology used to gather the data. It then examines the dollars appropriated for school infrastructure needs in the 1993–1994 school year compared to the 1998–1999 school year. The third section presents the state funding programs that were available in the 50 states during the 2001–2002 school year. Next, the use of bond issues to fund school infrastructure, debt limitations, and state aid directed toward debt retirement are explored. The fifth section discusses other funding options available to local school districts for their infrastructure needs. The chapter concludes with a discussion of issues that persist in funding school infrastructure.

METHODOLOGY

The data for this chapter were collected from several different sources. Indepth information on individual state funding can be found in *Public School Finance Programs of the United States and Canada, 1998–1999.*[1] The review process for the publication of these data was comprehensive. Each state chapter was reviewed by the editors and submitted to the United States Department of Education. The Department's adjudication process included an independent, external review by a person identified by the Department as knowledgeable about a particular state's funding. Chapters were then subject to the Department's internal review process. Another source of data for this chapter is *Highlights of the American Education Finance Association's Public School Finance Programs of the United States and Canada, 1998–1999,*[2] which includes summaries and extensive tables based upon data drawn from *Public School Finance Programs of the United States and Canada, 1998–1999.*[3]

To ensure that the data for this chapter were as current as possible, an extensive search was conducted of state department of education Web sites, seeking a description of the school infrastructure funding programs. From each state Web site, an individual was identified as an expert in school infrastructure funding and then contacted by email or by telephone. Individuals contacted were provided with a description of their respective state's 1998–1999 funding program and a summary of any new information gleaned from the Web site. They were then requested to confirm the accuracy of the information or to provide corrections and additional information. Forty-nine of 50 states responded, with the exception of Arizona.

STATE EFFORTS AT FUNDING INFRASTRUCTURE NEEDS

Capturing the amounts spent on school infrastructure is challenging for multiple reasons. For example, some states do not track what is spent. Other states find it difficult to separate local, state, and federal funding for infrastructure needs. Also, funding legislation may be approved in one fiscal year, but allocated and expended over a period of one to five years. A U.S. Government Accounting Office report, dated March 2000, stated:

> ...[T]here are no complete and current national data on how much funding for school construction is available annually to each local school district... There is wide variance among states in the degree to which they rely on local compared with state funding for school construction projects. Even within states, the amount of state or local funding can vary significantly from year to year.[4]

With these caveats, Table 2.1 presents the most accurate data available on state funding for school infrastructure for 1993–1994 and 1998–1999.

In 1993–1994, 24 states reported funding $4.128 billion for school infrastructure. Fifteen states reported no spending for school infrastructure, while the remaining 11 states were unable to report funding amounts. Of the 24 states reporting some level of funding, support for infrastructure as a percentage of total state school aid ranged from less than a fraction of a percent to 16.5%. In 1998–1999, 30 states reported funding $10.888 billion for school infrastructure. Eleven states, a decrease of four states from the 1993–1994, reported no funding for school infrastructure. The remaining nine states were unable to report the funding amounts. Support for infrastructure as a percentage of total state school aid ranged from a fraction of a percent to 18.6%. In 1998–1999, six states provided less funding as a percentage of state aid than they did in 1993–1994; increases as a percentage of state aid ranged from 1.3% to 13.4%.

Table 2.1.   State Funding for Infrastructure, 1993–1994 and 1998–1999 (in unadjusted dollars)

State	1993–94 $millions	1998–99 $ millions	Change in $ millions	1993–94 Percent State Aid	1998–99 Percent State Aid	Percent Change
Alabama	1.4	68.6	67.2	<1.0	2.6	2.0
Alaska	na	na	na	na	na	na
Arizona	na	310.0	na	na	12.0	na
Arkansas	0.0	35.7	35.7	0.0	2.3	2.3
California	882.0	6,000.0	5,118.0	5.9	na	na
Colorado	na	na	na	na	na	na
Connecticut	137.5	340.0	202.5	8.8	14.7	5.9
Delaware	na	na	na	na	na	na
Florida	544.0	419.0	−12.5	9.2	5.2	−4.0
Georgia	15.6	190.3	174.7	<1.0	4.4	4.0
Hawaii	94.7	89.3	−5.4	na	10.4	na
Idaho	0.0	0.0	na	0.0	na	na
Illinois	0.0	327.5	327.5	0.0	6.8	6.8
Indiana	na	35.6	35.6	na	<1.0	na
Iowa	0.0	0.0	na	0.0	0.0	na
Kansas	7.4	22.7	15.3	<1.0	1.0	na
Kentucky	53.7	300.0	246.3	2.7	10.3	7.6
Louisiana	0.0	0.0	na	0.0	0.0	na
Maine	47.9	54.1	6.2	7.7	7.0	−0.7
Maryland	84.1	79.3	−4.8	4.0	3.0	−1.0
Massachusetts	na	232.9	na	na	7.3	na
Michigan	0.0	0.0	na	0.0	0.0	na
Minnesota	118.0	237.0	119.0	4.8	6.1	1.3
Mississippi	na	na	na	na	na	na
Missouri	0.0	0.0	na	0.0	0.0	na
Montana	0.0	3.0	3.0	0.0	<1.0	na
Nebraska	<1.0	0.0	na	0.0	0.0	na
Nevada	0.0	0.0	na	0.0	0.0	na
New Hampshire	14.7	23.6	8.9	16.5	18.6	2.1
New Jersey	137.1	112.9	−24.2	2.8	1.9	−0.9
New Mexico	28.6	90.6	62.0	2.5	15.9	13.4
New York	452.0	850.9	398.9	4.8	7.0	2.2

Table 2.1.   (cont.)

State	1993–94 $millions	1998–99 $ millions	Change in $ millions	1993–94 Percent State Aid	1998–99 Percent State Aid	Percent Change
North Carolina	1,000.0	0.0	na	na	0.0	na
North Dakota	0.0	0.0	na	0.0	0.0	na
Ohio	46.6	0.0	na	1.2	na	na
Oklahoma	0.0	0.0	na	0.0	0.0	na
Oregon	0.0	0.0	na	0.0	0.0	na
Pennsylvania	184.0	253.8	69.8	3.9	3.0	–0.9
Rhode Island	17.0	22.7	5.7	4.5	4.5	0.0
South Carolina	15.4	46.7	31.3	1.1	2.4	1.3
South Dakota	0.0	0.0	na	0.0	0.0	na
Tennessee	na	315.1	na	na	14.2	na
Texas	na	na	na	na	na	na
Utah	9.0	30.9	21.9	<1.0	2.2	2.0
Vermont	10.0	17.0	7.0	4.6	2.6	2.0
Virginia	0.0	55.0	55.0	0.0	1.6	1.6
Washington	192.4	200.3	7.9	5.1	4.1	–1.0
West Virginia	35.4	123.7	88.3	3.2	9.0	5.8
Wisconsin	na	0.0	na	na	0.0	na
Wyoming	na	0.0	na	na	0.0	na
Total Amount	4,128.5	10,888.2	6,759.7			

Source: Compiled by the author from Steven D. Gold, David M. Smith, and Stephen B. Lawton, *Public School Finance Programs of the United States and Canada: 1993–1994* (Albany, New York: The Center for the States, 1995); and Catherine C. Sielke, John Dayton, C. Thomas Holmes, and Anne L. Jefferson, *Public School Finance Programs of the United States and Canada, 1998–1999*, Publication # NCES 2001-309 (Washington, D.C.: U. S. Department of Education, National Center for Education Statistics, 2001), http://www.nces.ed.gov/edfin/state_finance/statefinancing.asp.

STATE FUNDING PROGRAMS

Historically, school buildings have been symbols of local control. In the past, buildings were often the product of local cooperation and were erected with donated materials and time to meet the simpler needs of America's early schools.[5] However, some state funding of school buildings was occurring in the early 1900s. According to Thompson and Wood, between 1898 and 1927, eleven states—Arkansas, Delaware, Maine, Minnesota, Missouri, New York, Oklahoma, Pennsylvania, Rhode Island, Tennessee, and Wisconsin—offered capital outlay aid as an incentive for consolidation of smaller school districts. In 1903, Delaware and South Carolina provided aid for schools for black children. However, by as late as World War II, Thompson and Wood note that "only 12 states gave general aid for capital outlay and debt service to local schools."[6] Brimley and Garfield report that by 1965, "about 80% of the states had used some method of assisting local districts in financing capital outlays and debt service."[7] These methods, however, often consisted of loans rather than direct school aid. As later sections of this chapter will discuss, the voter-approved bond issue is very much in use in providing for school infrastructure needs.

Several conditions have pushed states to accept a greater role in funding education in general, and school infrastructure in particular. School finance litigation is one such impetus. While earlier litigation tended to focus on the provision of equitable basic educational programs, recent lawsuits have included the equitable and adequate facilities as essential to the education of America's children.[8] In addition, the nation is experiencing a tremendous growth in student enrollment, and many local school districts are unable to keep up with the demands for additional classrooms and schools. State-mandated class size reductions have also increased the need for more classrooms. Added to space needs are demands to upgrade older buildings to accommodate up-to-date technology and accessibility for the disabled.

Crampton's longitudinal research on state finance legislation found that while in 1994 only 18 bills affecting school infrastructure funding were passed by state legislatures and signed into law, that number increased dramatically to 70 bills in 1997.[9] Although the number of bills dropped to 60 in the 1998 legislative session, the number increased again in 1999 to 93. The overall increase in legislative activity speaks to the importance of the issue of infrastructure funding and also to greater involvement at the state level. As reported earlier, the number of states providing funding in 1998–1999 increased from 35 to 39, and the amount of reported funding increased by approximately 250%. By 2001–2002, the number of states providing funding increased once again to 42.

The basic funding mechanisms used by states to fund school infrastructure needs are the same as those used to fund basic educational programs: flat grants; equalized grants; full state funding; and categorical grants. Some states roll the funding for school infrastructure into their basic aid formula, and there are a few states that provide no fiscal support. Table 2.2 provides a brief description of each state's funding program(s) for the 2001–2002 school year. To aid in categorizing the type of funding support, the table contains columns labeled flat grant, equalized, basic support, full funding, categorical grant, and none.[10]

Table 2.2.   State School Infrastructure Funding Programs 2001–2002

State	State Funding Program	Flat Grant	Equalized	Basic Support	Full Funding	Categorical Grant	None
Alabama	Guaranteed tax yield for capital improvements.		X				
Alaska	Grants with required local contribution ranging from 5% to 35%.		X				
	Reimburses debt up to 70%. Debt must be pre-authorized.		X				
Arizona	Full state funding within required state standards.				X		
	Per pupil amount for "soft," short term capital needs.	X					
Arkansas	Provided within basic state aid: Average daily membership (ADM) x wealth index x $39.		X				
California	State provides approximately 55% to 66% of costs.					X	
Colorado	Included in Basic Support Program: $223–$800 per pupil.			X			
Connecticut	Equalized funding for 20% to 80% of eligible costs. Magnet schools receive 100%.		X				
	Additional funding for initiatives such as early childhood, reduced class size, full day kindergarten.					X	
Delaware	State pays 60% to 80% of costs. Equalized based on taxing ability.		X				
Florida	Public Education and Capital Outlay (PECO) funds projects based on need.					X	
Georgia	Equalized funding based on assessed valuation per pupil, ranging from 75% to 90%. Special local sales tax (SPLOST) funds are also included in the formula.		X				
	Grants for new classrooms, reduced class size initiatives.					X	
	Additional incentives available for low wealth district districts.					X	
Hawaii	Full state funding				X		
Idaho	Subsidies for debt retirement based on mill rate, health and safety issues.					X	

Table 2.2.   (cont.)

State	State Funding Program	Flat Grant	Equalized	Basic Support	Full Funding	Categorical Grant	None
Illinois	Equalized grants based on equalized assessed valuation (EAV) per pupil at the 90th percentile.		X				
	Grants for debt service equaling 10% of principal × grant index.		X				
Indiana	Flat grant of $40 per pupil in average daily attendance (ADA) in grades 1–12. Purpose is debt service	X					
Iowa	Grants based on enrollment size and inverse relationship with sales tax proceeds. Required local equalized match based on district fiscal capacity. Minimum match is 20%.		X				
Kansas	Weighting per pupil in basic aid of 0.25 for costs of new facility.	X					
	Grants for debt service equalized inversely to assessed valuation (AV) per pupil.		X				
Kentucky	Flat grant of $100 per pupil.	X					
	District levy of $0.05 per $100 of assessed valuation (AV) equalized if property wealth is less than 150 percent of state average.		X				
	Grants for debt service based on percentage of district unmet needs compared to state unmet needs.		X				
Louisiana	No state funding.						X
Maine	Funding for debt service based on local share for approved projects.		X				
Maryland	Funding based on state share of minimum foundation per pupil. Minimum is 50% of costs.		X				
Massachusetts	Reimbursement of 50% to 90% for approved projects. Funding based on calculation of property value, average income, district poverty level, and incentive points (type of construction, project manager, efficiency, maintenance history).		X				
Michigan	No state funding.						
Minnesota	Funding by weighted average daily membership (ADM) x ($173 + district average building age).					X	
	Equalized debt service aid.		X				
	Incentive grants such as $30 per year round pupil served, health and safety issues.					X	

Table 2.2.   (cont.)

State	State Funding Program	Flat Grant	Equalized	Basic Support	Full Funding	Categorical Grant	None
Mississippi	Flat grant of $24 per average daily attendance (ADA).	X					
	Other grants based on specific needs.					X	
Missouri	No state aid.						X
Montana	Funding for debt service only. Based on ratio of district mill value per pupil enrollment and the state mill value per pupil.		X				
Nebraska	Funding for accessibility and environmental issues: $0.052 per $100 assessed valuation (AV).					X	
Nevada	No state funding with the exception of special appropriations for two districts due to extreme need.						X
New Hampshire	State funds 30% to 55% of building costs depending on number of towns. Funding is not equalized.	X					
New Jersey	*Abbott* districts receive 100% funding						
	Non-*Abbott* districts receive equalized funding (minimum of 40%) based on district wealth (personal income and property tax base).		X				
	Some districts may be eligible debt service aid.					X	
New Mexico	Equalized funding for voter-approved two mill levy.						
	Grants for critical needs if district is bonded to 65 percent of capacity.						
New York	Equalized funding based on Building Aid Ratio and Approved		X				
	Building Expense.						
North Carolina	Funding provided based on average daily membership (ADM), growth, and low wealth.		X				
	Additional flat grant from proceeds of corporate income tax.	X					
North Dakota	No state funding.						X
Ohio	Funds Ohio School Facilities Commission.						
	Equity list developed based on three year average property wealth; local district must pass levies. State design manual requirements.		X				
Oklahoma	No state funding.						X

Table 2.2.   (cont.)

State	State Funding Program	Flat Grant	Equalized	Basic Support	Full Funding	Categorical Grant	None
Oregon	No state funding.						X
Pennsylvania	Funding (reimbursement) based on the greater of district's market value aid ratio, capital account reimbursement fraction, or density.		X				
Rhode Island	Funding for debt service. State share ratio = 1- ((district wealth per pupil/state wealth per pupil) × 62%). Minimum funding 30% of cost.		X				
South Carolina	Funding allocated per pupil based on available funding divided by K–12 average daily membership (ADM).	X					
South Dakota	No state funding.						X
Tennessee	Funding through the Basic Education Program. Based on cost per square foot per average daily membership (ADM) + 10% for equipment + 5% for architect fees + debt service at state bond rate.					X	
Texas	Guaranteed yield funding through the Instructional Facility Allotment which is based on size of district, property value, average daily attendance (ADA), and amount of annual debt service.		X				
Utah	Equalized funding based on local effort tax rate of $0.0024 per dollar of taxable value and need.		X				
Vermont	Funds about 30% of cost of project based on prioritized needs.					X	
	Debt service reimbursed based on the guaranteed yield provisions of the general aid formula.		X				
Virginia	Flat grant of $200,000 per district.	X					
	Remaining amount prorated based on enrollment and ability to pay.		X				
	Per pupil supplement for maintenance and debt service.	X					
Washington	Funding is based on eligible area, area cost allowance, and matching ratio. Required local effort (matching ratio) is determined by comparing district assessed valuation (AV) per pupil to state assessed valuation (AV) per pupil.		X				

Table 2.2.   (cont.)

State	State Funding Program	Flat Grant	Equalized	Basic Support	Full Funding	Categorical Grant	None
West Virginia	State funding is based on need: efficiency, adequate space, educational improvement, educational innovations, health and safety, and changing demographics.					X	
	Lottery money is dedicated to debt service.					X	
Wisconsin	Funding is included in the basic support program.			X			
Wyoming	State supplements mill levy if assessed valuation per average daily membership (AV/ADM) is below 150% of state average.	X					

Source: Compiled by the author using information from state departments of education and from Catherine C. Sielke, John Dayton, C. Thomas Holmes, and Anne L. Jefferson, *Public School Finance Programs of the United States and Canada, 1998–1999,* Publication # NCES 2001-309 (Washington, D.C.: U. S. Department of Education, National Center for Education Statistics, 2001), http://www.nces.ed.gov/edfin/state_finance/statefinancing.asp.

Ten states use the flat grant in funding school infrastructure needs. However, Indiana, New Hampshire, and South Carolina use the flat grant approach as the only mechanism to fund school infrastructure. New Hampshire's flat grant is based on towns because the school districts are fiscally dependent. Indiana funds on a $40 flat grant per pupil, and South Carolina divides available funding by the K–12 ADM (average daily membership). Other states use the flat grant in combination with other approaches. Arizona uses the flat grant per pupil for "soft" capital needs; Kentucky's $100 per pupil is the first tier of three levels of funding. Kansas provides a weighting per pupil (0.25) for infrastructure within its basic support grant. Virginia, a state with county school systems, provides a flat grant of $200,000 per district and a per-pupil supplement for maintenance and debt service; however, the bulk of funding is through equalized grants. While the flat grant, which is generally considered highly inequitable, is being used in state funding for infrastructure, it is often not the primary or only mechanism available.

The equalized grant is the most commonly used mechanism across the states. Twenty-seven states indicated that they provide equalized funding. Some states combine this funding with other mechanisms, such as the flat grant or the categorical grant. Although both Colorado and Wisconsin indicated that their funding is part of the basic support program, it can reasonably be argued that their funding is also equalized because their basic support funding formula is equalized, and the amount per pupil differs across school districts. The equalized grant provides the greatest equity in distribution of dollars because the formulas are designed to control for factors affecting fiscal capacity, such as property wealth.

While many states use a guaranteed yield approach using assessed valuation or income levels as the equalization factor, many other states have developed complex formulas that draw upon more variables. For example, Iowa, which provided no state aid for school infrastructure in 1998–1999, now uses a formula based on enrollment size and an inverse relationship with sales tax proceeds. Georgia, a state that has had a special local option sales tax for five years, passed legislation in 2001 that also includes the proceeds from this tax in its calculations for state funding. Massachusetts' formula includes property value, average income, district poverty level, and "incentive points," such as type of construction project manager and maintenance history, to reimburse approved projects. Minnesota's formula factors in building age. New Jersey's formula uses district wealth, which includes personal income and property tax base. North Carolina provides funding based on average daily membership, growth, and low wealth. Most equalized funding requires a local contribution. The addition of variables such as "need" and "incentive points" may influence judgments about equity as school finance researchers have defined it. In other words, the equalizing formulas used to distribute general or basic membership aid are generally purer because they include factors linked to fiscal capacity. The additional factors used to distribute equalized infrastructure aid tend to be attempts to remedy student population changes, the condition of current buildings, and health and safety needs.

Two states, Hawaii and Arizona, indicated having full state funding for facilities. Hawaii, since it is one school district, would quite naturally fall into this category. Arizona, as a result of its 1994 state supreme court decision,[11] created an entity outside the department of education to oversee school infrastructure needs, the Arizona School Facilities Board. Arizona now provides full state funding as long as school districts remain within the required state standards. School districts that wish to exceed these standards may do so through more traditional means, such as bonding.

Categorical grants by definition are monies targeted for specific policy goals or needs. Categorical grants for school infrastructure are frequently targeted at growth and/or health and safety issues. Some of the states have aggressive legislation to lower class size and, to further this policy goal, make funding for additional classroom space available. Connecticut provides infrastructure grants for their early childhood, full day kindergarten, and class size reduction programs. Minnesota is providing grants for year-round education pupils as well as health and safety issues. Nebraska, which is new to providing any state funding for infrastructure, now provides grants for implementing the Americans with Disabilities Act of 1990[12] and for environmental issues. West Virginia may be unique among the 50 states in that it is facing declining student enrollment; therefore grants are for need, based on efficiency, adequate space, educational innovations, health and safety, and changing demographics.

Eight states provide no funding for school infrastructure needs. Those states are Louisiana, Michigan, Missouri, Nevada, North Dakota, Oklahoma, Oregon, and South Dakota. The methods of funding school infrastructure needs in these states are covered in the next two sections which discuss bonding and other financing options for local school districts.

BONDING FOR SCHOOL INFRASTRUCTURE NEEDS

The voter-approved bond issue is still the major source of revenue for local school district infrastructure needs. Much of the equalized aid and other types of funding described above are used to pay debt service on bond issues. This debt may have existed prior to state funding, or the bond issue may have been needed to provide the required local contribution or to make up the difference between the state grant and the local project's cost. In a report published in 2000, the U.S. General Accounting Office "found no comprehensive database of the number or dollar amount of local school construction bond referendums that were voted on in 1998."[13] The report continued, stating: "Although most of the 50 states contacted in the telephone survey did not maintain comprehensive records of funds that localities provided for school construction, 19 states provided us data on the number and dollar amount of local school referendums that passed or failed in 1998."[14] Among these 19 states, 455 referendums, or 54%, passed. These referendums represented $9.052 billion, or 54%, of the total dollars requested.

The lack of voter support for the local bond issue means that school infrastructure needs continue to go unmet. In states that provide no support, there are few options left to provide the fiscal means for meeting infrastructure needs. In those states that require local effort to qualify for state aid, lack of support for the bond issue may render the local district unable to participate in the state funding program.

Table 2.3 presents data collected on bond issues, debt limitations, and debt service state aid. Only two of the 50 states do not allow local bond issues. Both Hawaii and Maryland allow bonding at the state level only. In addition, in a few states, bonds are approved and issued by entities other than the local school district. This occurs in states where school districts are dependent, and, therefore, the municipality or county assumes this responsibility. Some states require a supermajority for approval. Indiana

Table 2.3. Bond Programs and State Aid for Debt Service

State	Bonds	Conditions	Debt Limits	State Aid for Debt
Alabama	X	Municipality may issue bonds. Districts may issue revenue warrants.	None reported.	None.
Alaska	X	State approval.	None reported.	Reimburses up to 70%.
Arizona	X	Voter-approved for projects that exceed state standards.	10% for unified districts.	None.
Arkansas	X	Voter-approved second lien bonds.	30% of assessed valuation (AV).	None.
California	X	Voter-approved.	None reported.	None.
Colorado	X	Voter-approved.	None.	Part of basic program.
Connecticut	X	Issued by municipality, not school district.	None reported.	Limited.
Delaware	X	Voter-approved.	10% of assessed valuation (AV).	None.
Florida	X	Voter-approved.	Not reported.	None.
Georgia	X	Voter-approved.	10% of assessed valuation (AV).	Yes. (See Table 2.2).
Hawaii		Full state funding.		
Idaho	X	Voter-approved with super majority.	10–20 years.	Partial subsidy for interest.
Illinois	X	Voter-approved.	None reported.	10% of principal × grant index.
Indiana	X	No approval but subject to remonstration.	2%.	Flat grant: $40 per average daily attendance (ADA) in grades 1–12.
Iowa	X	Voter-approved with 60% majority.	5% of assessed valuation (AV); 20 years.	None.
Kansas	X	Voter-approved.	None reported.	Equalized grants based on assessed valuation (AV) per pupil.

Table 2.3. (cont.)

State	Bonds	Conditions	Debt Limits	State Aid for Debt
Kentucky	X	Districts sell bonds with state oversight.	20 years.	Yes. (See Table 2.2.)
Louisiana	X	Voter-approved.	10%–20% of assessed valuation (AV); 40 years.	None.
Maine	X	Voter-approved.	State approval.	Yes. (See Table 2.2.)
Maryland		Only state issued bonds.		
Massachusetts	X	Voter-approved.	2.5% of assessed valuation (AV).	Not reported.
Michigan	X	Voter-approved.	15% of assessed valuation (AV); 30 years.	None.
Minnesota	X	Voter-approved.	15% of market value	Equalized.
Mississippi	X	Voter-approved with 60% majority.	15% of assessed valuation (AV).	Included in flat grant; $24 per average daily attendance (ADA).
Missouri	X	Voter-approved.	15% of tax base; 20 years.	None.
Montana	X	Voter-approved.	45% of assessed valuation (AV).	Yes. (See Table 2.2.)
Nebraska	X	Voter-approved with 55% majority.	None.	None.
Nevada	X	Voter-approved.	15% of assessed valuation (AV).	None.
New Hampshire	X	Voter-approved with 60% majority.	None reported.	None.
New Jersey	X	Voter-approved.	None reported.	Formula considers debt service, district basic aid percentage, eligible costs, and school district fulfillment of maintenance requirements.
New Mexico	X	Voter-approved.	6% of assessed valuation (AV).	None.

Table 2.3. (cont.)

State	Bonds	Conditions	Debt Limits	State Aid for Debt
New York	X	Voter-approved.	Not reported.	Equalized funding available.
North Carolina	X	Voter-approved.	Not reported.	Yes. (See Table 2.2.)
North Dakota	X	Voter-approved with 60% majority.	10% of assessed valuation (AV)	None.
Ohio	X	Not reported.	Not reported.	None.
Oklahoma	X	Voter-approved with 60% majority.	10% of assessed valuation (AV).	None.
Oregon	X	Voter-approved by a 50% majority of 50% of voters.	Based on assessed valuation (AV) and school grade level.	None.
Pennsylvania	X	Voter-approved.	No limit.	Reimbursement based on approved payment schedule.
Rhode Island	X	Not reported.	Not reported.	State share calculated. Minimum state funding is 30%. (See Table 2.2 for formula.)
South Carolina	X	Voter-approved.	8% of assessed valuation (AV).	Not reported.
South Dakota	X	Voter-approved.	10% of assessed valuation (AV).	None.
Tennessee	X	Voter-approved. Issued by local municipalities, counties, etc.	None reported.	Part of basic state aid. (See Table 2.2.)
Texas	X	Voter-approved.	None reported.	Part of Instructional Facility Allotment. (See Table 2.2.)
Utah	X	Voter-approved.	40% of market value	Included in facility funding. (See Table 2.2.)
Vermont	X	Voter-approved.	None reported.	Based on guaranteed yield provisions of basic aid formula.

Table 2.3. (cont.)

State	Bonds	Conditions	Debt Limits	State Aid for Debt
Virginia	X	Voter-approved for county schools.	None.	Lottery allocation and Maintenance Supplement Program.
Washington	X	Voter-approved.	None reported.	
West Virginia	X	Voter-approved.	5% of assessed valuation (AV).	Lottery proceeds dedicated to debt service.
Wisconsin	X	Voter-approved.	10% of assessed valuation (AV); 20 years.	Part of basic state aid formula.
Wyoming	X	Voter-approved.	10% of assessed valuation (AV).	Supplements mill levy if assessed valuation (AV) per average daily membership (ADM) is less than 150% of state average.

Source: Compiled by the author using information from state departments of education and from Catherine C. Sielke, John Dayton, C. Thomas Holmes, and Anne L. Jefferson, *Public School Finance Programs of the United States and Canada, 1998–1999*, Publication # NCES 2001-309 (Washington, D.C.: U. S. Department of Education, National Center for Education Statistics, 2001), http://www.nces.ed.gov/edfin/state_finance/statefinancing.asp.

does not require voter approval, but the voters have the right of remonstrance if they disapprove of the board of education's actions. Debt limits vary widely across the states. While some debt limits are expressed in market value of property, the majority are a percent of assessed value. In addition, some states place year limitations for the bonding. Twelve states that provide state funding for school infrastructure do not allow that funding to be used for reimbursement of debt service.

OTHER FUNDING OPTIONS

Table 2.4 describes other funding options that states allow for school infrastructure. A number of states offer state loan funds. These loans are of particular benefit to low property wealth districts that may not otherwise be able to raise enough local funding to build a school due to debt limits or tax limitations. However, those funds must be repaid, which may mean reliance on the voter-approved bond issue or other voter-approved mill levies. Other state options are voter-approved mill levies that are earmarked for school infrastructure needs. Some states allow for lease-purchase options and/or rentals. There appears to be great interest in the developer or impact fee approach, particularly in areas of very high student enrollment growth. The local option sales tax is another new mechanism being used to fund infrastructure needs. Some states also allow for building reserve or sinking funds. And, of course, there is the pay-as-you-go approach, which is an option for the very wealthy school district or the one with few infrastructure needs.

The federal government has also joined in providing funding for school infrastructure needs. The Qualified Zone Academy Bond (QZAB) program is available in all states, and many states are using these funds in combination with their own funding to further meet their infrastructure needs. Areas in which the QZAB can be used are strictly defined.[15] Funding is for a school and not for a school district. The school needs to be in an Empowerment Zone or Enterprise Community or have at least 35% of students eligible for free or reduced-price lunch under the federal lunch program. Perhaps the biggest drawback to the QZAB funding is that it requires the passage of a bond issue. Districts that participate only have to repay the principal of the bonds; the federal government provides the buyers of the bonds with a federal income tax credit rather than interest on their investment. Given the approximately 54% pass rate of bond issues reported in 1998, it may be questionable as to which school districts are benefiting most from this federal initiative. More research is needed to analyze the impact of this program on bond issue passage rates.

Table 2.4.   Other School Infrastructure Programs

State	*Additional Funding Availability*
Alabama	Revenue warrants that do not exceed 80% of pledged revenue.
Alaska	None.
Arizona	None.
Arkansas	State loan program.
California	Developer fees.
Colorado	Voter-approved mill levies up to ten mills for three years.
Connecticut	State loan program.
Delaware	May assess a tax rate without referenda for state match requirements.
Florida	Up to two mill levy without voter approval; voter-approved $0.05 sales tax.
Georgia	Grants; voter approved $0.01 local option sales tax up to five years.
Hawaii	None.
Idaho	Two-thirds majority approved tax levies.
Illinois	None.
Indiana	Leases, rentals.
Iowa	County local option sales tax, $0.05 up to ten years.
Kansas	Additional mill levies with approval of State Board of Tax Appeals.
Kentucky	None.
Louisiana	None.
Maine	State revolving loan fund.
Maryland	None.
Massachusetts	None.
Michigan	State loan fund, sinking funds of five mills up to 20 years.
Minnesota	State loans.
Mississippi	Three mill levy up to 20 years without voter approval. State loan fund.
Missouri	Lease purchase up to 20 years.
Montana	Building reserves.
Nebraska	Voter-approved mill levies.
Nevada	Voter-approved mill levies, developer's fees.
New Hampshire	None.
New Jersey	Lease purchase.
New Mexico	None.
New York	None.
North Carolina	Local option sales tax.
North Dakota	Voter-approved building funds up to 20 mills annually.

Table 2.4.   (cont.)

State	Additional Funding Availability
Ohio	None.
Oklahoma	Mill levy up to five mills annually.
Oregon	None.
Pennsylvania	Some non-elected debt allowed.
Rhode Island	Leases, reserve funds.
South Carolina	Children's Education Endowment Fund. Funding based on total revenue available, basic aid support formula, weighted pupils, and need.
South Dakota	None.
Tennessee	Lease purchase, capital outlay notes.
Texas	Lease purchase.
Utah	Revolving loan fund.
Vermont	Sinking funds.
Virginia	Revolving loan fund; pooled bond issues.
Washington	Fund reserves; special levies.
West Virginia	None.
Wisconsin	State loan fund, sinking funds.
Wyoming	None.

Source: Compiled by the author using information from state departments of education and from Catherine C. Sielke, John Dayton, C. Thomas Holmes, and Anne L. Jefferson, *Public School Finance Programs of the United States and Canada, 1998–1999*, Publication # NCES 2001-309 (Washington, D.C.: U. S. Department of Education, National Center for Education Statistics, 2001), http://www.nces.ed.gov/edfin/state_finance/statefinancing.asp.

ANALYSIS AND CONCLUSIONS

Funding school infrastructure needs has not been a priority of the states; however, state support for funding has grown over the years. The data presented in this chapter show that the amount of funding for school infrastructure has definitely increased over the last eight to ten years. New mechanisms have developed, such as the special local option sales tax, providing districts with more ways to raise funding. More states have accepted responsibility for funding these initiatives. Dollars usually spell control. Although not reflected completely in the tables, many states are assuming more control with those dollars. For example, Arizona will fund projects at 100%, but only within state requirements. So those districts that wish to have more than the minimum requirements must still seek voter-approved bond issues. Many states, such as Georgia, offer incentives of more funding to districts that use state prototypical designs and state management of construction.[16] As one visits state Web sites for school facilities, one can only be surprised at the size of these departments, with planners, finance experts, construction managers, architects, and so forth all represented. Truly, school infrastructure has become such as issue that mini-bureaucracies have emerged within state departments of education. In two states, Arizona and Ohio, a separate entity completely in charge of school infrastructure needs sits outside of the department of education and receives separate funding from their legislatures.

A special issue of the *Journal of Education Finance* was devoted to school infrastructure issues in Fall 2001.[17] In the lead article, Crampton, Thompson, and Hagey argued that states need to develop short-term and long-term strategies to address the immense infrastructure needs. They stated: "In the short-term, those states with excess fiscal capacity might consider making an immediate investment in school infrastructure. A number of states have enjoyed a prolonged period of economic prosperity, allowing them to amass substantial surpluses and, at the same time to grant tax breaks to their citizens and businesses [and] … a portion of these funds might be utilized now for some of the most pressing infrastructure needs."[18] In the research conducted by the author for this chapter, state department of education experts indicated that state surpluses were being utilized in some instances to fund school infrastructure needs.

As the year 2002 begins, however, America is faced with a declining economy, and the effect this will have on school infrastructure funding is uncertain. As the economy slows, unemployment rises, and sales slump. These conditions are bound to negatively impact income and sales taxes, the mainstays of state revenue, and therefore funding for education. In past years, school systems, when faced with budget cuts, often deferred maintenance rather than cut educational programs. These actions are often blamed for the deplorable conditions chronicled in government and other reports.[19] In recent years, state legislators have been very active in the arena of accountability and high stakes testing, class size reduction, and the implementation of early childhood and pre-kindergarten programs. In the face of budget cuts, will states choose to reduce their investment in bricks and mortar in order to save educational programs?

Alexander and Salmon, in their 1995 work, listed several persistent problems in funding school infrastructure.[20] The first problem they identified is that state aid plans are only token in nature. That criticism probably still stands even though tremendous increases in appropriations have occurred. A possible illustration of this tokenism is the fact that while the U.S. General Accounting Office estimated in 1995 that schools' deferred maintenance costs alone were $112 billion,[21] research reported in a National Education Association publication[22] in 2000 placed the cost at approximately \$260 billion when new construction, renovations, and additions for enrollment growth and reform initiatives such as class size reduction were factored into the equation. While the \$10.8 billion shown in Table 2.1 for 1998–1999 shows a substantial increase over 1993–1994 funding, states are still falling short of the estimated required amounts.

The second persistent problem Alexander and Salmon identified was the lack of federal financial assistance.[23] In the past, the federal government has offered funding for certain infrastructure needs such as asbestos abatement, but that assistance has been minimal. In recent years, the federal government has made some funding available as part of the QZAB program. The program is limited to renovation and remodeling and cannot be used for new construction. In addition, the qualifying conditions limit the numbers and types of school districts that are eligible to participate in the program. Clark, in an analysis of funding for Texas school facilities, indicated that although "Texas was allocated \$32.5 million in QZAB bond authority for 2000, …the program is seldom used because it is difficult to establish."[24]

The third persistent problem identified by Alexander and Salmon is the existence of constitutional limitations and statutory provisions that limit the ability of local districts to fund projects or to participate in some state initiatives.[25] These include debt limits and tax limits. Because debt limits are often linked to assessed property values, districts with lower assessed property values are restricted in the amount of debt they can issue and may, therefore, be limited in the size and type of school facility they can build. In fact, in some instances, property values may be so low that the district cannot go into enough debt to even build a school building unless the state steps in and helps. Tax limits have the same effect. If the number of mills is limited and the property value is low, the district again finds itself unable to provide facilities for its students.

Coupled with these various limitations is the issue of voter support and the increased need for school construction. Almost all states allow voter-approved bond issues; in many instances bonding is required to either make up the difference between state support and dollars needed for the infrastructure project(s) or to provide the required local effort or match the state support system requires. The last several decades have witnessed a decline in voter support for education. In a recent report, the U.S. General Accounting Office found that nationally only 54% of bond issues were successful.[26] At the state level, Sielke found that only about 54% of bond issues were successful in Michigan in 1995, a state that has undergone substantial changes in funding education in recent years, but still provides no state aid for school infrastructure.[27] The Michigan research tested ten independent variables that might influence success of school bond issues and found that the most influential variable was the number of mills a district was already levying for debt service. The data suggested that an increase of one debt mill increased the odds ratio for passing a new bond issue by 39.8%. In other words, those who were already taxing themselves for facilities were willing to approve more bond issues. Even the federal QZAB program requires voter approval of bond issues as a prerequisite for funding. Further complicating the problem is the tremendous number of dollars that are needed to fund all of America's school infrastructure needs, amounts that the property tax base alone cannot support. While there is movement toward the use of other tax bases, the use of sales tax is limited. The local sales tax has been so successful in Georgia that most school systems now rely on it to fund their infrastructure needs instead of the bond issue.[28] However, the local option sales tax is only useful in districts that have retail bases; therefore, this form of funding is considered highly inequitable by rural communities. Because these areas lack a strong retail base, the citizens of these communities actually support neighboring school system infrastructure funding as they must shop in neighboring districts. The states that do allow the local option sales tax do, however, provide equalized funding and do include the sales tax proceeds within their formulas.

Even with all of the funding mechanisms available, the question of equity still arises, and it is a particularly complex issue when discussing school infrastructure needs. Alexander and Salmon[29] stated that the characteristics of an equitable state capital outlay program would be one in which the *Serrano*[30] principle is invoked; therefore the quality of the school facility should not be determined by fiscal capacity. The second characteristic would be an equitable measure of need. Alexander and Salmon tied fiscal need to educational program need. In reviewing state funding of school infrastructure, it appears that need most often means enrollment growth, physical condition of current buildings, and accessibility. The needs are so great that tying equity to educational programs and infrastructure funding is not yet as important as tying equity to physically acceptable buildings.

Looking into the future, several questions arise. Will voters continue to support bond issues, and even special option sales tax, to fund school infrastructure? Will the current economic downturn and the diminishing state fund balances cause state legislatures to decrease state funding for school infrastructure? Will those districts that have relied on local sales tax be unable to fund the infrastructure projects they planned if the economic downturn results in less sales tax revenue? Across the nation, states are teetering at the crossroads of making significant gains in funding school infrastructure while, at the same time, facing the possibility of being unable to fund their appropriations.

NOTES

1. Catherine C. Sielke, John Dayton, C. Thomas Holmes, and Anne L. Jefferson, *Public School Finance Programs of the United States and Canada, 1998–1999,* Publication # NCES 2001-309 (Washington, D.C.: U. S. Department of Education, National Center for Education Statistics, 2001), http://www.nces.ed.gov/edfin/state_finance/statefinancing.asp.

2. Catherine C. Sielke and C. Thomas Holmes, *Highlights of the American Education Finance Association's Public School Finance Programs of the United States and Canada, 1998–1999* (Washington D. C.: American Federation of Teachers, 2001).

3. Sielke et al., *Public School Finance Programs.*

4. U. S. General Accounting Office, *School Facilities: Construction Expenditures Have Grown Significantly in Recent Years,* GAO/HEHS-00-41 (Washington, D.C.: March 2000), 16.

5. David C. Thompson and R. Craig Wood, *Money & Schools,* 2d ed. (Larchmont, New York: Eye on Education, 2001), 267.

6. Ibid.

7. Vern Brimley, Jr., and Rulon R. Garfield, *Financing Education in a Climate of Change,* 8th ed. (Boston: Allyn & Bacon, 2002), 270.

8. For a fuller discussion of school finance litigation and the funding of school infrastructure, see Chapter 8 of this volume, "School Finance Litigation: One Strategy to Address Inequities in School Infrastructure Funding," by David C. Thompson and Faith E. Crampton.

9. Faith E. Crampton, "Financing Education in the Twenty-First Century: What State Legislative Trends of the 1990s Portend, *Journal of Education Finance* 27 (2001): 479–500; and Faith E. Crampton, "Education Finance Legislative Activity and Trends at the State Level," *Journal of Education Finance* 25 (Spring 2000): 597–607.

10. While the placement of any given state's funding program into these categories may appear straightforward, ambiguity in wording within some state statutes made the categorization less clear and required a judgment call on the author's part.

11. *Roosevelt Elementary School District No. 66 v. Bishop,* 170 Ariz. 233; 877 P.2d 806 (1994).

12. 42 U.S.C. § 12101 (1990).

13. U. S. General Accounting Office, *School Facilities,* 17.

14. Ibid., 18.

15. Further information on the QZAB program can be found at http://www.ed.gov/pubs/fixschools.

16. Catherine C. Sielke, "Georgia 2001 Legislative Session: Striving for Greater Equity," in *In Search of a More Equitable and Efficient Education System: The State of the States and Provinces 2001,* A monograph of the Fiscal Issues, Policy, and Education Finance Special Interest Group of the American Educational Research Association, Christopher Roellke, ed., (Poughkeepsie, New York: Vassar College, 2001), 55–58.

17. "The Crisis in School Infrastructure Funding," a special issue, Faith E. Crampton and David C. Thompson, eds., *Journal of Education Finance* 27 (Fall 2001): 625–746.

18. Faith E. Crampton, David C. Thompson, and Janis M. Hagey, "Creating and Sustaining School Capacity in The Twenty-First Century: Funding a Physical Environment Conducive to Student Learning," *Journal of Education Finance* 27 (Fall 2001): 644–645.

19. See, for example, U.S. General Accounting Office, *School Facilities: The Condition of America's Schools* (Washington, D. C.: February 1995); and Jonathan Kozol, *Savage Inequalities: Children in America's Schools* (New York: Harper Perennial, 1992).

20. Kern Alexander and Richard G. Salmon, *Public School Finance* (Boston: Allyn & Bacon, 1995), 345–347.

21. U. S. General Accounting Office, *School Facilities.*

22. *Modernizing Our Schools: What Will It Cost?* (Washington, D.C.: National Education Association, 2000) cited in Faith E. Crampton and David C. Thompson, "Introduction to the Special Issue," *Journal of Education Finance* 27 (Fall 2001): 629.

23. Alexander and Salmon, 345–347.

24. Catherine Clark, "Texas State Support for School Facilities, 1971–2001," *Journal of Education Finance* 27 (Fall, 2001): 696.

25. Alexander and Salmon, 345–347.

26. U. S. General Accounting Office, *School Facilities.*

27. Catherine C. Sielke, "Michigan School Facilities, Equity Issues, and Voter Response to Bond Issues Following Finance Reform," *Journal of Education Finance* 23 (Winter 1998): 309–322.

28. U. S. General Accounting Office, *School Facilities.*

29. Alexander and Salmon, 345–347.

30. *Serrano v. Priest,* 487 P.2d 1241 (Cal. 1971).

CHAPTER 3

CANADIAN APPROACHES TO THE FINANCING OF SCHOOL INFRASTRUCTURE

Vivian J. Hajnal
University of Saskatchewan

ABSTRACT

During the last ten years, governance and financial support for schools in Canada have changed. Most provinces have removed local school divisions' access to property taxes, and these taxes are now collected centrally. The financing of elementary and secondary programs has moved from dependence on local dollars to almost total government support. The funding programs for school infrastructure needs have also changed to reflect the programs used to fund the basic operating grants to schools and the lack of access to property taxes. Methods of providing capital funding to the school divisions vary greatly. The underlying issue for each school division and its constituents remains the adequacy of funding to support the school infrastructure needed to sustain a vibrant educational program.

Saving America's School Infrastructure, pages 53–66

INTRODUCTION

The purpose of this chapter is to describe the funding of school infrastructure in Canada. As Canada may be unfamiliar territory for some readers of this volume, several sections are provided for context. These include a description of the elementary and secondary school enrollments in the provinces and territories, numbers of schools, and school divisions. The chapter continues with information on funding processes, such as access to property taxes, statistics on capital expenditures, and considerations about litigation. The sources for most data were statistical series compiled by the Canadian Teachers' Federation and based on *Statistics Canada* data, as well as the Inter-Provincial Education Statistics Project of the British Columbia Ministry of Education.

Needs for capital expenditures in Canada mirror those in the United States. Resources for renovation and replacement of existing buildings, construction of new and expanded facilities, and accumulated deferred maintenance are required. In support of changing program needs and enrollments, local jurisdictions experience additions; new schools; replacements; alterations; renovations; deferred maintenance; changes in building safety or health requirements; and decommissioning. No Canadian studies have examined the level of need for capital expenditures across Canada; however, individual provinces, such as Quebec, have initiated studies on the state of their school facilities.[1]

Almost all provinces and territories face the challenges associated with remote and sparsely populated school divisions. Rural depopulation, a partial result of uneconomic farm conditions and a lower birth rate, is increasing the need to close schools. In some circumstances, schools built to accommodate 300 students now have 50. To keep travel times to school at a manageable level, some small schools are a necessity. The case of the small school and the diseconomies of scale can be significant.[2] Migration of families to urban areas is increasing the need for new schools there. The growth in First Nation populations is also increasing the need for schools in isolated locations.[3] The same provincial jurisdiction may well face all of the above issues.

THE CANADIAN CONTEXT

In Canada, consisting of ten provinces and three territories,[4] education is primarily a provincial responsibility. The provinces and territories serve 92.7% of elementary and secondary student enrollments. Approximately 1.5% of total student enrollments are the responsibility of the federal government. Private schools serve 5.8% of school enrollments. The public, private, and federal elementary and secondary school enrollments (estimated)[5] for the years 1999–2000 and 2000–2001 are provided in Table 3.1.

Table 3.1. Elementary-Secondary Enrollments and Schools by Province/Territory, 1999–2000 and 2000–2001

Province/Territory	Year	Enrollments				Schools			
		Public	Private	Federal	Total	Public	Private	Federal	Total
Newfoundland and Labrador	1999–2000	93,985	488	—	94,568	345	7	—	353
	2000–2001	90,434	579	—	91,106	324	9	—	334
	Change	–3,551	91	—	–3,462	–21	2	—	–19
	% Change	–3.8%	18.6%	—	–3.7%	–6.1%	28.6%	—	–5.4%
Prince Edward Island	1999–2000	24,127	264	49	24,440	67	3	1	71
	2000–2001	25,809	279	50	26,138	67	3	1	71
	Change	1,682	15	1	1,698	0	0	0	0
	% Change	7.0%	5.7%	2.0%	6.9%	0.0%	0.0%	0.0%	0.0%
Nova Scotia	1999–2000	157,768	2,617	1,776	162,161	468	27	15	510
	2000–2001	157,607	2,713	1,949	161,269	465	27	17	509
	Change	–1,161	96	173	–892	–3	0	2	–1
	% Change	–0.7%	3.7%	9.7%	–0.6%	–0.6%	0.0%	13.3%	–0.2%
New Brunswick	1999–2000	127,301	775	907	128,983	344	19	10	373
	2000–2001	125,521	778	914	127,213	335	18	10	363
	Change	–1,780	3	7	–1,770	–9	–1	0	–10
	% Change	–1.4%	0.4%	0.8%	–1.4%	–2.6%	–5.3%	0.0%	–2.7%
Quebec	1999–2000	1,011,958	102,484	7,191	1,122,187	2,648	304	37	2,996
	2000–2001	1,009,152	102,083	7,467	1,119,249	2,643	303	37	2,990
	Change	–2,806	–401	276	–2,938	–5	–1	0	–6
	% Change	–0.3%	–0.4%	3.8%	–0.3%	–0.2%	–0.3%	0.0%	–0.2%
Ontario	1999–2000	2,022,506	93,960	16,178	2,133,267	4,595	746	113	5,458
	2000–2001	2,017,278	98,188	17,660	2,133,740	4,521	791	121	5,437
	Change	–5,228	4,228	1,482	473	–74	45	8	–21
	% Change	–0.3%	4.5%	9.2%	0.0%	–1.6%	6.0%	7.1%	–0.4%
Manitoba	1999–2000	191,414	14,615	16,807	222,999	708	95	57	862
	2000–2001	190,881	15,036	17,382	223,470	708	96	58	864
	Change	–533	421	575	471	0	1	1	2
	% Change	–0.3%	2.9%	3.4%	0.2%	0.0%	1.1%	1.8%	0.2%

Table 3.1. (cont.)

Province/Territory	Year	Enrollments				Schools			
		Public	Private	Federal	Total	Public	Private	Federal	Total
Saskatchewan	1999–2000	192,637	2,467	14,212	209,316	789	36	69	894
	2000–2001	191,729	2,330	14,716	208,775	783	34	69	886
	Change	–908	–137	504	–541	–6	–2	0	–8
	% Change	–0.5%	–5.6%	3.5%	–0.3%	–0.8%	–5.6%	0.0%	–0.9%
Alberta	1999–2000	533,796	26,128	12,016	572,024	1,627	183	67	1,879
	2000–2001	538,007	27,149	12,623	577,863	1,630	185	72	1,889
	Change	4,211	1,021	607	5,839	3	2	5	10
	% Change	0.8%	3.9%	5.1%	1.0%	0.2%	1.1%	7.5%	0.5%
British Columbia	1999–2000	618,142	61,655	5,036	684,833	1,669	325	109	2,103
	2000–2001	625,522	64,218	5,089	694,829	1,686	338	110	2,134
	Change	7,380	2,563	53	9,996	17	13	1	31
	% Change	1.2%	4.2%	1.1%	1.5%	1.0%	4.0%	0.9%	1.5%
Yukon	1999–2000	6,297	—	—	6,297	28	—	—	28
	2000–2001	6,417	—	—	6,417	28	—	—	28
	Change	120	—	—	120	0	—	—	0
	% Change	1.9%	—	—	1.9%	0.0%	—	—	0.0%
Northwest Territories and Nunavut	1999–2000	18,053	—	—	18,053	90	3	—	93
	2000–2001	18,419	—	—	18,419	90	2	—	92
	Change	366	—	—	366	0	–1	—	–1
	% Change	2.0%	—	—	2.0%	0.0%	–33.3%	—	–1.1%
Canada	1999–2000	4,997,984	305,453	74,453	5,379,409	13,378	1,748	480	15,622
	2000–2001	4,995,776	313,353	78,155	5,388,793	13,280	1,806	497	15,599
	Change	–2,208	7,900	3,702	9,384	–98	58	17	–23
	% Change	0.0%	2.6%	5.0%	0.2%	–0.7%	3.3%	3.5%	–0.1%

Source: Canadian Teachers' Federation, *Economic Service Notes*, September 2001–5.

At Confederation, Roman Catholics in Ontario and Protestants in Quebec were afforded constitutional guarantees with respect to the ability to provide denominational education. These guarantees were reaffirmed for additional provincial jurisdictions. As a result, three provinces currently provide public funding of Catholic separate schools: Alberta, Ontario, and Saskatchewan.[6] With guaranteed choices available, the need for other private schools was less evident. Consequently private schools serve a very small portion of the education system in Canada, forming 4.6% of the total elementary and secondary school enrollments in 1987–1988 and 5.8% in 2000–2001.[7]

The federal government is responsible for providing educational services to First Nations students who are living on reserves in the provinces and to children of armed forces personnel at home and abroad. At 1.5% of the total student enrollments, the federal students are primarily students from First Nations. By province, the proportion of First Nation on-reserve students enrollment ranged from 0.0% in Newfoundland to 7.8% in Manitoba. Between 1999–2000 and 2000–2001, federal elementary and secondary school enrollments increased by 5.0% from 74,453 to 78,155. This total growth reflected increases between 1.1% and 9.7% in each of the nine provinces which have federal students and can be attributed to the increase in school population on the First Nation Reserves. However, many Aboriginal students are not located on reserves, and these Aboriginal students are the responsibility of the provincial jurisdictions.

Public school elementary and secondary enrollments declined slightly from 4.998 million in 1999–2000 to 4.996 million in 2000–2001, with seven out of ten provinces experiencing declines in 2000–2001. Only the provinces of Prince Edward Island, Alberta and British Columbia and the territories, Yukon and Northwest Territories/Nunavut, experienced increases in public school enrollment.

Total public, private, and federal elementary and secondary school enrollments remained relatively stable at the national level, increasing slightly from 5.379 million in 1999–2000 to 5.389 million in 2000–2001. Nevertheless, these modest changes mask more dramatic changes at the provincial and local levels where urban school enrollments are increasing; rural school enrollments are decreasing; and First Nations enrollment on reserves are increasing rather dramatically.

The changes in total enrollments from 1999–2000 to 2000–2001 are similar to the patterns from 1991–1992 to 1998–1999.[8] Over the eight years, enrollments declined in Newfoundland by 22.16%; Nova Scotia by 3.27%; New Brunswick by 8.31%; Quebec by 3.57%; Manitoba by 0.62%; and Saskatchewan by 2.57%. Prince Edward Island enrollment remained almost unchanged, with a slight increase of 0.33%. Enrollments increased in Ontario by 6.90%; Alberta by 9.04%; British Columbia by 13.94%; Yukon by 0.46%; and a combined Nunavut/Northwest Territories by 19.17%. Ontario and Prince Edward Island are the two provinces which appear to have somewhat different patterns. The 2000–2001 estimates suggest that Ontario's long-term growth in enrollment may ameliorate, and Prince Edward Island may experience an increase in enrollment.

Table 3.1 also includes the statistics on the number of schools in each of the jurisdictions. While the total number of public, private and federal schools declined by 0.1%, public schools declined from 13,378 in 1999–2000 to 13,280 in 2000–2001, a decrease of 0.7%. Only British Columbia and Alberta had more public schools in 2000–2001 than in the previous year. The number of federal schools increased by 3.5% while private schools increased by 3.3%.

The number of school divisions in each province/territory is indicated in Table 3.2. There has been a large reduction in the number of school divisions in almost all provincial jurisdictions, primarily achieved through amalgamation. The number of school divisions in Manitoba was further reduced to 37 in 2002, under the stated mandate of reducing administrative costs. In Saskatchewan, the Minister of Education has strongly requested a reduction of 24 school divisions to 72 by 2003. In 1998, Lawton suggested that the provincial school systems had become leaner and more centralized in the 1990s as a result of policies adopted to fight deficits, at the provincial and federal levels, and the recession.[9]

Table 3.2.   School Divisions and Their Funding Sources

Province/Territory	School Divisions	Administrative Units	Education Funding
Newfoundland and Labrador	11	10 Anglophone 1 Francophone	From general revenues (100%).
Prince Edward Island	3	2 Anglophone 1 Francophone	From general revenues (100%).
Nova Scotia	8	5 Regional 2 District 1 Francophone	From general revenue (83%) and mandatory property taxes collected by municipalities (17%).
New Brunswick	14	9 Angophone 5 Francophone	From general revenues (100%).
Quebec	72	9 English 60 French 3 First Nations	From provincial grants (85%) and local property tax levies (15%).
Ontario	72	Public: 31 Anglophone 4 Francophone Catholic: 29 Anglophone 8 Francophone	From general revenues and provincial property taxes. Boards lost the right to local taxation in 1998.

Table 3.2.   (cont.)

Province/Territory	School Divisions	Administrative Units	Education Funding
Manitoba	54	53 Public 1 Francophone	From general revenues and a provincial levy on property (67%). From a school board levy on property (33%).
Saskatchewan	96	75 Public 19 Catholic 1 Francophone 1 Protestant	From general revenue through provincial foundation grant (40%). Boards generate 60% of funding from property tax base.
Alberta	62	41 Public 16 Catholic 5 Francophone	From general revenues and provincial property taxes. Boards may seek elector approval to levy tax up to 3% of their budget allocation.
British Columbia	60	59 Public 1 Francophone	From general revenue and provincial property taxes. Local access to property tax through referenda (rarely used).
Yukon		1 Central Administration 1 Francophone	From general revenues (100%).
Northwest Territories	10	8 DivisionalEducational Councils (DECs) 2 Yellowknife District Educational Authorities (DEAs)	The Yellowknife DEAs level local property taxes to cover at least 25% of their expenditures. The territory collects taxes for the DECs and then allocates 100% of the funds.
Nunavut		1 Central Administration	From general revenues (100%).

Source: Adapted from "Education Across Canada," Chart 1 (Canadian School Boards Association, 2001), http://www.cdnsba.org.

PROVINCIAL/TERRITORIAL FUNDING PROGRAMS FOR SCHOOL INFRASTRUCTURE NEEDS

During the last ten years, governance and financial support for schools in Canada have changed. Most provinces have removed local school divisions' access to property taxes, and these taxes are now collected centrally. The financing of elementary and secondary programs has moved from dependence on local dollars to almost total government support. The funding programs for school infrastructure needs have also changed to reflect the programs used to fund the basic operating grants to schools and the lack of access to property taxes. Table 3.2 provides details on the sources of revenue for elementary and secondary education.

Saskatchewan is the only remaining province which allows school divisions to collect unbridled property taxes. In Saskatchewan, approximately 40% of the educational burden is shouldered by the province, and 60% is supported by the property taxes that are collected for the local school divisions. Since the province has an equalizing formula, there are some school divisions which receive no provincial operating grant while there are others that receive as much as 80% of their expenditures from the province. Similarly, there are differences in the proportion of funds that the province provides for infrastructure, with the range of contributions from the local school divisions expected to be from 14% to 53%, determined by the division's ability to pay. As approximately 20 school divisions receive no provincial operating grant and are considered to be "negative grant" school divisions, the central authority is currently re-examining its property taxation stance and will be forced to make changes to ensure equity considerations.

In all provincial/territorial jurisdictions, the central authority decides which capital expenditures will be incurred. Although there are differences among the provinces, the main approach is similar. School divisions must provide a list of their needs and required information to the central authority. Based on available funding, the central authority uses this information to decide which projects will be funded. There are many more requests than there is funding. In British Columbia, the School Finance and Capital Plan Board ranks the projects, and in Newfoundland, the ranking is completed by the Newfoundland and Labrador Education Investment Corporation. Although many central authorities require annual five year capital plans, the lists of needed projects may actually be incomplete. Because school divisions know they will have little chance for success in receiving a capital project, they may not bother to report their needs.

Decisions on funding specific projects are always difficult, and jurisdictions try to ensure equity in the educational program space provided to students province-wide. Priorities vary among provinces but include such items as health; fire; safety; critical space shortage; structural repair/systems/restoration; non-critical space shortage; joint use initiatives; reduction in number of on-site portables; and site accessibility.

Methods of providing capital funding to the school divisions vary greatly. For example, in British Columbia capital funding to the school divisions is accomplished through prepaid capital advances from the province and are recorded as deferred revenue in the capital fund. The deferred capital revenue is recognized over the expected life of the capital asset. In Manitoba, the capital expenditures are financed through 20 year debentures, with repayment of principal and interest costs totally supported by the province through annual operating and capital grants.

The reported capital expenditures for the provinces and territories are provided in Table 3.3.[10] These capital expenditures include expenditures for physical assets of a fixed or permanent nature with a useful life of more than one operating year that are not financed by debt services. They also include expenditures of an annual or cyclical nature for major repairs and upgrades but exclude expenditures for non-major repairs, which would be included in operating expenditures. They do include principal and interest payments and sinking fund payments. Given the wide variation in provincial population, it is not surprising that 1999–2000 capital expenditures across the provinces range from $10.3 million to $1.05 billion. The within-province fluctuations indicate jurisdictions, such as Quebec, Manitoba, and New Brunswick, where capital budgets changed little over the years. In others, like Newfoundland and Prince Edward Island, there is more variability.

Table 3.4 provides the reported capital expenditures per student and displays a very wide range of expenditures reported among the provinces and territories. Newfoundland has the lowest reported expenditure per student at $138, while Yukon has the highest reported expenditure at $1,998. No attempt was made to account for regional cost factors, but it can be assumed that one of the determinants responsible for the large expenditures per pupil in the territories is regional cost. A second determinant would be diseconomies of scale. On a per student basis, the coefficient of variation is highest for Newfoundland and Prince Edward Island, and lowest for Quebec.

As might be expected, jurisdictions experiencing declining enrollments have the lowest expenditures per student, and jurisdictions with increasing enrollments have the highest. (See Table 3.5.) The correlation coefficient between enrollment changes and capital expenditure per student is .66 and the R^2 is .44. The only province which appears to be particularly anomalous is New Brunswick at $978 per student. With a decreasing enrollment, New Brunswick has the third highest capital expenditure among the provinces/territories.

LITIGATION

Litigation concerning school finance, which is so prevalent in the United States, has been relatively uncommon in Canada.[11] Most provinces have not been sued for concerns about equitable or adequate funding. Consequently, much interesting financial data, more readily available in the United States, is not available in Canada. As well, the accuracy of data that is available has not been tested, and there is little discussion of capital expenditure issues. Lawton speculates that the court cases in the United

Table 3.3. Reported Capital Expenditures by Year (in millions of dollars)

Province/Territory	*1991–1992*	*1992–1993*	*1993–1994*	*1994–1995*	*1995–1996*	*1996–1997*	*1997–1998*	*1998–1999*	*1999–2000*
Newfoundland and Labrador	42.4	45.0	22.7	21.3	18.3	26.8	9.9	12.5	12.6
Prince Edward Island	12.9	14.0	13.2	14.8	1.9	4.3	6.7	10.0	10.3
Nova Scotia	66.1	70.5	63.0	69.7	67.2	63.0	52.7	54.1	45.6
New Brunswick[a]	101.0	104.9	112.6	112.4	113.4	119.5	119.2	120.2	124.2
Quebec	444.8	389.9	433.6	456.8	437.7	423.6	440.1	435.0	434.3
Ontario[b]	1,085.1	1,056.7	729.9	1,091.8	1,101.6	783.1	973.8	1174.0	1050.4
Manitoba	64.0	63.7	69.6	69.1	65.9	65.9	76.5	71.7	71.3
Saskatchewan	93.9	67.9	74.3	66.1	68.6	65.8	75.9	87.9	71.1
Alberta	533.3	529.3	496.0	453.7	382.1	320.9	403.4	406.3	404.5
British Columbia	283.2	310.6	378.6	407.2	475.1	455.2	494.8	494.8	512.2
Yukon	na	14.8	5.3	6.8	10.3	10.7	13.9	9.2	11.5
Northwest Territories and Nunavut[c]	na	26.3	18.8	33.8	27.7	29.2	35.1	30.5	15.0

[a] New Brunswick figures for 1996–1997 are for a nine month period only.

[b] In 1993–1994, there was a significant reduction in expenditures in Ontario, resulting from the introduction of a loan-based financing system.

[c] In 2000, Northwest Territories was divided into two territories. This explains the inconsistency in Northwest Territories data from that year. Nunavut data were not available.

Source: Data from Inter-Provincial Education Statistics Project for the years 1997–1998 and 1999–2000. Italicized figures are estimates.

Table 3.4. Reported Capital Expenditures per Student[a]

Province/Territory	1991–1992	1992–1993	1993–1994	1994–1995	1995–1996	1996–1997	1997–1998	1998–1999	1999–2000
Newfoundland and Labrador	$350	$381	$198	$194	$171	$260	$100	$132	$138
Prince Edward Island	533	575	545	610	77	175	278	416	429
Nova Scotia	400	424	380	424	410	384	325	338	288
New Brunswick	717	749	812	823	840	n/a	906	931	978
Quebec	407	358	399	422	402	389	394	390	394
Ontario[b]	584	559	383	566	560	402	494	590	524
Manitoba	518	458	487	375	357	356	414	387	375
Saskatchewan	498	359	394	352	366	352	409	477	390
Alberta	1,112	1,080	1,001	928	763	631	781	776	767
British Columbia	539	582	692	726	831	778	834	835	865
Yukon	na	2,659	961	1,223	1,758	1,747	2,252	1,562	1,998
Northwest Territories and Nunavut[c]	na	1,842	1,241	2,177	1,702	1,772	2,135	1,811	1,598

[a] Enrollment numbers used were full-time equivalent (FTE) enrollments as determined for the Interprovincial Education Statistics Project (Public Schools).
[b] In 1993–1994, there was a significant reduction in expenditures in Ontario, resulting from the introduction of a loan-based financing system.
[c] In 2000, Northwest Territories was divided into two territories. This explains the inconsistency in Northwest Territories data from that year. Nunavut data were not available.

Source: Data from Inter-Provincial Education Statistics Project for the years 1997–1998 and 1999–2000. Italicized figures are estimates.

Table 3.5.   Relationship Between Change in Enrollment and Per-Pupil Expenditure on Capital

Province/Territory	Change in Student Enrollment	Capital Expenditures per Pupil
Newfoundland and Labrador	−22.16	138
New Brunswick	−8.31	978
Quebec	−3.57	394
Nova Scotia	−3.27	288
Saskatchewan	−2.57	390
Manitoba	−0.62	375
Prince Edward Island	−0.33	429
Ontario	6.90	524
Alberta	9.04	767
Yukon	10.46	1998
British Columbia	13.94	865
Northwest Territories and Nunavut	19.17	1598
Correlation	.66	
R^2	.44	

Sources: Change in student enrollment was derived from the Inter-Provincial Education Statistics Project for the years 1997–1998 and 1999–2000. Per-pupil expenditure on capital was derived from Inter-Provincial Education Statistics Project for the year 1999–2000.

States may be moving state school systems to more centralized control, just as legislative actions have in Canada.[12]

A move to limit the ability of school divisions in Alberta to collect property taxes did result in a legal challenge, and the Supreme Court of Canada found the new funding scheme to be constitutional.[13] At issue was the differences in treatment between the Catholic separate school boards and the other public school boards, and it was found that public boards did not have to mirror equality rights of the separate school boards. While the plaintiff was the Alberta School Boards' Association, intervenors included several school divisions in Saskatchewan; trustee associations in Ontario, Saskatchewan, and British Columbia; and the Attorneys General for Ontario, Quebec, New Brunswick, Manitoba, British Columbia, and Saskatchewan.

It seems unlikely that there will be a parallel growth in Canadian litigation to that which has occurred in the United States since the 1970s. Given the minimal access to property taxes for the local school divisions and the heavy reliance on provincial and territorial governments for funding of operating and capital expenditures, disparities in funding between school divisions are less evident. Nevertheless the vast geographical areas, differing needs, and varying costs provide a potential growth area for litigation concerning adequacy. In a time of teacher shortage, the inability of some remote communities to attract teachers will exacerbate the adequacy arguments.

CONCLUSION

The purpose of this chapter was to describe the funding of school infrastructure in Canada. In many provinces, recent changes have removed the right of school divisions to access property taxes. Consequently, capital expenditures are centrally funded by the provinces and territories. Issues become the level of capital funding available to local school boards to provide for the needs of their school divisions and the consequent animosity between school boards and the provincial government, and among the school boards themselves, when only a limited number of projects are funded. The underlying issue for each school division and its constituents remains the adequacy of funding to support the school infrastructure needed to sustain a vibrant educational program. A study which examined the level of needs for school infrastructure across Canada would add much needed information to complete this portrait.

NOTES

1. Gilles Marchand, Director of "*La direction de l'equipment scolaire*," in the Ministry of Education of Quebec, reported a study of current school facilities would be complete at the end of 2001 or early in 2002.

2. In the Yukon, a public K–9 school is established in each rural community for 25 or more school age children if the children are further away than 60 kilometers or 36 miles from their nearest school. For details on each province and territory, see Catherine C. Sielke, John Dayton, C. Thomas Holmes, and Anne L. Jefferson, eds, *Public School Finance Programs of the United States and Canada: 1998–99* (Washington, D.C.: U.S. Department of Education, National Center for Education Statistics, 2001), http://www.nces.ed.gov/edfin/statefinance/statefinancing.asp.

3. In Saskatchewan on the Big River First Nation, there are 566 students in grades K–12 and 40 students in nursery school in 2001–2002. There are 22,000 square feet of school area, including 26 classrooms. This compares to the average school enrollments in Saskatchewan of 236 students.

4. The three territories are Yukon, Northwest Territories and Nunavut. As Nunavut was separated from the Northwest Territories in 2000, in most instances data from Nunavut are not yet available. See Table 3.2 for a list of the provinces.

5. Canadian Teachers' Federation, 2001, "Growth in Full-time Teaching Force Lower in Public than Private Schools," *Economic Service Notes*, September 2001–5, 8–10.

6.   See the second column of Table 3.2 for school division denominations.

7.   Private school enrollments are described in *Statistics Canada, 2001*, "Trends in the Use of Private Education," *The Daily*, July 4, 2001, 1–4, http://www.sstatcan.ca/Daily/English/010704/d010704b.htm; and Canadian Teachers' Federation, 8–10.

8.   Increases were calculated using data from 1991–1992 to 1998–1999 obtained from the British Columbia Inter-Provincial Education Statistics Project, Final Edition, for the years 1997–1998 and 1999–2000, http://www.bced.gov.bc.ca/schools/interprovincial/interp01.pdf.

9.   Stephen B. Lawton, "Trends in Canadian Educational Expenditures: Is the Worst Over?" *Journal of Education Finance* 24 (Fall, 1998): 220–236.

10.   Data for Tables 3.3 and 3.4 were obtained from the British Columbia Inter-Provincial Education Statistics Project for the years 1997–1998 and 1999–2000. The author wishes to recognize the British Columbia Ministry of Education for its Inter-Provincial Education Statistics Project. This project fills a small void in a very large abyss.

11.   For a fuller discussion of the history of school finance litigation and school infrastructure funding issues in the United States, see Chapter 8 of this volume, "School Finance Litigation: A Strategy to Address Inequities in School Infrastructure Funding," by David C. Thompson and Faith E. Crampton.

12.   Lawton, 220–236.

13.   Supreme Court of Canada, *Public School Boards' Association of Alberta v. Alberta (Attorney General)*, 2000 SCC45. File No. 26701, http://www.lexum.umontreal.ca/csc-scc/en/pub/2000/vol2/html/2000scr2_0409.html.

CHAPTER 4

FINANCING CAPITAL FACILITIES IN HIGHER EDUCATION

Mary P. McKeown-Moak
MGT of America, Inc.

ABSTRACT

Capital funding for higher education is a large, complex, and confusing activity. Although the capital resources of the nation's campuses are critically important and represent a huge investment by the states' citizens, the magnitude of these resources has largely been ignored by legislators and other state policymakers. Prospective students, faculty, and staff base a major part of their decisions to become part of a campus on the quality and appearance of the campus facilities. In 1996, it was estimated that a backlog of $26 billion of accumulated deferred maintenance needs existed on U.S. campuses. Five years later, the backlog appears to have gotten larger, and evidence has mounted that the nation's college and university campuses are in deteriorating condition.

Saving America's School Infrastructure, pages 67–99

INTRODUCTION

In Fiscal Year 2002, the estimated value of land, buildings, and equipment at U.S. colleges and universities exceeded $280 billion.[1] The operation of college and university facilities, including buildings, grounds, utilities, and equipment, is a complex management function. This function involves not only the physical assets of the college or university, but also the institution's financial and human resources, accounting for approximately 10% of institutional operating budgets. The physical plant is a critical component of a college or university's resources. The condition of a campus' buildings and grounds reflects their place in the values of institutional leadership. Prospective students, faculty, and staff base a major part of their decision to become part of a campus on the quality and appearance of the campus facilities. Many research studies over the past 20 years have found that the condition and appearance of campus buildings and grounds were very important in the selection of a college or university for more than 50% of high school students.[2] Despite the importance of the physical plant, for the last twenty years college and university administrators have decried the condition of their campus physical plants and equipment to anyone who would listen. The U.S. Congress and state legislatures have heard that academic buildings and equipment are deteriorating and becoming obsolete faster than colleges and universities can respond, and there is evidence that this contention may be correct.

In 1988, Rush and Johnson, working with the National Association of College and University Business Officers (NACUBO) and the Association of Physical Plant Administrators (APPA), studied the capital renewal and deferred maintenance needs of U.S. colleges and universities and concluded that a multi-billion dollar crisis existed.[3] In 1996, Kaiser and Davis updated the Rush and Johnson study, re-examining the huge backlog ($26 billion) of accumulated deferred maintenance needs on U.S. campuses.[4] Five years later, the backlog appears to have gotten larger, and evidence has mounted that the nation's college and university campuses are in deteriorating condition. Nearly 25% of college and university space was constructed before 1950, and another 25% was constructed between 1950 and 1965.[5] This means that about half of all campus buildings and space now are over 35 years old. Since the "useful life" of most buildings is estimated to be 40 years, the evidence suggests that almost half of all campus buildings have outlived their useful lives and are now obsolete. These problems leave many institutions unable to carry out their mission and place capital assets and the safety of students, faculty, staff, and visitors at risk.

What are the components of the capital assets of colleges and universities? How are the nation's college and university capital needs funded? What state policies control how funding is provided to acquire, construct, renovate, or expand campus facilities? This chapter attempts to answer those questions. Capital funding for higher education is a complex and often confusing activity. Although significant attention has been paid to the operating revenues and expenditures (also called current operating budgets) of institutions of higher education, little information is available on funding for the physical plant. This is due, in part, to the nature of fund accounting in higher education. Under fund accounting, revenues and expenditures for capital facilities are reported in the "Plant Fund" category, instead of in current operating funds. Legislatures are more likely to focus attention on the operating budget. In addition, most states provide funding for capital assets "off-line" or out of the "capital budget" instead of the "state operating budget." Consequently, annual financial reports focus on the current operating budget, although the plant fund may be included as a separate component of consolidated financial statements. In addition, operating budget costs are reported under very close guidelines dictated by the American Institute of Certified Public Accountants (AICPA), the National Association of College and University Business Officers (NACUBO), and the Governmental Accounting Standards Board (GASB). Guidelines for reporting capital revenues and expenditures are far less clear.

DEFINITION OF "CAPITAL ASSETS" AND "PHYSICAL PLANT"

In this chapter, the terms "physical plant" and "capital assets" are used interchangeably. "Capital assets" or "physical plant" is used here to mean the buildings, land, infrastructure, and equipment that have been purchased, modified, operated, and maintained by institutions of higher education. Typically, capital expenditures are defined as those for items that exceed a certain dollar amount threshold or have an expected life of longer than a single fiscal year.[6] Construction of a new building is the most common example of a capital expenditure. Other types of capital expenditures include renovations of existing buildings, purchase of land or an existing building, major equipment purchases (those that exceed specified dollar amounts and are expected to last longer than one year, such as a mainframe computer), and infrastructure improvements, including roads and utility tunnels.

However, notwithstanding the definitions used here, some states define expenditures for major equipment not as a capital expenditure but as an operating budget expense. Expenditures for major renovation and building renewal may be paid for from the operating budget. Because of this difference in definition, generalizations about capital funding in higher education are difficult to make. In addition, states and individual institutions may fund capital expenditures either through the operating budget or through the capital budget. These issues are discussed in more detail in the following sections.

DATA SOURCES

Because little information is available from reliable sources, two surveys were completed to collect data for this chapter. The first survey of all the states' higher education financial officers (SHEFOs) was conducted in February, 2001, collecting information on the sources of funding for capital assets, as well as total state appropriations for physical plant. The purposes of this survey were not only to collect information on the nature and magnitude of state funding for the physical plant, but also to determine if states had begun to address the deteriorating condition of campuses. This survey built upon the results of an earlier survey of SHEFOs completed by Filipic at the Ohio Board of Regents, which set a baseline of funding against which progress (or regress) on funding capital facilities needs could be measured.[7] This survey supported the contention that substantial variations exist in state practice on funding of capital projects. The second survey, completed in December 2001, interviewed state chief budget officers, SHEFOs, or whomever was designated the most knowledgeable person regarding the funding and condition of college and university physical plants in each state. Particular attention was paid to state policies on funding various types of campus activities. The results of the surveys were used to provide all data in the tables and figure in the chapter.[8]

REVENUE SOURCES FOR CAPITAL PROJECTS

Unlike elementary and secondary school districts, the majority of colleges and universities do not have the power to levy taxes to fund capital projects. The exceptions to this rule include certain local universities, such as Washburn University of Topeka, Kansas, and local community colleges that have taxing powers, although not all community colleges have taxing authority. All other private and public colleges and universities have to rely upon other sources of revenue for funding capital items.

Revenues to fund capital expenditures may come from several different sources: operating budget surpluses; private gifts and grants; state or local appropriations; state or local bonding; certificates of participation; or institutional bonding (usually with a requirement that the state legislature give permission to issue bonds). In addition, if state appropriations are made for capital items, the appropriation may be made to the institution's operating budget or capital budget; or to the operating or capital budget of another state agency, like a state department of general services or state department of planning.

Capital projects cover a wide range of higher education functions, including instruction, research, public service, and institutional operations. These functions are commonly referred to as Education and General (E & G) operations. Other functions include student activities, athletics, and auxiliary enterprises such as residence halls, parking structures, and bookstores. In addition, some universities operate golf courses and other recreation facilities.

Historically, revenue-generating activities like residence halls and parking structures that are not essential to instructional services or E & G functions had to be self-supporting, and any capital items were funded out of their own revenues. College and university facilities that are used for academic instruction, research, public service, and institutional functions, such as libraries, student services, or institutional support, that support the institution's primary missions have been funded primarily through state or local sources. Those state or local sources include appropriations and state or local general obligation bonds, although other funds collected and appropriated by the state and often dedicated by statute or state constitution are included in this category. States with limited bonding authority also have used student fees as a bonding mechanism, replacing the student fee revenue with state appropriations for operations. Public institutions that have local bonding authority (mostly community colleges) often are required to use local bonding for E & G buildings. In addition, some states require the use of grant and contract research overhead monies to fund buildings that house research laboratories.

Student fees traditionally have funded facilities that house student activities. These facilities include student unions, student activity centers, and buildings that house student government or other student-run operations. Often the construction costs for the facilities are financed through revenue bonds, with student fees pledged as debt support.

Revenue generated from athletic events has been used to fund athletic facilities. Institutions with large athletic programs, generally National Collegiate Athletic Association (NCAA) Division 1 universities, may not be permitted to use state funds for the athletic facilities. However, institutions with smaller athletic programs or institutions that are responding to Title IX issues may be permitted to use state funds for athletic facilities and equipment.

Revenue bonds typically fund facilities that house auxiliary enterprise activities, and the debt service on these bonds is paid from revenues generated by the auxiliary enterprise. Activities that generally are in this category include bookstores, student housing, and food service. However, at smaller colleges, state or local revenues may fund facilities and equipment for these functions.

The above distinctions may be blurred by different interpretations of what is included in "E & G." In numerous instances, especially for new institutions, small and rural colleges, or under strong political consideration, athletic, auxiliary, and student activity facilities may be eligible for state funding. A further complication is a facility or equipment that serves multiple functions. Facilities containing E & G operations also may house athletic facilities or student housing. Because of the location of some student activity facilities like student unions, certain student services functions of the institution may be co-located in these facilities. The mixing of functions and facilities results in the blurring of traditional capital financing lines. The states using each form of funding are displayed in Table 4.1, and each funding source is discussed in the paragraphs that follow. Because all states permit institutions to receive gifts for capital items, and some institutions may be able to carry forward surplus operating budget funds for capital items, those two sources are not displayed in Table 4.1.

Operating Budget Surpluses

Some institutions are fortunate enough to generate operating budget surpluses that fund capital investments, but this is the source of funding in only a small minority of cases. Because capital expenditures, especially for the construction of new buildings, generally involve millions of dollars, institutions typically have to plan and "save" resources over more than one fiscal year to have sufficient funds for construction or major renovations.

In some states, institutions may carry forward funds from the end of one fiscal year into subsequent years that would permit funding of capital items. In other states where statute does not permit carrying forward of state funds, institutions either will carry forward tuition and fees, or other operating budget revenues from sources other than state appropriations; or the institution will transfer funds out of the current operating budget into Plant Funds. The transfer of operating funds to Plant Funds is considered an expenditure during the current fiscal year in the operating funds' budget. Unexpended funds transferred from operating accounts may be held in Plant Funds indefinitely until expended. There is some danger in transferring funds and holding those funds in "fund balances" for financing major capital projects. For example, in a year when Arizona was facing operating budget deficits, the state "swept" unexpended and unencumbered fund balances into the state treasury. Some school districts and universities lost millions of dollars that had been planned for use in building projects.

Table 4.1. Sources of Capital Funding for Public Higher Education

State	Funding for 4-year Institutions				Funding for 2-year Institutions			
	State Appropriation	State Bonding	Institutional Bonding	Other	State Appropriation	State Bonding	Institutional Bonding	Local Appropriation or Bonding
Alabama	1	1	1		1	1	1	
Alaska	1		1		1		1	
Arizona	1		1				1	1
Arkansas	1	1	1		1	1	1	
California	1	1	1			1	1	1
Colorado	1		1		1		1	
Connecticut		1	1			1	1	
Delaware	1	1	1	1	1	1	1	1
Florida	1		1		1		1	
Georgia	1	1	1		1	1	1	
Hawaii	1	1	1		1	1	1	
Idaho	1		1		1		1	
Illinois	1	1	1		1	1	1	1
Indiana		1	1			1	1	
Iowa	1	1	1				1	1
Kansas	1	1	1				1	1
Kentucky		1	1			1	1	
Louisiana		1	1	1		1	1	1

Table 4.1.   (cont.)

State	Funding for 4-year Institutions				Funding for 2-year Institutions			
	State Appropriation	State Bonding	Institutional Bonding	Other	State Appropriation	State Bonding	Institutional Bonding	Local Appropriation or Bonding
Maine	1	1	1		1	1	1	
Maryland	1	1	1		1	1	1	1
Massachusetts	1	1	1		1	1	1	
Michigan	1	1	1		1	1	1	1
Minnesota	1	1	1			1	1	
Mississippi	1	1	1				1	1
Missouri	1		1				1	1
Montana	1	1	1				1	1
Nebraska	1	1	1				1	1
Nevada	1		1		1		1	
New Hampshire	1	1	1			1	1	
New Jersey	1	1	1	1	1	1	1	
New Mexico	1	1	1		1	1	1	1
New York		1	1		1	1	1	1
North Carolina	1	1	1		1	1	1	1
North Dakota	1	1	1	1	1	1	1	
Ohio	1	1	1		1	1	1	
Oklahoma	1	1	1	1	1	1	1	

Table 4.1.   (cont.)

State	Funding for 4-year Institutions				Funding for 2-year Institutions			
	State Appropriation	State Bonding	Institutional Bonding	Other	State Appropriation	State Bonding	Institutional Bonding	Local Appropriation or Bonding
Oregon	1	1	1		1		1	1
Pennsylvania	1	1	1		1	1		1
Rhode Island	1	1	1			1	1	
South Carolina	1	1	1			1	1	1
South Dakota			1				1	
Tennessee	1		1		1		1	
Texas		1	1			1	1	1
Utah	1	1	1		1	1	1	1
Vermont		1	1			1	1	
Virginia	1	1	1		1	1	1	1
Washington		1	1	1		1	1	1
West Virginia	1	1	1		1	1	1	
Wisconsin		1	1			1	1	1
Wyoming	1		1	1	1		1	1
TOTAL	40	40	50	7	29	34	49	25

Gifts and Donations

Some capital expenditures are made through contributions to the institution as major gifts from private donors or corporations. So-called "capital campaigns" to raise private gifts are a common method of raising funds to build, expand, or enhance facilities. Occasionally, the federal government will provide funding for capital equipment or buildings as a form of "gift" or "donation." However, this is extremely rare, and generally federal government funding of capital items is made only for research universities.

State General Operating Revenues

Another form of capital funding for public institutions is through the state's budget process. In some states, the legislature has designated certain revenue sources, such as lottery funds, for capital purposes. In these states, capital budget requests from those agencies with access to the funds are evaluated each year or biennium in light of projected available revenues and the total competing needs.

Other states fund capital projects with unbudgeted surpluses from the general revenue fund or with budgeted general revenue funds. The use of budget surpluses reached a peak in Fiscal Years 1999, 2000, and 2001, when many states had the luxury of greater-than-anticipated state revenues. In Fiscal Year 2002, 40 states indicated that state appropriations could be used to fund capital projects at four-year colleges or universities, and 29 states indicated that state appropriations could be made to fund capital items at two-year institutions. Although this might seem like significant amounts of state appropriations were available for higher education capital projects, not all states actually appropriated state revenues for capital projects. Actual state appropriations are discussed in the next section.

Bonding

The most common method of funding capital projects is through bonding, with state or local general obligation bonds; certificates of participation; or institutional, state, or local revenue bonds. Under state or local general obligation bonds (GOBs), general revenues of the state or local taxing district are pledged to fund the debt service on the bonds. Under revenue bonds, specific revenues (either state, local, or institutional) are pledged to fund the debt service. In Fiscal Year 2002, 40 states provided state general obligation bonding authority for four-year public colleges and universities, while 34 states provided state GOBs for two-year institutions.

The amount of state debt may be limited by constitutional or statutory provisions. In most states that have provisions limiting state debt, the debt limit is set as a percentage of state revenues. When revenues are increasing, additional debt may be issued each year. However, when revenues decline, as happened in 2002 following expanded state revenues in 1999–2001, Kentucky and several other states found themselves in the position of having more debt than the debt limit would permit. Consequently, some of the already scarce state revenues had to be used to buy down debt until the debt limit was reached.

Bond rating firms, such as Standard and Poor's, usually give higher ratings to general obligation bonds (GOBs) rather than to institutional or local revenue bonds. GOBs and state revenue bonds are tied to the "full faith and credit" of the state issuing the bonds, and such bonds may receive the highest bond rating. When state revenues decline, however, bond rating agencies may downgrade the institution's credit rating. A lower credit rating means that the institution may have to pay higher interest rates to secure the "loan" and adds to the costs of construction. A downgrade from an AAA to an A+ rating may result in a difference of 1.875% in the cost of the loan.

All states permit institutional bonding authority to four-year institutions for capital projects, and only Pennsylvania did not indicate that two-year institutions had institutional bonding available. Alaska, Colorado, Florida, Indiana, Nevada, South Dakota, and Tennessee do not permit state or local GOBs to generate revenues for capital projects at two-year institutions. In these states either state appropriations, gifts, and/or institutional bonding provide funding for capital expenditures. Long-term debt is the primary institutional method of funding capital projects that house auxiliary enterprise activities. Auxiliary enterprises include dining halls, residence halls, bookstores, and, in some cases, student unions. A portion of the revenue stream from operations can be dedicated to repayment of the debt. In private universities and for academic buildings at public colleges and universities, a portion of the revenue stream from tuition and fees may be dedicated to repayment of debt service. For example, prior to 1997, tuition at any State University of New York (SUNY) institution was used to fund the debt service on academic capital projects, including purchase of major equipment.

State and institutional budget/financial officers prefer that bonds be general obligation bonds rather than revenue bonds because interest rates on GOBs typically are lower than interest rates on revenue bonds. It is very unlikely that a state would default on GOBs, but revenue streams can become constricted, causing a lowering of credit ratings and an increase in the cost of the bond offering.

Specialized Fees

Another method of raising revenues for capital projects is through specialized fees. For example, students at an institution may decide to fund a building such as a campus recreation center by imposing a fee on themselves to be used exclusively for the construction and maintenance of a building; or the board of trustees may determine that the institution will charge a fee for facilities renewal, and all funds generated by the fee will be used for capital projects. Recreation centers, tennis courts, playing fields, student unions, campus lighting, and child care centers are examples of capital projects that have been constructed or improved by special fees.

Other Sources of Revenue

In addition to the methods of raising revenue discussed above, seven states indicated that institutions in their state used some other form of financing capital projects. One form of "funding" is a lease-purchase arrangement. In a lease-purchase, the college or university enters into an agreement with a private contractor to build a facility on land held by the college or university, and the institution then leases back the building constructed by the private contractor. At the end of a specified period of time, the building becomes the property of the college or university. This type of "funding" pays for the building out of current operating funds; it is used most commonly for parking structures or residence halls where there is a revenue stream to fund the lease payments, but it also has been used for lecture halls and research facilities. Another source of revenues for capital funding is a special "endowment" fund. Here, the state sets a fund for use in the capital budget. Revenues for the fund may come from some windfall, like the tobacco settlement, and are dedicated to the special purpose of capital expenditures.

STATE FUNDING OF CAPITAL PROJECTS

Each state funds higher education capital projects differently. Indeed, there are different relationships between the capital and operating budgets, and which budget includes which items. For example, in Alabama, all appropriations are made to the operating budgets of the institutions. The institutions must then determine how to allocate the resources among the operating and capital budgets. In Idaho, the legislature appropriates funds to both the capital and operating budgets, and funds for the capital budget may not be used for operating budget items. In California, the legislature also appropriates funds to both the capital and to the operating budgets. In addition, the state may appropriate funds to service debt or pay bondholders directly. In Maryland, the legislature appropriates operating funds to the institutions, but appropriations for the capital budget go directly to another state agency to be used for projects at higher education institutions. In Kentucky, capital funding includes major building projects, repairs and renovations, and major equipment while operating budget funding includes utilities. (This is the most common method of allocating resources between the capital and operating budgets.) In contrast, other states include only major building projects in the capital budget; and equipment, repairs and renovations, and utilities are included in the operating budget.

In addition, state spending for capital items varies from year to year. One state may provide significant amounts for capital items in one year and none the next. In one year, direct state appropriations from general revenues may fund capital items, and, in the next, all capital projects require bonding. For example, Minnesota provided $102 million in 1992 but only $5.2 million in 1993 and no funds at all in 1995. The $5.2 million in 1993 was a direct appropriation for construction, while the $102 million in 1992 was a combination of bonding and direct appropriations.

Figure 4.1 displays state capital spending for the ten year time period 1991 to 2000. In this graph, state capital spending is defined to include state bond funds as well as appropriations from state special or general revenues. These data are from 19 states that responded to the first SHEEO survey.[9] In these states, total state capital spending increased from $1.9 billion in 1991 to $3.1 billion in 2000, reaching a low point of $1.3 billion in 1995. In 2000, only $700 million of the total $3.1 billion was in the form of appropriations, and the remaining $1.8 billion was in the form of state bond funds. The data cannot be extrapolated to reach a total amount for the nation because the 19 responding states likely are not representative of the other states, particularly because the two largest states, Texas and California, provided data.

To make matters more confusing, states may appropriate funds for capital items into the operating or capital budgets of either the institution or another state agency. As was indicated earlier, states fund capital items in both operating budgets and in separate capital budgets. States, such as Illinois and Maryland, provide funding for capital to the budgets of agencies other than colleges and universities or their governing boards. Other states provide funding directly to the institution but may make the appropriation to the operating budget rather than to the capital budget. The funds may be used for new construction; repair and renovation; infrastructure such as roads and utility tunnels; equipment; or debt service. Debt service is the repayment of bond interest and principal. States often require institutions

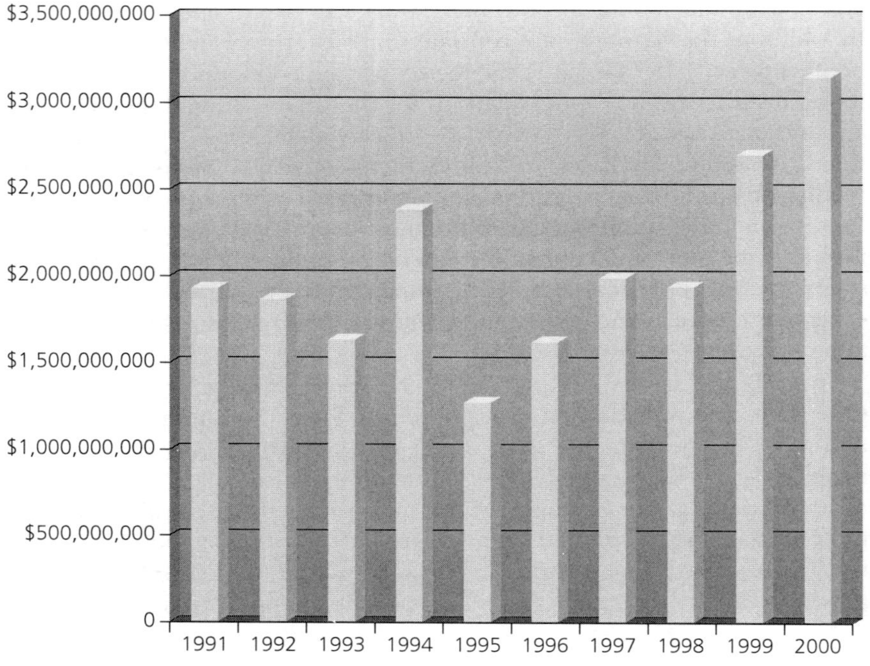

Figure 4.1.   State Capital Spending, 1991–2000

to bond to obtain funds for capital projects but will provide state appropriations to cover the debt service requirements.

Tables 4.2 and 4.3 display information on Fiscal Year 2001 state appropriations for capital items in 37 states by type of project and by budget receiving the appropriation. These data may not be representative of all states, but it safely may be concluded that over $5 billion was appropriated for capital expenditures during Fiscal Year 2001. This number is significantly greater than appropriations in prior years because states were enjoying large budget balances in a good economy. It appears that many states remembered the lessons of earlier in the 1990s when budget shortfalls occurred and appropriated budget surpluses for one-time expenditures on capital. As state budgets become tighter and states experience budget shortfalls, it is unlikely that capital appropriations will continue at this level. In fact, during Fiscal Year 2002, Virginia stopped construction on a number of higher education construction projects because the state was experiencing budget shortfalls.

In Fiscal Year 2001, the 37 states responding to the survey indicated that total state appropriations for higher education capital expenditures totaled $4.5 billion. No state appropriations for higher education capital expendi-

Table 4.2. Fiscal Year 2001 State Appropriations for Capital by Use

State	Institutional Operating Budget				Operating Budget of Another Agency		
	New Construction	Repair/Renovation	Infrastructure	Debt Service	New Construction	Repair/Renovation	Debt Service
Alabama							
Arizona						8,800,000	
Arkansas							
California							
Connecticut							
Delaware							
Florida	235,770,898	26,492,798			223,602,938	16,232,170	
Georgia							
Hawaii							
Idaho							
Illinois							
Indiana				106,500,000			
Iowa							
Kansas							
Louisiana							
Maryland							
Massachusetts	35,816,800						
Missouri							
Nevada							

Table 4.2.   (cont.)

State	Institutional Operating Budget				Operating Budget of Another Agency		
	New Construction	Repair/Renovation	Infrastructure	Debt Service	New Construction	Repair/Renovation	Debt Service
New Hampshire							
New Jersey							
North Carolina							19,000,000
North Dakota		8,097,514					
Ohio							
Oklahoma							
Pennsylvania		31,275,000	6,230,000				
Rhode Island		2,501,068			10,153,227	8,898,967	
South Carolina							
Tennessee							
Texas							
Utah							
Vermont							
Virginia							
Washington							
West Virginia							
Wisconsin							
Wyoming						4,200,000	
TOTAL	271,587,698	68,366,380	6,230,000	106,500,000	233,756,165	38,131,137	19,000,000

Table 4.3.   Fiscal Year 2001 State Appropriation for Capital by Receiving Budget

	Institutional Capital Budget					Capital Budget of Another Agency				Grand Total, All Appropriations
State	New Construction	Repair/ Renovation	Infrastructure	Equipment	Debt Service	New Construction	Repair/ Renovation	Equipment	Debt Service	
Alabama										0
Arizona	1,200,000									10,000,000
Arkansas	62,000,000				24,000,000					86,000,000
California	100,000,000									100,000,000
Connecticut	127,000,000									127,000,000
Delaware										0
Florida										502,098,804
Georgia	3,100,000	3,939,980		34,195,000						41,234,980
Hawaii	36,510,000	62,950,000	10,968,000	6,091,000						116,519,000
Idaho	21,000,000									21,000,000
Illinois	245,700,000	71,600,000								317,300,000
Indiana	44,100,000	32,200,000	11,400,000							194,200,000
Iowa	3,000,000	13,150,000								16,150,000
Kansas		8,000,000			15,000,000					23,000,000
Louisiana	481,198,424									481,198,424
Maryland						348,200,000				348,200,000

Table 4.3. (cont.)

State	Institutional Capital Budget					Capital Budget of Another Agency				Grand Total, All Appropriations
	New Construction	Repair/ Renovation	Infrastructure	Equipment	Debt Service	New Construction	Repair/ Renovation	Equipment	Debt Service	
Massachusetts										35,816,800
Missouri	92,706,958	40,626,950								133,333,908
Nevada		5,000,000			10,000,000	199,500,000	10,000,000			224,500,000
New Hampshire	4,200,000									4,200,000
New Jersey	75,000,000									75,000,000
North Carolina	46,000,000								201,000,000	266,000,000
North Dakota	17,915,000	7,713,544	5,443,000							39,169,058
Ohio										260,842,798
Oklahoma	10,477,282									10,477,282
Pennsylvania		15,000,000					39,345,000			91,850,000
Rhode Island									16,153,215	37,706,477
South Carolina	78,000,000									78,000,000
Tennessee	51,285,000	31,723,000								83,008,000
Texas						28,000,000	54,425,000	79,100,000	13,475,000	175,000,000
Utah						11,358,800	17,356,000			28,714,800
Vermont	5,100,000									5,100,000

Table 4.3. **(cont.)**

State	Institutional Capital Budget					Capital Budget of Another Agency				Grand Total, All Appropriations
	New Construction	Repair/ Renovation	Infrastructure	Equipment	Debt Service	New Construction	Repair/ Renovation	Equipment	Debt Service	
Virginia	53,475,400	115,132,950	24,512,000	12,354,000						205,474,350
Washington	490,000,000									490,000,000
West Virginia	0									0
Wisconsin	100,000,000									100,000,000
Wyoming										4,200,000
TOTAL	2,148,968,064	407,036,424	52,323,000	52,640,000	49,000,000	587,058,800	121,126,000	79,100,000	230,628,215	4,471,451,883

tures were made in Alabama, Delaware, and West Virginia. Of the total appropriated, $743.6 million were appropriated in operating budgets and the remaining $3.7 billion in capital budgets. A total of $3.2 billion was appropriated to institutions, and $1.3 billion were appropriated to other agencies for capital expenditures at institutions of higher education. From a different perspective, $3.2 billion or 72.5% were appropriated for new construction; $635 million or 14.2% for repair and renovation; $405 million or 9.0% for debt service; $131.7 million or 3.0% for equipment; and only $58.6 million or 1.3% for infrastructure. These appropriations are summarized in Table 4.4.

To determine if there is a relationship between state appropriations for the operating budget and state funding for capital expenditures for Fiscal Year 2001, the simple correlation between the two was calculated.[10] The correlation between state capital funds for higher education per capita and state appropriations for the operating budgets of higher education per capita was 0.0171, which was not statistically significant. Therefore, it was concluded that capital support appears to be unrelated to state support for the operating budgets of institutions.[11] It follows then that states that support higher education through their operating budgets are not more likely to provide support for capital budgets. In addition, support for operating budgets did not offset support for capital items or vice versa.

Similarly, capital support appears to be unrelated to demographic projections. The simple correlation between the projected change in high school graduates between 1996 and 2008 and total capital support for higher education between 1991 and 2000 was calculated and was equal to 0.0037. States projecting substantial growth in their public high school graduating classes were not any more likely to spend more for capital projects than states that were projecting no growth or even reduced enrollments in higher education. For example, Arizona predicted a 50% increase in enrollments at public institutions between 1995 and 2010 but appropriated less than $15 million for capital projects in any one year. On the other hand, Wisconsin projected fairly flat enrollments but expended, on average, $70 million per year for higher education capital projects. This evidence may suggest that states like Wisconsin have been dedicating resources to improvement of the condition of campus facilities.

STATE POLICIES ON FUNDING OF CAPITAL PROJECTS

Each state has a different set of policies and practices that governs what facilities and equipment the state will fund and where the funding will be appropriated. There has been a wide variety of funding approaches used in higher education capital funding, and, over time, space for different activi-

Table 4.4. Summary of Fiscal Year 2001 State Appropriations for Higher Education Capital Expenditures

Appropriations Made to:	New Construction	Repair/ Renovation	Infrastructure	Equipment	Debt Service	Total, All Uses
Institutional Operating Budgets	271,587,698	68,366,380	6,230,000	0	106,500,000	452,684,078
Institutional Capital Budgets	2,148,968,064	407,036,424	52,323,000	52,640,000	49,000,000	2,709,967,488
Subtotal, Institutional Budgets	2,420,555,762	475,402,804	58,553,000	52,640,000	155,500,000	3,162,651,566
Other Agency Operating Budgets	233,756,165	38,131,137	0	0	19,000,000	290,887,302
Other Agency Capital Budgets	587,058,800	121,126,000	0	79,100,000	230,628,215	1,017,913,015
Subtotal, Other Agency Budgets	820,814,965	159,257,137	0	79,100,000	249,628,215	1,308,800,317
Total, All Budgets	3,241,370,727	634,659,941	58,553,000	131,740,000	405,108,215	4,471,451,883
Total as a % of Grand Total	72.5%	14.2%	1.3%	3.0%	9.0%	100.0%

ties and functions has been funded in many different ways and from a variety of sources. There are some general practices or policies across all the states related to some types of activities or buildings as was mentioned in a previous section of this chapter. For example, dormitories or residence halls typically are funded from self-generated resources, but this may be a state policy, or it may be practice. As was demonstrated earlier, capital budgets are not "clean" in that what one state funds in the capital budget may be funded in the operating budget of another state or not funded at all.

Over time, higher education facilities have moved away from distinct functions within a building and from state funding only for the educational and general components of the institution. In many states, the policy used to be that instruction and instructional-related buildings and activities were funded by state funds (or local funds for community colleges) while student-related non-instructional activities were funded by student fees. However, building uses have become mixed. In addition, campus buildings are deteriorating, and questions arise about how preservation and maintenance of buildings should be funded. Should building maintenance be funded through operating budgets or through the capital budget? Should the state fund maintenance of facilities that were constructed with other than state funds? Should the use of the building determine how maintenance should be funded? How should it be determined that a campus requires additional space? Should there be space standards that are used to evaluate the need for additional space on a campus? If there is a need for construction of additional space or for renovation, are there guidelines or standards that should be used to determine the cost per square foot of construction or renovation? Should those construction cost guidelines consider the different uses of the space? Should space standards and construction cost guidelines differ for research universities, regional universities, and community or technical colleges?

Although combining different functions into the same facility often is effective and efficient, questions also arise about funding the facility. With so many different combinations possible, it generally is not practical to develop standards for every combination. However, it is practical to develop policies and general guidelines that both the state and institution can use when requesting funding. Table 4.5 lists each state and summarizes how each major type of facility is funded. The facilities are separated into categories for four-year and two-year institutions. The solid block indicates that the facility would be funded by state funds, while the empty block indicates no state funds. Note that solid blocks are present in the E & G category and virtually disappear in the auxiliary category. Almost all states provide funds for E & G facilities, while little state funding is provided to facilities that serve clear auxiliary enterprise functions. Facilities that contain student activities and athletics may receive some state funding, but these facilities are funded primarily from sources other than state funds.

Table 4.5. Funding Sources for Different Facilities: Four-Year Institutions and Community Colleges (CC)

State/Province	E & G Facilities		Student Activity Facilities		Athletic Facilities		Clear Auxiliary Enterprises Facilities	
	4-Year	CC	4-Year	CC	4-Year	CC	4-Year	CC
Alabama	◧	◧	◧	◧	◧	◧	◧	◧
Alaska	■	■	□	◧	◧	◧	□	□
Arizona	■	□	◧	□	□	□	◧	□
Arkansas	■	■	◧	◧	■	■	□	□
British Columbia	■	■	◧	□	□	□	□	□
California	■	◧	□	□	□	□	□	□
Colorado	■	■	◧	◧	□	□	□	□
Connecticut	■	■	□	◧	◧	—	□	◧
Delaware	■	■	◧	◧	◧	◧	◧	◧
Florida	■	■	□	□	□	□	□	□
Georgia	■	■	◧	◧	◧	◧	□	□
Hawaii	■	■	■	■	■	■	□	□
Idaho	■	■	◧	◧	◧	■	□	□
Illinois	■	◧	□	□	□	□	□	□
Indiana	■	■	◧	◧	◧	◧	□	□
Iowa	■	□	□	□	□	□	□	□
Kansas	◧	□	□	□	□	□	□	□
Kentucky	■	■	◧	◧	□	□	□	□
Louisiana	■	■	□	□	◧	◧	◧	◧
Maine	■	■	□	□	□	□	□	□
Maryland	■	◧	□	□	◧	□	□	□
Massachusetts	◧	◧	◧	◧	◧	◧	□	□
Michigan	◧	◧	□	□	□	□	□	□
Minnesota	◧	■	□	□	□	□	□	□
Mississippi								
Missouri								
Montana	◧	□	□	□	□	□	□	□
Nebraska	◧	□	◧	□	□	□	□	□
Nevada	■	■	□	□	◧	◧	□	□
New Hampshire	■	■	◧	◧	◧	◧	□	□
New Jersey	◧	◧	◧	◧	◧	◧	□	□

Key: ■ = State Funds   ◧ = State and Other   □ = Other

Table 4.5.   (cont).

State/Province	E & G Facilities		Student Activity Facilities		Athletic Facilities		Clear Auxiliary Enterprises Facilities	
	4-Year	CC	4-Year	CC	4-Year	CC	4-Year	CC
New Mexico	■	■	□	■	□	□	□	□
New York	■	◧	■	◧	◧	◧	□	◧
North Carolina	■	◧	◧	◧	□	□	◧	◧
North Dakota	■	■	■	■	■	■	◧	◧
Ohio	■	■	◧	◧	◧	◧	◧	◧
Oklahoma	■	■	◧	◧	◧	◧	□	□
Ontario	◧	◧	□	□	□	□	□	□
Oregon	◧	□	□	□	□	□	□	□
Pennsylvania	◧	◧	□	□	◧	◧	□	□
Rhode Island	■	■	□	■	□	■	□	■
South Carolina	◧	◧	◧	◧	◧	◧	◧	◧
South Dakota	◧	—	□	—	□	—	□	—
Tennessee	■	■	◧	◧	□	□	□	□
Texas	◧	◧	◧	◧	◧	◧	□	□
Utah	◧	◧	□	□	□	◧	□	□
Vermont	■	■	□	□	□	□	□	□
Virginia								
Washington	■	■	□	□	◧	◧	□	□
West Virginia	◧	◧	□	□	□	□	□	□
Wisconsin	■	□	□	□	□	□	□	□
Wyoming	◧	◧	□	□	□	□	□	□

Key: ■ = State Funds   ◧ = State and Other   □ = Other

All the states from which information was obtained indicated that state funds in some form are used for the funding of E & G facilities at four-year colleges and universities. Thirty-two states fund four-year E & G facilities primarily from state sources, while another 17 states fund these facilities by a combination of state and other funding. For two-year community and technical colleges, 25 states fund E & G facilities primarily from state sources, and seven states do not provide any state capital funding. Sources other than state funds primarily funded facilities that housed auxiliary enterprises. In fact, only eight states reported that they provide some state capital funds for auxiliary enterprise facilities or equipment at four-year institutions, and ten states provide state capital funds for auxiliary enterprises at two-year institutions. One state, Rhode Island, funds all community college facilities from state sources. Student activities and athletic facilities are more likely to receive state support. About half the states provide some capital funding. These states indicated that state support is provided for these facilities either because of the size or the location of the institutions.

Many situations are less clear-cut than structures that contain only academic functions or auxiliary functions. State policies related to funding for multi-purpose buildings may tie the source of funding for a facility to its use(s) or function(s). States were asked if a policy or consistent practice exists relating the fund sources to the uses of the facility. For example, state capital facilities staff members were asked if student unions that house enrollment management functions could be constructed or renovated from different fund sources than student unions that housed only student activity functions. Thirty-three states responded that policies or well-defined practices on funding exist, but only 29 states follow their policies consistently. Only 27 states have policies that state that maintenance costs for a facility constructed from a non-state funding sources must be paid by non-state funds.

Tables 4.6 and 4.7 identify state practices or policies on various multi-use facilities. The types of facilities are grouped to easily identify of states that vary policies or practices based on the function of the facility. For four-year institutions, state funds are provided for education and general facilities and in many states for portions of facilities that are related to the E & G functions of the institution. The same general principle is in place for community or technical colleges where state or local revenues fund E & G buildings and also the E & G-related portions of student activities, athletic, or auxiliary facilities. However, for community colleges, fewer distinctions are made between state or local funding for portions of buildings that might house auxiliary or student activity functions. When buildings are devoted entirely to student activities, intercollegiate athletics, or an auxiliary enterprise such as a bookstore, usually no state funding is provided. When the facility is a mixed-use building, there is no clear pattern of funding among the states.

State staff members were asked how the state determines the need for additional space and if cost-per-square-foot standards exist for construction or renovation. The most common method of determining the need for additional space is to use a standard for different types of space set by the Council for Educational Facilities Planners International (CEFPI) that relates square footage needs to the number of students, staff, and programs that an institution has. The calculated "need" then is compared to a space inventory that is maintained by type of space. Space is classified into classrooms, laboratories, offices, library space, greenhouses, dormitories,

Table 4.6.   State Policies or Practices on Capital Funding for Facilities on Four-Year Campuses

State/Province	General Academic w/Research	Library w/ Student Commons	Student Union w/ Enrollment Mgnt	Student w/o Enrollment Mgnt	New Football Practices Facility	Multi-use Athletic Facility	New Bookstore in Academic Building	Addition to Bookstore	Building for Childcare	Building for Wellness Center	Renovation of Central Plant
Alabama	◧	◧	◧	◧	◧	◧	◧	◧	◧	◧	◧
Alaska	■	■	■	□	◧	◧	■	◧	■	□	■
Arizona	◧	◧	◧	□	□	□	◧	◧	□	◧	◧
Arkansas	■	■	■	◧	■	■	◧	□	■	■	■
British Columbia	◧	◧	□	□	□	◧	◧	□	□	◧	◧
California	◧	◧	◧	□	□	□	◧	□	□	□	◧
Colorado	◧	◧	◧	◧	□	◧	◧	□	□	□	□
Connecticut	■	—	□	□	◧	◧	◧	■	◧	□	■
Delaware	◧	◧	◧	◧	◧	◧	◧	◧	◧	◧	◧
Florida	◧	◧	◧	□	□	◧	◧	◧	◧	—	■
Georgia	◧	◧	◧	◧	◧	◧	◧	◧	—	—	◧
Hawaii	◧	■	■	■	■	■	◧	□	■	—	■
Idaho	■	◧	◧	◧	◧	◧	□	□	□	◧	■
Illinois	◧	◧	□	□	□	◧	◧	□	◧	□	◧
Indiana	◧	◧	◧	□	□	◧	◧	□	◧	□	■
Iowa	◧	—	◧	□	□	◧	—	□	◧	□	□
Kansas	◧	—	—	□	□	□	—	□	□	□	◧

Key: ■ = State Funds   ◧ = State and Other   □ = Other

Table 4.6.   (cont.)

State/Province	General Academic w/Research	Library w/ Student Commons	Student Union w/ Enrollment Mgnt	Student w/o Enrollment Mgnt	New Football Practices Facility	Multi-use Athletic Facility	New Bookstore in Academic Building	Addition to Bookstore	Building for Childcare	Building for Wellness Center	Renovation of Central Plant
Kentucky	◧	—	◧	◧	□	◧	◧	□	□	□	■
Louisiana	◧	◧	—	□	◧	◧	◧	◧	◧	—	■
Maine	◧	◧	◧	□	□	□	◧	□	—	—	□
Maryland	■	■	■	□	◧	◧	◧	□	□	□	■
Massachusetts	◧	◧	◧	◧	◧	◧	□	□	◧	—	—
Michigan	◧	◧	◧	◧	□	◧	□	□	◧	—	□
Minnesota	◧	◧	◧	□	□	◧	◧	□	◧	□	◧
Mississippi											
Missouri											
Montana	◧	◧	—	□	□	◧	◧	□	□	□	◧
Nebraska	◧	◧	◧	□	□	◧	—	□	◧	□	◧
Nevada	◧	◧	◧	□	◧	◧	◧	□	□	—	◧
New Hampshire	◧	◧	◧	◧	◧	◧	◧	◧	◧	◧	◧
New Jersey	◧	◧	◧	◧	◧	◧	◧	◧	◧	—	◧
New Mexico	■	◧	◧	□	□	◧	◧	□	◧	—	■
New York	■	◧	■	■	◧	◧	□	□	◧	■	■
North Carolina	◧	◧	◧	◧	□	◧	—	□	□	□	◧

Key: ■ = State Funds   ◧ = State and Other   □ = Other

Table 4.6.   (cont.)

Key: ■ = State Funds   ◧ = State and Other   □ = Other

State/Province	General Academic w/Research	Library w/ Student Commons	Student Union w/ Enrollment Mgnt	Student w/o Enrollment Mgnt	New Football Practices Facility	Multi-use Athletic Facility	New Bookstore in Academic Building	Addition to Bookstore	Building for Childcare	Building for Wellness Center	Renovation of Central Plant
North Dakota	■	■	■	■	■	■	■	■	◧	■	■
Ohio	◧	◧	◧	◧	◧	◧	◧	◧	◧	◧	◧
Oklahoma	■	◧	◧	◧	◧	◧	◧	◧	◧	◧	◧
Ontario	◧	◧	◧	□	□	◧	◧	□	□	□	◧
Oregon	◧	◧	◧	◧	◧	◧	◧	◧	◧	—	◧
Pennsylvania	■	◧	□	□	◧	◧	◧	□	—	□	□
Rhode Island	■	□	□	□	□	□	□	□	□	□	□
South Carolina	◧	◧	◧	◧	◧	◧	◧	◧	◧	◧	◧
South Dakota	◧	◧	□	□	□	□	□	□	□	□	□
Tennessee	■	◧	◧	□	□	◧	—	□	—	—	◧
Texas	◧	◧	◧	□	◧	◧	■	◧	◧	□	■
Utah	◧	◧	◧	□	□	◧	◧	□	□	◧	◧
Vermont	■	◧	◧	□	□	□	◧	□	□	◧	■
Virginia											
Washington	◧	◧	◧	□	◧	◧	◧	◧	◧	—	◧
West Virginia	◧	◧	◧	□	□	◧	◧	□	—	—	◧
Wisconsin	◧	◧	—	□	□	◧	◧	□	◧	—	□
Wyoming	◧	◧	□	□	□	□	□	□	□	□	□

Key: ■ = State Funds   ◧ = State and Other   □ = Other

Table 4.7. **State Policies or Practices on Capital Funding for Facilities on Two-Year Campuses**

State/Province	Library w/ Student Commons	Student Union w/ Enrollment Mgmt	Student w/o Enrollment Mgmt	New Football Practices Facility	Multi-use Athletic Facility	New Bookstore in Academic Building	Addition to Bookstore	Building for Childcare	Building for Wellness Center	Renovation of Central Plant
Alabama	◧	◧	◧	◧	◧	◧	◧	◧	◧	◧
Alaska	■	■	□	◧	◧	■	◧	■	□	■
Arizona	□	□	□	□	□	□	□	□	□	□
Arkansas	■	■	◧	■	■	◧	□	■	■	■
British Columbia	◧	□	□	□	◧	◧	□	□	◧	◧
California	◧	◧	□	□	□	□	□	□	□	□
Colorado	◧	◧	◧	□	◧	◧	□	□	□	□
Connecticut	—	□	□	—	—	◧	◧	◧	□	■
Delaware	◧	◧	◧	◧	◧	◧	◧	◧	◧	◧
Florida	◧	◧	□	□	◧	◧	◧	◧	—	■
Georgia	◧	◧	◧	◧	◧	◧	◧	—	—	◧
Hawaii	■	■	■	■	■	◧	□	■	—	■
Idaho	◧	◧	◧	■	■	□	□	□	◧	■
Illinois	◧	□	□	□	◧	◧	□	◧	□	◧
Indiana	◧	□	□	□	◧	□	□	◧	□	■
Iowa	—	□	□	□	□	—	□	□	□	□
Kansas	—	—	□	□	□	—	□	□	□	□
Kentucky	—	◧	◧	□	◧	◧	□	□	□	■

Key: ■ = State Funds　◧ = State and Other　□ = Other

Table 4.7. (cont.)

State/Province	Library w/ Student Commons	Student Union w/ Enrollment Mgnt	Student w/o Enrollment Mgnt	New Football Practices Facility	Multi-use Athletic Facility	New Bookstore in Academic Building	Addition to Bookstore	Building for Childcare	Building for Wellness Center	Renovation of Central Plant
Louisiana	◧	—	◧	◧	◧	◧	◧	□	—	■
Maine	◧	◧	□	□	□	◧	□	—	—	□
Maryland	□	□	□	□	□	□	□	□	□	◧
Massachusetts	◧	◧	◧	◧	◧	□	□	◧	—	—
Michigan	◧	◧	◧	□	◧	□	□	◧	—	□
Minnesota	◧	◧	□	□	◧	◧	□	◧	□	◧
Mississippi										
Missouri										
Montana	□	—	□	□	□	□	□	□	□	□
Nebraska	□	□	□	□	□	—	□	□	□	□
Nevada	◧	◧	□	◧	◧	◧	□	□	—	◧
New Hampshire	◧	◧	◧	◧	◧	◧	◧	◧	◧	◧
New Jersey	◧	◧	◧	◧	◧	◧	◧	◧	—	◧
New Mexico	◧	◧	□	□	◧	◧	□	◧	■	◧
New York	◧	◧	◧	◧	◧	◧	◧	◧	◧	◧
North Carolina	◧	◧	◧	□	◧	—	□	□	□	◧
North Dakota	■	■	■	■	■	■	■	◧	■	■
Ohio	◧	◧	◧	◧	◧	◧	◧	◧	◧	◧

Key: ■ = State Funds   ◧ = State and Other   □ = Other

Table 4.7.   (cont.)

State/Province	Library w/ Student Commons	Student Union w/ Enrollment Mgnt	Student w/o Enrollment Mgnt	New Football Practices Facility	Multi-use Athletic Facility	New Bookstore in Academic Building	Addition to Bookstore	Building for Childcare	Building for Wellness Center	Renovation of Central Plant
Oklahoma	◧	◧	◧	◧	◧	◧	◧	◧	◧	◧
Ontario	◧	◧	□	□	◧	◧	□	□	□	◧
Oregon	□	□	□	□	□	□	□	□	—	□
Pennsylvania	◧	□	□	◧	◧	◧	□	—	□	□
Rhode Island	■	■	■	■	■	■	■	■	■	■
South Carolina	◧	◧	◧	◧	◧	◧	◧	◧	◧	◧
South Dakota	n/a	n/a	n/a	n/a	n/a	n/a	n/a	n/a	n/a	n/a
Tennessee	◧	◧	□	□	◧	—	□	—	—	◧
Texas	◧	◧	□	◧	◧	■	◧	◧	□	■
Utah	◧	◧	□	□	■	◧	□	□	◧	◧
Vermont	◧	◧	□	□	□	◧	□	□	◧	■
Virginia										
Washington	◧	◧	□	◧	◧	◧	◧	◧	—	◧
West Virginia	◧	◧	□	□	◧	◧	□	—	—	◧
Wisconsin	◧	—	□	□	◧	◧	□	◧	—	□
Wyoming	◧	□	□	□	□	□	□	□	□	□

Key: ■ = State Funds   ◧ = State and Other   □ = Other

etc. Thirty-eight states collect and maintain space inventory information, but not all of those states maintain the data in a format that provides information on the uses of the space. Evaluation of space needs on a campus is quite difficult if information on the current space and the uses of the space is not available. Only seven states require institutions to follow cost guidelines in the construction or renovation process. Firms, such as Means, produce annual cost guidelines at such detailed levels that it is possible to differentiate between a classroom with windows and a classroom without windows.

CONCLUDING COMMENTS

Capital funding for higher education is a large, complex, and confusing activity. Although the capital resources of the nation's campuses are critically important and represent a huge investment by the states' citizens, the magnitude of the resources has largely been ignored by legislators and other state policymakers. An extreme diversity of policies, practices, and funding methods has evolved in each of the states. These are the result of factors unique to each state, including the presence of absence of bonding authority; availability of dedicated revenue streams; the size and diversity of the public higher education system; the availability of local tax sources; and the political traditions of the state. No single state can be said to have a "model" or "best practices" method of funding capital activities that would work in another state. In recent years, the states have earmarked substantial revenues (over \$5 billion in Fiscal Year 2001) to the acquisition, construction, renovation, and improvement of capital assets. Approximately 20% of the funding in that one year alone was dedicated to the repair and renovation of existing facilities. At that rate, it would take over 25 years to erase the backlog of accumulated deferred maintenance needs on U.S. campuses. The revenue picture for many states has changed considerably since July 1, 2001. States that were able to use budget surpluses to fund capital facilities needs are now faced with revenue shortfalls. In this environment, it is unlikely that states will be able to continue funding capital facilities at the Fiscal Year 2001 levels. Institutions will have to seek alternate revenue sources to maintain the capital assets that are so important to carrying out their missions. It is hoped that the capital needs of institutions of higher education will continue to receive priority funding.

NOTES

1. Estimated by the author from data in *Digest of Education Statistics, 2000* (Washington, D.C.: National Center for Education Statistics, 2001).

2. See, for example, Carnegie Foundation for the Advancement of Teaching, "How Do Students Choose a College?" in *Change* (January/February 1986): 29–32.

3. Sean C. Rush and Sandra L. Johnson, *The Decaying American Campus: A Ticking Time Bomb* (Arlington, Virginia: APPA (Association of Higher Education Facilities Officers), 1989).

4. Harvey H. Kaiser and Jerry S. Davis, *A Foundation to Uphold* (Arlington, Virginia: APPA (Association of Higher Education Facilities Officers), 1996).

5. Harvey H. Kaiser, *Crumbling Academe: Solving the Capital Renewal and Replacement Dilemma* (Washington, D.C.: Association of Governing Boards of Universities and Colleges, 1984).

6. J. Kent Caruthers and Daniel T. Layzell, "Capital Master Planning and Capital Budgeting," in Lucie Laposky and Mary McKeown-Moak, eds., *Roles and Responsibilities of the Chief Financial Officer,* Number 107, New Directions for Higher Education (San Francisco, California: Jossey-Bass Publishers, 1999).

7. Matthew V. Filipic, "Capital Survey," Paper presented at the Annual Professional Development Conference of the State Higher Education Executive Officers (SHEEO), Portland, Oregon, 2000.

8. Data from the first survey were first reported in Mary P. McKeown-Moak, *Third Annual Report on the State of the States* (Denver, Colorado: State Higher Education Executive Officers, 2001). The December 2001 survey was completed by J. Kent Caruthers, Denis Curry, Tom Jons, and Mary McKeown-Moak of MGT of America, Inc. for the Governor's Office, State of Washington.

9. Filipic, "Capital Survey."

10. Data on state appropriations per capita were obtained from *Grapevine*. *Grapevine* data are available at http://www.coe.ilstu.edu/grapevine/

11. Filipic, "Capital Survey."

Part II

CURRENT CHALLENGES TO FUNDING OF SCHOOL INFRASTRUCTURE

CHAPTER 5

CAPITAL NEEDS AND SPENDING IN URBAN PUBLIC SCHOOL SYSTEMS

Policies, Problems, and Promises

James G. Cibulka
University of Kentucky

Bruce S. Cooper
Fordham University

ABSTRACT

After decades of piecemeal policies in which states have reluctantly and halt-ingly played a limited role in addressing the infrastructure needs of urban school systems, it is time to recognize a national problem requiring a federal response. Some critics may argue that this is appropriately a state and local responsibility. Yet the perceived dangers of a heavy federal hand are consid-erably less in the area of facilities assistance than in federal aid flows to sup-port specific education programs or widespread school testing. In the case of capital spending, the rationale for federal involvement is clearly consistent with decades of federal education policy: to address the needs of special underserved populations and resource-challenged schools; and to improve the capacity of state and local policymaking systems to address a critical national need. Where state and local policy makers have been unable or unwilling to act to address an enduring crisis, the justification for federal involvement is clear and compelling.

Saving America's School Infrastructure, pages 103–128

INTRODUCTION

The supply of adequate facilities for schooling children in urban systems continues to be a major national problem. As the U.S. General Accounting Office explained:

> The nation has invested hundreds of billions of dollars in school infrastructure to create an environment where children can be properly educated and prepared for the future. Almost exclusively a state and local responsibility, this infrastructure requires maintenance and capital investment. However, public concern is growing that while laws require children to attend school, some school buildings may be unsafe or even harmful to children's health.[1]

For all its importance, however, researchers who study school finance have overlooked the capital side of the ledger, concentrating instead upon operational finances and equity. As differentiated from the "operations" budget, Garms, Guthrie, and Pierce explain that: "Capital expenses are usually limited to the purchase of items of a permanent nature, normally divided into the categories of land and improvements, buildings and equipment."[2]

Yet the management of capital in urban school systems is a critical component of urban education finance because as student populations grow and change, buildings and equipment age and become obsolete; and educational needs and requirements shift, creating the need for plant upgrading or replacement. In addition, capital spending is the largest single "physical" item in most school districts' budgets, dominating public attention and forcing decision-makers to increase their district's spending, to borrow money, and to service the debt.

Although research on financing and economics of public education is well developed, the understanding of the dynamics of the financing of urban school facilities is less well analyzed or predictable.[3] Capital budgeting has qualities that confound researchers and make the practice of capital finance and management more difficult. The confusion stems from the nature of planning, managing, constructing, and improving the physical plant and systems of education; it is neither readily predictable nor highly rational. Yet school finance as a field of research and management is dominated by a rational decision-making model informed by the paradigms utilized in economics and finance. At every turn, we see risks and the unexpected. For example, schools can suddenly, unpredictably leak, catch fire, suffer seismic shock, and break down. Such contingencies can be planned for only within limits.

Also, plans to rebuild facilities may take years longer than predicted, increasing the costs. Changes on the demand side, with large influxes of new students or significant outflows and declines, make the base unit (enrollment or average daily attendance) changeable. Further, student needs change, putting pressures on the physical plant and facilities to keep pace. Garms, Guthrie, and Pierce noted:

> An important characteristic of capital expense is the unevenness of expenditures. Construction of a school in one year may cost several million dollars, with expenditures in succeeding years being almost zero. Unlike the operating budget in which the largest single cost is personnel (salaries and benefits), capital is not so readily divisible or controllable, since buying land, hiring and paying contractors, and fixing buildings are neither easily broken into salary units nor managed with great surety. Only the largest districts, such as New York and Chicago, can manage to even out these expenditures and spend about the same amount each year.[4]

Despite the dominance of a rational decision-making model in this field of study—with its emphasis on technical planning—capital budgeting and management are highly political phenomena. Bond referenda, school closings, location decisions for new schools, efforts to obtain legislative authorizations, and legal demands for equity and access—to name only some examples—are all inherently political components of the capital budget, further contributing to the level of difficulty in understanding and predicting the capital budget. In discussing and illustrating these irrational points, we can learn much about how capital management works and how to research and improve it.

THE STUDY

Given these complexities, we need a more accurate descriptive model that captures the range of factors influencing both the demands that lead to the need for capital spending and the factors that influence how those needs are supplied. This chapter, then, has two purposes: First, we seek to establish a political economy model for balancing the demand side for new and improved facilities with the complexities of the supply side. In laying out the model, we review research evidence supporting the role played by the following factors: (a) educational; (b) economic; (c) political; and (d) institutional factors. In presenting these factors taxonomically, we recognize that in the real world these four categories are not discrete and that it often is difficult to disentangle several factors that operate together.

Second, we explore case studies of the environments where this move toward greater equity of capital support occurs, involving both state and local jurisdictions. We discuss urban school systems within their state jurisdiction because we believe that the state context is absolutely critical for understanding urban school infrastructural challenges—an argument we shall make in more detail later in the chapter. Included are data from Maryland, New Jersey, and Washington concerning just how the states and a sample city in each state have attempted to fund local facilities costs and needs—using Baltimore, Passaic, and Seattle as examples—and how state involvement has complicated the financing of school facilities on both the supply and demand side of the equation.

THE MODEL

This chapter attempts to make sense of the capital management of urban schools in the United States by positing a model that distinguishes between factors influencing demand for capital spending from those factors that influence its supply. Four categories of cause and effect influence demand and supply. First, new educational demands and requirements influence the need for school facilities. Second, economic causes, such as demands on the tax base, land use practices, zoning policies, etc., provide pressures on both the demand and supply side.

Third, since capital funding has become part of a larger movement toward educational equity, and the states have taken on more of the responsibility for funding and regulating facilities' use and construction, we treat capital within a larger political framework. This focus involves the states, the courts, and even the federal government—a major change from the mainly local nature of capital construction support in the middle of the 20th century. Mediating and sometimes confusing these influences are the local, county, state, and even federal political systems that determine how funds for capital are to be raised and spent. Indeed, the role played by these political factors, in addition to the institutional factors mentioned below, causes us to describe this model as a political economy model.

Finally, since capital is a key part of the structure of schools, we take an institutional view of how capital fits into the larger organizational framework, focusing on the crucial relationship among capital construction and local zoning, land-use, labor relations agreements—the whole apparatus of schools, and their urban settings, as governmental units. These educational, economic, political, and institutional pressures operate on both the demand-side and the supply-side. As shown in Table 5.1, school districts face two competing sets of influences, supply-side and demand-side pressures, when promoting change, growth, and improvements in their educational facilities.

Below, we discuss these demand and supply influences, citing briefly previous research that establishes their importance. After that discussion, we turn to the question of how these factors play out in our cases of urban school system settings.

Table 5.1. Modeling the Causal Factors Affecting Urban School Infrastructure As Demand and Supply

Causes	Demand Factors	Supply Factors	Requirements for Balancing Demand and Supply to Meet Capital Funds
Educational	• Enrollment increases, programmatic shifts, and changing student needs. • Declining enrollments (lead to higher marginal costs). • Private school demand. • Outdated facilities. • Changing educational and social priorities.	• Appropriate facilities. • Strategic decisions about program resources.	• Enrollment changes, programmatic shifts, and changing student needs are anticipated in a long-term capital/facilities plan, which is revised as above factors change.
Economic	• Municipal overburden. • Land use and development decisions.	• Limited local tax base. • Zoning policies. • High cost of land and construction.	• Adequate local tax base.
Political	• Political support for quality public education.	• Inadequate state funding. • Patronage in contracts and/or jobs. • Citizen opposition to closing schools.	• Strong local political support.
Institutional	• Fiscal dependence on city. • Legal limitations on debt service. • Required voter approval. • Collective bargaining contracts. • Increasing state regulation and intrusion into local policymaking, e.g., state education program standards.	• Bureaucratic mismanagement, e.g., poor planning leads to backlog of facilities needs. • Political and legal controls on funding.	• Bureaucratic capacity to manage needs.

DEMAND-SIDE FACTORS

Educational Causes

Demographic trends

Fluctuations in student enrollment are a major factor shaping demand for capital facilities.[5] Population growth or declines are influenced by in-migration and out-migration from neighborhoods and the community; changes in birth rates; age profiles of demographic groups; and retention policies for students. Authorities do census reviews, demographic studies, and future projections, providing fuel for those who argue the need for more schools, better schools, newer schools, and more attractive schools. While demographic growth leads to demands for more spending on facilities, demographic declines leave a surfeit of space associated with increased per-pupil costs for facilities and space use inefficiencies.

A post-World War II perspective shows a long period in which demands for expanding expenditures for public schools were dominant. Buildings and infrastructure were ramped up to handle the amazing growth of the post-war student population and the extension of school upward through high school (for more students) and downward into kindergarten and now into preschool education, creating what is called the P–12 or even P–16 system.[6] As Garms et al. noted, "During the period from World War II to the end of the 1960s, an unprecedented number of new schools were built. The rapid increase in student population, combined with migrations from farms to city and suburbs, made necessary the construction of thousands of new schools."[7]

Changing demographics also leads to a possible influx of students who are disabled, bilingual, and from poverty backgrounds. These changing demographics not only promote increased costs for providing appropriate educational programs,[8] but also can affect demand for facilities because of smaller class sizes, more special equipment, and the like.

Private school demand and supply

Public school facility needs are influenced by demand for private schools and supply of those schools in particular communities. Urban school systems traditionally have had large percentages of the school-age population attending parochial schools,[9] depressing the demand for public school facilities. However, in recent decades many parochial schools have closed due to changes in the parishes that sponsored them or because of changing commitments of dioceses or religious orders that owned and ran these schools. This contraction in the private sector often increased demand for public school facilities. At the same time, the growing demand for private schools in inner-cities and tuition support for low income families to attend these schools has been a counteracting influence; it has had an effect on public school enrollments in those neighborhoods. Obviously, consumer demand for private schools and the changing supply of those schools are important factors affecting public school capital needs.

Outdated facilities

The age and condition of buildings can be a source of demand, independent of demographic trends. Buildings have a limited life span beyond which they become obsolete, unsafe, or simply too costly to maintain.

Changing educational and social priorities

Facilities demands are influenced by a variety of educational and social priorities. The need to desegregate racially separate schools led to the dismantling of dual school systems and efforts to foster racial desegregation, new school programs, and expanded student needs and accessibility. State and federal laws providing access to public education for students with special needs led to demands on school buildings to accommodate these pupils. A variety of other needs have been addressed, e.g., for the gifted and talented, for those with special language needs, and for "least restrictive," and "barrier-free" access. Specialists have been hired and programs developed to meet these needs, all of which create demands for additional space. The growing recognition of the importance of early childhood programs in promoting the cognitive and emotional growth of young children increased pre-school and kindergarten programs. Educational technology has influenced use of school space. To some extent, these priorities are influenced by social custom. For example, the nine-month school year leads to underutilization of school facilities,[10] although in a few places such as California the severe shortage of school facilities necessitated year-round use of facilities in many communities. The inefficient use of our school facilities has the effect of artificially raising demand for the facilities by causing more schools to be built than otherwise would be the case.

Economic Causes

Municipal overburden

In urban areas, the demand for noneducational services is great, particularly when compared with relatively affluent suburbs. The costs of providing transportation, public housing, social welfare, and police services all act as drains on the available tax dollar.[11] Municipal overburden, while it remains controversial among economists, arguably has the effect of depressing economic demand for public school facilities and programs even if the city appears to have property wealth on paper.

Land use and development decisions

The demand for school facilities is influenced by economic decisions in the private marketplace. New residential development leads to the need for additional schools. Construction of commercial buildings in heretofore residential neighborhoods can drive up the cost of housing, causing current residents to flee, thus either accelerating other commercial development or leading to new residents who may be older (reducing demand for public school spaces) or younger (increasing demand). Commercial developments, such as shopping centers can also change the fabric of neighborhoods by making "Mom and Pop" small businesses unprofitable. The absence of local institutions can in turn contribute to higher crime and greater mobility. Schools do not directly control these private market decisions and priorities; yet these choices can profoundly affect the demand for and quality of public education. Such decisions can be regulated by municipalities, of course, which is why we have listed zoning policies as a supply-side factor.

Political Causes

Support for quality public education

Public support for quality public education may be the most important political factor influencing demand for school facilities, proving to be a major problem in cities. A very small percentage of the population uses public schools because of relatively large concentrations of the elderly in many central cities. At the same time, the movement of poor immigrants and others to the cities increases the costs of providing services in these jurisdictions.[12] The perceived quality of urban public schools has declined, and costs have risen, accelerating middle-class flight to private schools and to the suburbs. This out-migration has diminished taxpayer support for increased public school spending, leading to a downward spiral where those with the ability to flee do so.

At the same time, the politics in urban settings and in the nation, more generally, support improvements in public schooling. The business community has been a strong voice in creating sustained pressure for improvements in exchange for increased financial support. The accountability movement of the 1990s has garnered strong support from the nation's political establishment, including the nation's governors. The enactment of President Bush's *No Child Left Behind Act* by the U.S. Congress in 2001 symbolizes the bipartisan political consensus that both more accountability and more resources are important strategies for school improvement.[13] A new breed of urban mayors also recognizes the need to improve public schools as a vital component of the economic resurgence of cities.[14]

Institutional Causes

Fiscal dependence on city

Across the country, only a limited number of school districts are fiscally dependent on other jurisdictions. Urban districts constitute a disproportionately large number of these districts. Historically, urban school systems were run by mayors. Even where reformers succeeded in separating schools from municipal government, suspicious state legislatures often required budgetary review by the city council. This oversight is especially true in the case of capital funding, where the city government may be the only entity with authority to borrow funds for school construction.

Legal limitations on debt service

Even where urban districts have fiscal independence, their borrowing authority may be statutorily limited by the state. This limit also reflects an anti-urban bias, although in some states such limits are imposed on all units of local government as well.

Required voter approval

One way of restricting local authority to borrow is to require voter approval for exceeding a statutorily limited mill rate for capital expenses or even to require all borrowing to go to voters for approval. During the 1970s and 1980s, voters often turned down such levy campaigns, responding to inflationary cycles and declining enrollments. Political resistance to perceived high government spending grew in the 1970s, and school board elections and bond referenda are two of the few, limited avenues citizens have to express their discontent.

Collective bargaining contracts

The construction trade is highly unionized. Union wage rates and negotiated work rules, while perhaps defensible from the point of view of the employees, do drive up the costs of construction. These prevailing rates in urban service areas are among the highest in the country.

Increasing state regulation and intrusion into local policymaking

States play a bigger and bigger role, not only in setting the rules for financing school capital but also for issuing and repaying debt and bonds, and for the procedures determining how these construction resources will be made available to school systems. There is a plethora of state requirements for construction and for education programs. First, all states impose, to varying degrees, health and safety standards, square footage requirements, open land requirements, and the like that influence the costs of new construction and remodeling. Second, state education program standards, such as required programs, mandated class size reductions, and the use of specialists, all have implications for building usage.

SUPPLY-SIDE FACTORS

Educational Causes

Appropriate facilities

The critical question in supplying school facilities to students is: To what degree is the facility (building, classroom, equipment) effective in supporting student learning and the activities of teachers? For example, a chemistry class or a biology class that must be delivered in an outdated, poorly supplied laboratory may affect both students and their teachers by: (1) depriving youth of opportunities to practice principles of science rather than acquire their knowledge only from a textbook, thereby discouraging critical problem solving; and (2) weakening the opportunity for teachers to engage and motivate students with sound pedagogy. Also, libraries with inadequate holdings or inadequate space for computer searches consign students to a second-class education.

Strategic decisions about programmatic resources

School systems have been slow to develop strategies for relating facilities to programs. Buildings may conform to architectural whims and local inspectors but rarely to what teachers and students want and need. Districts and states have been irresponsibly slow in building capital finance policies that relate curriculum and learning to building design and equipment. For example, Passaic, New Jersey, to be discussed later in the chapter, must submit to the state a five-year facilities management plan. The state mandates consideration of all of the following variables in setting priorities and allocating resources:

- Grade configuration at each school;
- Enrollment projects by level, neighborhood, and school;
- Class size and range;
- Dedicated specialty spaces for art, music, laboratories, media centers, resource rooms, small group instruction, administrative offices, nurse suite, parent resource room, and faculty room;
- Community services, such as family counseling, recreation, parenting, libraries, health clinics, and nutritional services;
- Technology, including integration, opening and closing schools, and trailers and leased facilities.

With so many needs and demands, school district decision-makers find it difficult to balance the supply and demands of the system and to set strategic, rational decisions in a highly political, constrained environment. For example, as this is written, the state of New Jersey faces a $4 billion shortfall in its school budget.

Economic and Political Causes

Limited local tax effort and tax bases

The supply of resources is directly related to sources of income, whether from the state, local district, or special construction and development authority. Local wealth and effort are key factors in determining the supply of funds for facilities.

The traditional reliance on local tax levies for facilities funding has failed to keep pace. As Burrup et al. explain, "The uncomplicated and formerly satisfactory system of financing public school capital outlays with funds raised almost solely by local property taxes is obsolete and impractical for present-day use."[15] In prior eras, fewer school-age children attended school for such long periods of time. Now pre-school through high school have increased the student populations and concomitant demand for more space. Costs of construction were lower, and schools facilities were simpler and cheaper. Buildings less often became overcrowded or obsolete; and the resources available per pupil for education (and capital) were more favorable in earlier times.

Cities were once considered property-wealthy jurisdictions. Today, most are below average in per-capita or per-pupil valuations. This supply-side reality worsens when one takes into account the problems on the demand side which already were mentioned. In addition, municipal overburden and declining local support for urban schools simply aggravate the problems of financing facilities from local property taxes.

Zoning policies

School officials are limited by local zoning policies that are often set in response to private market pressures, such as the need for commercial and industrial development. These policies impose limitations on where schools can be built and the cost of obtaining land where zoning is amenable.

High cost of land and construction

A related factor is that the general cost of living in urban areas drives up the cost of land, planning, building materials, and highly unionized construction trades.

Inadequate state support for capital spending

Among school finance reformers, so much attention has been devoted to school operating cost equity that capital funding issues have been virtually ignored until recently. Walter G. Hack explained that "many states have mounted studies and enacted legislation to provide more equity in educational programs and financing. In much of the reform legislation which has been enacted, *little or no modification has been made in the system to finance capital outlay* (emphasis added)."[16] Some data presented in this article actually showed that state interference in the way capital is raised has actually worked to the detriment of those districts it was avowedly designed to help, e.g., poor districts could not afford increased local taxes to pay off bonds or other borrowed capital funds.

Many of these problems arising from a wave of school finance equity lawsuits, for example, from *Serrano v. Priest* in California in 1971[17] through the latest iteration of *Abbott v. Burke* in New Jersey,[18] are now affecting the capital side of the ledger.[19] We know much less about the effects of state equity requirements on financing of facilities than about the support of equitable school operational funding. However, according to Burrup and coauthors, the supply side of funding facilities is being affected by a number of important changes: (1) states bearing the major and ultimate responsibility for the funding of school capital development; (2) equity being difficult to incorporate into the varied capital outlay debt encumbered by districts across the state; (3) high debt not being carried by districts for long periods of time as it cuts into funding available for other programs and services; and (4) some districts being limited by their ability to raise funds for capital and debt service because of lower property values and weaker ability to raise local taxes (on property).[20]

In fact, applying the notion of fiscal neutrality,[21] many states have been much slower to guarantee districts the resources to provide equal facilities than in equalizing school operating spending across systems. While the demand for more and better school facilities has increased, the ability of districts—and their states—to supply funds in an efficient and equitable manner has not kept pace. Barr and Wilkerson explain the problem as follows:

> Funding of facilities, except in a few states, has been a low-priority item in public school finance. Sophisticated formulas have been devised for cooperative state and local financing of current operation, of special programs, and of some specific services, but equal diligence has not be exerted in many states in devising feasible programs for state and local support of capital outlay and debt service.[22]

Much has happened since 1965 when this statement was made. States have been under rising pressure to provide more funding for capital programs; and state courts have ruled increasingly that equal education funding includes more than just operations. The state thus has an abiding constitutional responsibility to help the poorer communities to build new buildings, repair old ones, and to meet the space needs of districts, recognizing that local communities that are property-poor cannot pay for these capital improvements by raising the local property tax rates.

Patronage in contracts and/or jobs

In some cities there is anecdotal evidence that high costs of supplying school facilities are related to patronage. Allegedly, lucrative contracts are awarded to developers and contractors who are friends of public officials, and jobs are provided for political supporters, not to mention the political clout of the construction unions that demand higher wages in exchange for their political support. At one time, powerful political machines in American cities did control such decisions. This is less true today. The decline of political machines has been fueled by a vigilant press, new political coalitions, a better educated citizenry, and changes in laws pertaining to contract procurement. Nonetheless, such influence-peddling still exists in varying degrees and, where it exists, inflates facilities costs.

Citizen opposition to closing schools

School systems saddled with old facilities and declining enrollments usually have a need to close facilities. However, this step is particularly difficult politically. Neighbors fear a decline in property values, and school alumni retain sentimental loyalties to their underutilized alma maters. Those who advocate school closings have few political allies in such conflicts. As a result, school officials often find it easier to leave open half-empty and outdated facilities, driving up per-pupil costs.

Institutional Causes

Bureaucratic mismanagement

One of the complications of supplying adequate facilities results from poor planning and management. Given the insularity of many urban school bureaucracies, the professional qualifications of personnel are not always the primary factor in recruiting individuals to head facilities planning departments in these school systems. In addition, these departments are often understaffed, reflecting other priorities. Bureaucratic inefficiencies lead to backlogs of facilities needs and favoritism in awarding contracts.

Political and legal controls on funding

Restrictions exist on supplying funds for facilities such as debt service, capital, indebtedness, sinking funds (if legal), constructions permits, and land use restrictions. All affect the ability of communities to raise capital funds.

GENERALIZATIONS AND CASE EXAMPLES

The above model suggests the complex array of causal factors affecting both demand for capital expenditures in urban areas and the adequacy with which such demands are supplied. Ultimately, it is the political system that must mediate between competing demand and supply forces but, as the model illustrates, the political system is more than a mediator. It is deeply engaged in generating the shape of demand and supply, quite apart from its mediating function. Drawing upon the model, our analysis of capital funding for schools in a number of jurisdictions points up four major generalizations:

1. Big city capital costs (per-pupil capital expenditures and debt service) vary widely.

2. Many urban school systems continue to suffer from underfunding of school facilities due to long-term enrollment declines. Some others, however, are now witnessing increasing enrollments. This pupil growth or decline profile generates very different dynamics and should be viewed as a critically important element shaping demand for spending on infrastructure.

3. Despite greater state support for capital spending, funding continues to be inadequate and has led to greater state control and complex regulatory oversight. The shift from general support to equity-driven and needs-driven funding has proven problematic.

4. Local management of capital planning and spending continues to be inefficient and impedes urban school systems from adequately responding to capital demands.

Because of space limitations, we shall draw selectively on our cases to illustrate these trends in this chapter.

Big City Capital Costs: A Comparison

A survey of six U.S. school districts indicates the variation in urban spending on capital for schools, standardized by district size (enrollments), showing capital spending and debt service. As presented in Table 5.2, New York City Public Schools has a 2002 capital budget of approximately $2 billion and in Fiscal Year 2002 (the most recent year for which data are available) total debt service was $537 million. Los Angeles Unified School District is even higher at $2.293 billion for capital, with debt service of $330.0 million, although district spent only approximately 24% of its capital budget in 2002.

The Chicago Public Schools' capital budget is $569 million and debt service is $240 million. Seattle Public Schools, the smallest district among the six with 47,432 students, has a total capital budget of $175 million, as well as debt service of $1.0 million. The Passaic, New Jersey, public schools has a facilities budget of $285 million and debt service of $1.7 million. While the state of New Jersey has promised to provide the resources to finance school repairs and construction ($285 million), the amount actually spent last year was only $1.7 million, illustrating how state intervention can become ensnared in red tape and bureaucracy.

Table 5.2 also shows that when taken comparatively on a per-pupil basis, the New York City school system has a capital budget of $1,812 per student, and the Los Angeles Unified School District's capital budget is $3,173 per pupil. The Chicago Public Schools' is $1,307 per pupil, while the Seattle Public Schools—spending the least overall—has the highest per-pupil capital budget at $3,685. The Baltimore City school system has a relatively large capital expenditure budget (after many years of spending nearly nothing), but its debt service is low, as will be explained below. Comparatively, Passaic budgeted $2,714 per student for capital improvements, and $161 per student for debt service in 2002. These data underscore the considerable variation among urban school districts in their per-pupil capital spending and debt service.

Table 5.2.   Capital and Debt Service Total and Per Pupil for Sample Districts for Fiscal Year 2002

District	*Total Capital Budget*	*Per Pupil Capital*	*Total Debt Service*	*Per Pupil Debt Service*
New York Board of Education	$2.001 billion	$1,812	$537 million	$486
Los Angeles Unified School District*	2.293 billion	3,173	330 million	456
Chicago Public Schools	0.569 billion	1,307	240 million	551
Seattle Public Schools	0.175 billion	3,685	1 million	22
Houston Independent School District	0.248 billion	1,188	107 million	512
Baltimore City Schools	0.175 billion	3,685	1 million	21
Passaic Public Schools, New Jersey	0.285 billion	2,714	1.7 million	161

*In 2000-01, the district spent only 23.6% of its capital budget.

Overcoming Declining Enrollments as a Brake on Demand

What are some of the factors that contribute to variation in capital spending and debt service costs? One is that school systems have recovered to varying degrees from the "politics of decline" associated with diminishing enrollments. These enrollment declines often have been sharper and/or more lengthy than those in suburban and rural school districts due to out-migration from the city, a relatively older population, and greater flight to private schools.

Cities suffering enrollment decline have to resolve a political obstacle, creating the perception that the system should be reducing its expenditures. Thus, they must garner wider political support for school construction. In Chicago, this was resolved through strong mayoral intervention as the school system has suffered from a long-term enrollment decline. Dating back as far back as the 1960s, school officials had difficulty garnering public support for building construction, prompting the first Mayor Richard Daley to create a building commission with bonding authority to avoid having to gain voter approval for new schools. After the Illinois state legislature in 1995 gave the second Mayor Richard Daley authority to run the public schools, he initiated an ambitious building campaign. Because of this previously large building effort, which was managed by former schools chief Paul Vallas, the capital budget shown in Table 5.2 is lower per student than the other big cities, although Chicago consequently has the highest debt service per pupil at $551.

Seattle also overcame a legacy of underinvestment associated with enrollment decline, but in a very different manner than Chicago. The reform character of the political culture in that city relied on voter approvals; so direct support of the electorate had to be a key strategy for reinvesting in the district's infrastructure. Seattle Public Schools is a relatively middle-class district that attempted racial integration through busing and witnessed a dramatic reduction in student enrollments between 1975 and 1995 from 98,212 to 44,321 although it has maintained about 94 schools despite the decline in students. During the 1970s and 1980s school closings were the primary issue, not new school construction. Levies were rarely passed.

However, in the 1990s Seattle Public Schools was very successful in passing levies to pay for school facilities; the taxpayers have been willing, at least until very recently, to raise the local property tax levy to cover both operating costs and construction. The capital budget of $174.8 million for 2001–2002 is funded through three levies approved by the voters of Seattle. The levies are as follows: (a) Building Excellence I for $330 million, passed in 1995, with a debt service yearly of about $66 million; (b) Building, Technology, and Athletic Fields for $150 million, passed in 1998, which is in its fourth year of a six year loan cycle; and (c) Building Excellence II, the newest effort, at $398 million, passed in 2001.

Because the district has been very successful in passing levies, very little debt is incurred through the issuance of bonds and loans. The last bond issue was in June 2001 for $53 million to provide funds to build a new Seattle Public Schools Administration Center, near the Seattle football and baseball stadiums and funds to support the acceleration of technology infrastructure. Seattle Public Schools has only $21 per student budgeted for debt service, totaling $2.8 million. (See Table 5.2.) The small size of the debt service also reflects the reality that the district actually has too many schools and needs to close and consolidate them, rather than build a raft of new schools. The state of Washington has contributed $185 million for general facilities aid and $63 million for special building projects. The state required the community to contribute $89 million, as "state matches."

State Aid with Strings Attached

States have stepped in to provide additional aid to urban districts, creating a downside as shown in two brief cases: a small district, Passaic, New Jersey, and a large one in Baltimore, Maryland.

The Passaic Public Schools is an interesting district for comparison and contrast with the Seattle Public Schools for several reasons. First, the Passaic Public Schools is located in an old-style inner-city district in the industrial "rust belt" of Northern New Jersey, with 85% students in poverty and 79% non-English speaking. Second, Passaic Public Schools operates in a state with a strong succession of school equity court cases[23] that not only mandated major state aid for school operations but prevented the local impoverished *Abbott* districts, 30 statewide, from raising the capital funds locally. New Jersey is required by the state's high court to fund 100% of Passaic Public Schools' school capital construction and renovations costs. Passaic cannot raise local funds for construction and must await help from the state under court mandates. As such, the state has inserted itself into the equalization of school facilities spending, a trend that has been noted by other researchers.[24] Consequently, Passaic provides a good starting point for understanding the growing complexities of state-aided, equity-driven facilities finance in the U.S., as a set of dynamics are in motion that tend to cripple the ability of states to fund facilities—and local districts to get the capital projects completed in a timely and economical fashion.

Third, Passaic Public Schools has many of the geographic and land-use problems associated with urban districts: congestion; a shortage of available land; and an increase in student population averaging about 8% per year. In fact, in 2001–2002, the district grew from about 10,300 students to

13,201, mainly because the state required poor districts to offer full-time kindergarten and full- or part-time pre-school to all children, bringing a large influx of students, ages three to five, into the system. At the same time, despite being impoverished, Passaic shows vitality.

Reflecting its optimism as a growing district, Passaic Public Schools has done extensive analysis of its facilities needs, using a most complex set of dimensions: land available and use; building capacity and shortcomings; modernization plans; and special program demands on the capital of the district. As stipulated in state regulations, called the "*Abbott* criteria," the capital plan is no longer restrained by local poverty.

In response to the court order, New Jersey has taken steps to equalize funding of capital. Under the Educational Facilities Construction and Financing Act (S–200), the state laid down four stipulations that affect districts such as Passaic: First, the state authorized the borrowing of $6 billion to be used in the 30 poorest (*Abbott*) districts, $2.5 billion for non-*Abbott* projects, and $100 million for county vocational school construction. Second, the law provides for 100% state funding of eligible school construction costs in the *Abbott* districts. Bonds were issued for a total of $8.5 billion by the New Jersey Economic Development Authority.

The New Jersey Supreme Court ordered the state to provide school facilities that would include health and safety; educational adequacy and efficient construction; design; management; and construction. This new aid was accompanied by increased regulation by a variety of state agencies, including the New Jersey Department of Education and the Economic Development Authority to help raise the money; the Department of Labor to monitor the "prevailing wages" of all school construction projects; the Office of the Attorney General, Unit of Fiscal Integrity, to prevent fraud and corruption; the Department of Community Affairs to handle the contracts; and the Department of the Treasury to ensure the hiring of minority and women contractors in order to meet the state's requirements for affirmative action and to coordinate spending of the state's $8.6 billion in "state-contract-backed debt." What was once a primarily local matter—the raising of funds, purchase of land, and construction and renovation of buildings—has now become a highly complex, cumbersome, and laborious state-level activity

Delays in receiving the money have led to serious problems in Passaic and other *Abbott* districts. While the state forbade *Abbott* districts from spending their own money on capital, debt services, or repairs, New Jersey was slow in funding these 30 *Abbott* districts. Ironically, the new state policies actually made it easier for the non-*Abbott* districts, who were no longer required to seek a positive bond election to borrow money. Only a simple vote by the local board of education would do for these non-*Abbott* districts to take on the debt and start their renovations. Passaic struggled to house its growing student base, to incorporate new demands for state-required pre-school and kindergarten classes. Sixty portable classroom trailers were delivered but stored empty because they were ruled unsafe. Meanwhile the wealthier districts were building and renovating with impunity. In short, state red-tape has ensnared the poorest districts, more than the state has helped.

In the Baltimore City Public Schools, additional state aid has proven to be an inadequate incentive to spur needed capital construction despite a 1997 city-state partnership agreement to help the district. The state of Maryland had threatened a takeover of the school district, citing poor management of the school system and low educational performance of Baltimore school children. Under a consent decree, the district agreed to undertake significant managerial and governance reforms directed at improving student achievement; and, in return, the state agreed to provide $230 million in aid over a five year period. It also promised to provide 90% state funding for the first $10 million of capital construction for the five years. Spending above that is reimbursed at 75%.[25] For the Fiscal Years 2002 and 2003, the provision was extended and increased to $20 million.

For years, the spending had been pathetically low, reflecting the decade-long enrollment decline of the school system. The school system's facilities plan estimates a $600 million need to bring current buildings up to standards. Yet as recently as four years ago, the school system was spending only $1 million on facilities needs. The city-state partnership agreement has increased state and local spending on capital improvements for schools. However, the state's promise has fallen short. In Fiscal Year 2003, it will fund only 12 of 41 projects requested by the school system, authorizing only $11.3 million rather than the requested $17.5 million.[26]

Also, Baltimore City, like other school systems in Maryland, is constrained by being fiscally dependent. It must obtain Board of Estimate approval (consisting of the mayor, city council, and comptroller) before it can sell its own bonds. For every $10 million in state funds received, the city must match with $1.1 million. The city government has been reluctant to authorize borrowing for schools, preferring to fund downtown redevelopment and economic development projects. Locally, this unwillingness reflects limited political support for school facilities expenditures in the city. Baltimore City Public Schools is still caught in a cycle of decline. While elementary level test scores have risen for several years, and political confidence in the school system appears to be rebuilding, the improvements are still fragile. The Baltimore case illustrates the complex interconnection between fiscal needs and garnering the political support to address them. While the objective data support the need for increased capital expenditures, neither local political support nor state support is sufficient to supply the required funds.

FISCAL MISMANAGEMENT

The Baltimore City Public Schools case also illustrates a problem on the supply side. Urban school systems do not always have facilities planning departments which can be relied upon to provide competent planning. Despite state intervention in 1997, until recently the school system has been plagued by scandals. For example, the school board's first choice of a chief executive officer, Robert Booker, failed to prevent embarrassing scandals involving his chief financial officer and other business officials. The school board has had difficulty gaining control of the personnel recruitment process, and it would appear that vestiges of a patronage or "friends and neighbors" appointment system continue to survive several years after ties with city hall have been severed.[27] As a result, turnover of personnel on the business side of the organization has been high, including a new director in the Department of Facilities Planning and School Construction.

Other urban school systems have suffered from similar management problems. For example, when David Adamany was appointed interim CEO of the Detroit Public Schools in a state takeover of the school district in 1999, he discovered that $1.395 billion (93%) of a $1.5-billion plan voters approved in 1994 remained unspent. He found it necessary to renew old bonds. Even after his intervention, however, more than $900 million in construction bonds remained unspent. While the $1.5 billion will not cover all the needed repairs and construction, the school system was unable to demonstrate the capacity to spend even the resources that voters had approved.[28]

FUTURE RESEARCH

More research is needed to learn just how funds are raised for building construction and renovation. Four common questions are being asked:

1. Does the school system have direct fundraising capacity for buildings and renovations? We know, for example, that New York City has a construction authority that is independent of the New York City Board of Education, and the Houston Unified School District can raise capital directly through bond elections to meet increased demands for space and improvement.

2. What have been the trends affecting capital development in the district? In contrast to New York City, the Seattle Public Schools has faced a major drop in enrollment over the last 20 years, requiring fewer schools, while New York City has grown in size, placing pressure on the city to provide more land and space for schools.

3. What is the bond rating of the various districts, based on what key factors? Districts raise capital funds in different ways, based on different factors.

4. What effect have capital costs and spending had on resources available for operations, programs, and schools? Is there "drainage" out of operating costs to pay for capital and debt service or interest?

In answering these and other questions, in an attempt to find an equilibrium point between the demand for new, more, and better facilities, and the ability of communities and states to supply these physical resources, we realize that the process will never be rationalized or truly balanced. Too many unintended and unanticipated forces intervene on both sides of the equation.

FOUR NOT-SO-MODEST PROPOSALS

Given the highly complex, confusing picture of urban school infrastructure policy outlined in this chapter, we should try new policy approaches, both as a spur to innovation and to improving the adequacy of funding. We do not endorse still another decade or two of hobbling along with current structures and policies while the infrastructure of urban schools continues to deteriorate and students are schooled in unsafe, unsavory, and/or overcrowded buildings. We recognize that the proposals we offer here are anything but modest and are likely to be controversial. However, the current situation calls for dramatic action, not mere ameliorative responses. These proposals speak to who constructs and manages school facilities, where school facilities are located, and how to rationalize the capital funding structure:

1. *Experiment with outsourcing.* The problem of supplying adequate school facilities is at least partially a bureaucratic one, as developments in Baltimore, Passaic, and other cities clearly establish. The entrenched nature of urban school bureaucracies and the micromanagement of school funding decisions by school boards, which introduce a variety of particularistic demands, have impeded rational planning and management. While accountability for the expenditure of public monies is essential, the current system could benefit from the application of greater private sector involvement in this arena. Some examples include:
   - Creation of urban school capital funding authorities in cities which would have responsibility for long-term capital planning, initiating and managing school construction and renovation, and

making school closing decisions. The membership of the boards of these authorities could include financial experts as well as public officials, appointed by the mayor and/or governor. Provision should be made for regular review of the operations of the authorities and appeals of their decisions, but, in general, they should be able to function with much more autonomy than is the case under existing statutes and practices applying to school board decision-making.

- The private sector could be invited to build schools and then lease them back to the local school system or to a building authority created to act on behalf of the school system as discussed above. State and federal tax policies should be examined to offer favorable terms for expensing costs, depreciation write-offs, and related considerations. These policies have been applied to construction of other kinds of government buildings and to other areas of social policy such as housing.

- Consider outsourcing management of school facilities. This approach has been tried for building maintenance in some cities, but it could be extended to structural upkeep of the facilities over the period of the lease in terms specified initially in the lease arrangement. This privatization would encourage long-term planning, realistic assessment of needs, and currency of facilities maintenance, perhaps increasing quality and controlling costs.

- The state could simply take over the building of schools and other education buildings, could underwrite the bonds necessary, or could provide resources to meet the debt services incurred by local districts. These approaches would not only simplify the process of building construction, as the Passaic Public Schools' situation illustrates, but also relieve the extra strain on impoverished communities that would have great difficulty floating bonds and paying them off without raising local taxes and overburdening poor local citizens and businesses.

2. *Integrate approaches to land-use and the location of schools.* School planning could benefit from closer coordination with state and urban development decisions. The problems of providing quality educational experiences for urban school children are related to other critical infrastructure needs, such as access to quality housing, transportation, recreation, and jobs, and the availability of social services. Despite decades of discussion and abortive public policies, urban development policies and programs remain highly fragmented. They are constrained by lack of public authority to guide development decisions, outdated or counterproductive zoning and taxing policies, and narrowly constructed "silo" bureaucracies incapable of

addressing the interdependent needs of urban neighborhoods and urban populations.

One possible approach to ending this fragmentation, much discussed but seldom tried, would be to encourage more mixed land use, where schools could be located within or adjacent to commercial buildings, near affordable housing, or as the first few floors in an office building. For example, the famous Friends Central School in Philadelphia occupies the first few floors of an office building, with revenues from the property supporting the school. This mixing and integrating of spaces would provide effective use of facilities and cost-efficient public-private partnerships. If planned in conjunction with potential employers in these commercial buildings, this strategy could provide access to nearby jobs, affording parents and caregivers opportunities to become involved in the schools that their children attend, and even offer childcare for parents working in the commercial firms nearby. Such mixed land-use—locating schools and housing near commercial buildings and services—should also encourage greater safety in urban neighborhoods, a major concern of inner-city residents and an impediment to anchoring working class and middle class residents in the central city and urban schools.

3. *Strengthen regional planning for school facilities needs.* Decision-makers need to coordinate strategic planning for school facilities on a regional basis. The current district-by-district approach leads to provincial decisionmaking and tends to ignore the larger, regional shifts and changes in demography, industry, technology, pedagogy and programs which will affect schools throughout a regional service area. Such planning bodies should not supplant the authority of local school districts but rather could inform and strengthen local decision-making. Regional planning should help inform strategic options undertaken by each district and may provide incentives for shared use of facilities across district lines. Many states do have regional service agencies that might undertake this function.

4. *Rationalize the revenue structure for urban school infrastructure needs.* After decades of piecemeal policies in which states have reluctantly and haltingly played a limited role in addressing the infrastructure needs of urban school systems, it is time to recognize a national problem requiring a federal response. Heretofore, federal assistance in addressing capital spending needs of urban school systems has been very limited. While the Federal Housing Authority (FHA) may not be the appropriate analogue in terms of structural response to this problem, the FHA has nonetheless created a large federal presence in national housing policy. A similar dramatic response is now

required to assist in the construction and renovation of urban schools. Perhaps, a Federal Education Facilities Initiative (FEFI) could be created: (a) to offer technical support; (b) to help underwrite local capital costs; and (c) to set benchmarks and standards for funding and building new schools for the 21st century. Already, we see the spreading effects of E-Rates, a federal program to wire schools for technology, as districts worked to make schools technologically ready and to increase interschool communications with federal financial support.

Some critics may argue that this capital development is appropriately a state and local responsibility. Yet the perceived dangers of a heavy federal hand are considerably less in the area of facilities assistance than in federal aid flows to support specific education programs or widespread school testing, as is found in the recent federal education act, *No Child Left Behind.*[29]

In the case of capital spending, the rationale for federal involvement is clearly consistent with decades of federal education policy: to address the needs of special under-served populations and resource-challenged schools; and to improve the capacity of state-and local policymaking systems to address a critical national need. Where state and local policy makers have been unable or unwilling to act to address an enduring crisis, the justification for federal involvement is clear and compelling.

NOTES

1. United States General Accounting Office, "School Facilities: Conditions of American Schools," *Report to Congressional Requesters* (Washington, D.C.: February 1995), 2.

2. Walter I. Garms, James W. Guthrie, and Lawrence C. Pierce, *School Finance: The Economics and Politics of Public Education* (Englewood Cliffs, New Jersey: Prentice-Hall, 1978), 262.

3. See Garms et al., (1978); and Percy E. Burrup, Vern Brimley, Jr., and Rulon R. Garfield, *Financing Education in a Climate of Change,* 7th ed. (Boston: Allyn and Bacon, 1999).

4. Garms et al., 363.

5. Ibid., 311–313.

6. Bruce S. Cooper, Miriam R. Cilo, and Bruce L. Baker, "Bridging the Gap Between School and College: An Analysis of K–16 Education in New York City," *Educational Administration Quarterly* (in press).

7. Garms et al., 363.

8. Burrup et al., 34.

9. Ibid., 237.

10. Ibid., 42.

11. Seymour Sacks, *The Municipal Overburden* (Syracuse, New York: Syracuse University Research Corporation, 1974).

12. Ibid., 155.

13. Public Law 107–110.

14. James G. Cibulka, "State and Federal Intervention to Improve Baltimore and Washington, D.C.'s Public Schools," In James G. Cibulka and William L. Boyd, eds., *A Race Against Time: Responses to the Crisis in Urban Schooling* (Weston, Connecticut: Ablex/Greenwood Press, in press).

15. Burrup et al., 255.

16. Walter G. Hack, "School District Bond Issues: Implications for Reform in Financing Capital Outlay," *Journal of Education Finance* 2 (Fall 1976): 156.

17. *Serrano v. Priest*, 487 P.2d 1241 (Cal. 1971).

18. *Abbott v. Burke*, 798 A.2d 602 (NJ. 2002).

19. For a fuller discussion of the history of school finance litigation and school infrastructure funding issues, see Chapter 8 of this volume, "School Finance Litigation: A Strategy to Address Inequities in School Infrastructure Funding," by David C. Thompson and Faith E. Crampton.

20. Burrup et al., 256–257.

21. John E. Coons., William Clune III, and Stephen D. Sugarman, *Private Wealth And Public Education* (Cambridge, Massachusetts: Belknap Press of Harvard University Press, 1970), 36.

22. W. Montford Barr and William R. Wilkerson, "State Participation in Financing Local School Facilities," *Trends in Financing Public Education* (Washington, D.C.: National Education Association, 1965), 3.

23. *Robinson v. Cahill*, 303 A.2d 273 (N.J. 1973); *Abbott v. Burke* (1998).

24. David C. Thompson, William E. Camp, Jerry G. Horn, and G. Kent Stewart, *State Involvement in Capital Outlay Financing: Policy Implications for the Future* (Manhattan, Kansas: Center for Extended Services and Studies, Kansas State University, 1988); Barr and Wilkerson (1965); David S. Honeyman, "School Facilities and State Mechanisms that Support School Construction: A Report From The Fifty States," *Journal of School Finance* 16 (Fall 1990): 233–251.

25. Cibulka (in press).

26. Interview with Yale Stenzler, Maryland State Department of Education, January 9, 2002.

27. Interview with school board member, April 2001.

28. Peggy Walsh-Sarnecki, "Schools to Revive Bond Project; Detroit Seeks New Buildings and Upgrades," *Detroit Free Press*, 24 March 2000, http://www.freep.com.

29. Public Law 107–110.

CHAPTER 6

FUNDING SCHOOL INFRASTRUCTURE IN RURAL AMERICA

Jeffrey Maiden
University of Oklahoma

ABSTRACT

Providing a comparable physical environment to children schooled in communities with small populations or to those living in areas isolated from larger population centers typically is costlier than in other settings. For rural schools, the problem is particularly complex. School facilities in rural areas are usually older and in worse condition than those in non-rural areas, but, at the same time, rural school districts have less property wealth upon which to draw for financing infrastructure needs through bonded indebtedness. To exacerbate the problem, few states provide significant fiscal support for school infrastructure. Taken together, the data presented in this chapter suggest a significant and growing crisis in infrastructure funding needs in rural school districts. While additional research on the diseconomy of scale rural schools face in financing infrastructure is clearly needed, it is incumbent upon states to create more adequate and equitable school infrastructure funding systems for all children, regardless of geographic location.

Saving America's School Infrastructure, pages 129–146

INTRODUCTION

School children across the nation are being educated in physical facilities that are inadequate.[1] Widespread problems, such as the inability of older schools to support educational technology; backlogs of deferred maintenance; lack of fiscal and physical capacity to meet the demands of increasing student enrollments; and the overall need to bring educational facilities into full compliance with legal mandates have been brought repeatedly to the attention of policymakers and the public alike.[2] Approximately $112 billion is needed just to make the nation's educational facilities safe and accessible.[3] This estimate does not even take into consideration the infrastructure needs attaching to future increases in enrollment.

Much of the difficulty in maintaining adequate, safe, and compliant facilities may be traced to states' failure to fund school infrastructure. Local school districts' infrastructure funding needs, addressed in a series of national reports on school facilities, accelerated with the educational reform movement that swept the nation in the early 1980s, resulting in a plethora of new educational mandates from the federal and state levels. At the same time, growth of educational programs for special needs students increased school districts' fiscal stress. In order to be successful, many of these reforms and mandates necessitated new construction, repair, and renovation of school facilities, but they were not given the financial priority they deserved. Exacerbating the problem is the wide range of circumstances in which school districts throughout the nation currently find themselves. For example, the challenges in funding infrastructure are real for both rural and urban schools, but they may require differing solutions, given characteristics unique to each setting.[4]

The challenge faced by the rural educational community in financing safe, adequate, and compliant facilities is the focus of this chapter. First, the chapter provides a national context for understanding the depth of the problem by exploring the magnitude of rural educational facilities funding needs in relation to the number and concentration of rural students and the condition of rural schools. The discussion then turns to an analysis of the provisions for funding school infrastructure in a cross-section of states with substantial concentrations of rural schools and students. The third section presents a case study of a rural state that typifies the central themes of the chapter, with an interdistrict analysis of rural schools' capacity to fund school infrastructure. The chapter concludes with recommendations for further inquiry.

INFRASTRUCTURE FUNDING CHALLENGES FACING RURAL SCHOOL DISTRICTS

The literature documenting the diseconomy of scale faced by rural education is extensive.[5] Providing a comparable educational experience to children schooled in communities with small populations or to those living in areas isolated from larger population centers typically is costlier than other settings. While the majority of studies have focused on the multiple and varied effects of diseconomy of scale on the general education program, the diseconomy in meeting the infrastructure needs of rural schools is no less real although it may not be as well documented. In fact, one might posit that diseconomy relating to fiscal support for school facilities is more pronounced because state support for current operations, flowing primarily through state aid funding formulas, is far more generous than state support for school infrastructure and debt service. For rural schools, the problem is particularly complex given the magnitude of their educational infrastructure funding needs.

An overview of national and state-by-state data helps to place the challenges facing rural school districts in perspective. Nationally, 27.4% of the total school population, or 12,777,183 students, reside in rural school districts. (See Table 6.1.) State-by-state data on student enrollments in rural schools and their percentage of total student enrollments are also presented in this table. In 15 states, rural school enrollments represent a substantial percentage of total student enrollments. For example, in nine states, rural school enrollments constitute between 50% and 60% of total enrollments. These states, with the percentage of rural student enrollments in parentheses, are: Arkansas (57.0%); Idaho (58.7%); Iowa (55.7%); Kentucky (55.6%); Nebraska (52.7%); New Hampshire (52.5%); North Carolina (50.3%); North Dakota (57.9%); and West Virginia (58.6%). Rural school enrollments represent more than two-thirds of states' school enrollments in the following six states: Maine (73.9%); Mississippi (68.5%); Montana (72.8%); South Dakota (70.6%); Vermont (83.4%); and Wyoming (68.3%). In contrast, states with the highest numbers of rural students may not necessarily have the highest concentrations. For example, Texas has the largest number of rural students in the nation at 830,027; but rural students comprise only 20.8% of the student population.

While data on the number and percentage of rural students in the United States provide important background information, further data on the level of poverty among rural students is essential in order to gain a better understanding of the critical importance of funding school infrastructure. In the United States, 8,896,867 children, aged 5–17, live in families considered below the poverty rate. (See Table 6.2.) Of these, 1,165,141, or 13.10%, are rural children. Sixteen states have substantial concentrations

Table 6.1.   Rural School Enrollment and Percentage by State, 1999

State	Total	Rural	Rural as % of Total	Non-Rural	Non-Rural as % of Total
Alabama	729,988	315,826	43.3	414,162	56.7
Alaska	134,391	62,071	46.2	72,320	53.8
Arizona	851,226	127,357	15.0	723,869	85.0
Arkansas	450,985	256,965	57.0	194,020	43.0
California	5,952,598	326,496	5.5	5,626,102	94.5
Colorado	708,109	161,258	22.8	546,851	77.2
Connecticut	554,002	120,291	21.7	433,711	78.3
Delaware	112,836	33,529	29.7	79,307	70.3
District of Columbia	77,194	0	0.0	77,194	100.0
Florida	2,381,480	272,834	11.5	2,108,646	88.5
Georgia	1,422,762	597,136	42.0	825,626	58.0
Hawaii	185,860	0	0.0	185,860	100.0
Idaho	245,016	143,800	58.7	101,216	41.3
Illinois	2,027,600	399,969	19.7	1,627,631	80.3
Indiana	988,289	395,176	40.0	593,113	60.0
Iowa	494,962	275,529	55.7	219,433	44.3
Kansas	465,223	225,868	48.6	239,355	51.4
Kentucky	629,193	350,087	55.6	279,106	44.4
Louisiana	756,044	225,459	29.8	530,585	70.2
Maine	209,091	154,508	73.9	54,583	26.1
Maryland	846,582	101,002	11.9	745,580	88.1
Massachusetts	971,425	189,598	19.5	781,827	80.5
Michigan	1,659,184	542,914	32.7	1,116,270	67.3
Minnesota	854,303	296,757	34.7	557,546	65.3
Mississippi	500,716	342,910	68.5	157,806	31.5
Missouri	914,010	379,817	41.6	534,193	58.4
Montana	158,477	115,370	72.8	43,107	27.2
Nebraska	288,261	151,975	52.7	136,286	47.3
Nevada	325,547	39,767	12.2	285,780	87.8
New Hampshire	206,783	108,500	52.5	98,283	47.5
New Jersey	1,288,570	164,857	12.8	1,123,713	87.2
New Mexico	324,489	122,883	37.9	201,606	62.1
New York	2,886,153	486,990	16.9	2,399,163	83.1

Table 6.1.   (cont.)

State	Total	Rural	Rural as % of Total	Non-Rural	Non-Rural as % of Total
North Carolina	1,275,954	642,292	50.3	633,662	49.7
North Dakota	112,751	65,282	57.9	47,469	42.1
Ohio	1,886,018	611,002	32.4	1,275,016	67.6
Oklahoma	627,032	271,246	43.3	355,786	56.7
Oregon	545,075	179,024	32.8	366,051	67.2
Pennsylvania	1,816,716	585,737	32.2	1,230,979	67.8
Rhode Island	156,454	23,773	15.2	132,681	84.8
South Carolina	666,780	286,734	43.0	380,046	57.0
South Dakota	130,988	92,446	70.6	38,542	29.4
Tennessee	897,526	323,916	36.1	573,610	63.9
Texas	3,991,783	830,027	20.8	3,161,756	79.2
Utah	478,910	94,374	19.7	384,536	80.3
Vermont	104,559	87,250	83.4	17,309	16.6
Virginia	1,132,673	353,691	31.2	778,982	68.8
Washington	1,002,361	264,635	26.4	737,726	73.6
West Virginia	291,811	170,973	58.6	120,838	41.4
Wisconsin	877,753	344,284	39.2	533,469	60.8
Wyoming	92,300	62,998	68.3	29,302	31.7
United States	46,688,793	12,777,183	27.4	33,911,610	72.6

Source: U.S. Bureau of the Census, http:// www.census.gov.

of poor children living in rural areas. In seven states, approximately half of all poor children live in rural areas. These states, with the respective percentages in parentheses, include: Kentucky (40.92%); Maine (42.45%); Montana (42.30%); North Dakota (48.54%); South Dakota (58.20%); Vermont (45.89%); and West Virginia (45.02%). In Alaska and Mississippi, approximately one-third of poor children live in rural areas, at 32.67% and 36.63% respectively. In the remaining seven states, approximately one-fourth of poor children reside in rural areas: Arkansas (24.19%); Idaho (26.84%); Iowa (24.97%); Nebraska (29.20%); New Hampshire (24.35%); North Carolina (29.15%); and Virginia (25.69%). Texas, however, has the largest actual number of rural children living in poverty, at 68,263; and North Carolina has the second largest population of poor rural children at 66,354.

Table 6.2.   Children Aged 5–17 in Families Below Poverty Rate, 1999

State	Total Number of Children	Number of Rural Children	Percentage of Children in State in Rural Areas
Alabama	187,565	38,596	20.58
Alaska	15,224	4,974	32.67
Arizona	187,039	24,792	13.25
Arkansas	119,178	28,829	24.19
California	1,349,016	36,618	2.71
Colorado	87,634	8,660	9.88
Connecticut	74,177	4,399	5.93
Delaware	16,732	2,476	14.80
District of Columbia	25,758	0	0.00
Florida	522,558	35,312	6.76
Georgia	307,316	49,703	16.17
Hawaii	26,107	0	0.00
Idaho	33,563	9,008	26.84
Illinois	362,225	20,983	5.79
Indiana	140,362	23,238	16.56
Iowa	61,977	15,477	24.97
Kansas	65,999	13,858	21.00
Kentucky	166,110	67,964	40.92
Louisiana	256,468	30,127	11.75
Maine	31,580	13,406	42.45
Maryland	107,724	9,906	9.20
Massachusetts	141,146	7,987	5.66
Michigan	327,993	47,133	14.37
Minnesota	94,113	17,827	18.94
Mississippi	155,334	56,903	36.63
Missouri	179,861	39,568	22.00
Montana	33,001	13,961	42.30
Nebraska	33,430	9,760	29.20
Nevada	35,773	1,797	5.02
New Hampshire	14,411	3,509	24.35
New Jersey	178,238	6,583	3.69
New Mexico	106,556	13,267	12.45
New York	396,091	31,607	7.98
North Carolina	227,593	66,354	29.15

Table 6.2.   (cont.)

State	Total Number of Children	Number of Rural Children	Percentage of Children in State in Rural Areas
North Dakota	17,828	8,653	48.54
Ohio	325,187	53,870	16.57
Oklahoma	150,267	29,684	19.75
Oregon	72,235	9,695	13.42
Pennsylvania	332,820	37,024	11.12
Rhode Island	26,535	993	3.74
South Carolina	154,271	21,603	14.00
South Dakota	26,691	15,533	58.20
Tennessee	176,748	31,640	17.90
Texas	966,236	68,263	7.06
Utah	38,046	3,094	8.13
Vermont	12,930	5,934	45.89
Virginia	173,002	44,445	25.69
Washington	133,596	18,522	13.86
West Virginia	83,281	37,495	45.02
Wisconsin	126,605	21,779	17.20
Wyoming	12,737	2,332	18.31
United States	8,896,867	1,165,141	13.10

Source: U.S. Bureau of the Census, http://www.census.gov.

Table 6.3 offers another way in which to view rural children in poverty. Nearly one-third, or 31.4%, of children residing in rural communities are members of families living below the national poverty level. The highest percentages are found in the following five states: Arizona (52.97%); Louisiana (50.96%); Mississippi (53.30%); New Mexico (66.59%); and South Carolina (57.59%). In these states, more than half of all school-aged children living in rural communities are poor, and, in New Mexico, the percentage is a shocking two-thirds.

Because poor children and poor facilities often go hand-in-hand, a sense of the current condition of the school facilities in which rural students are being educated is important. On average, school facilities in rural school districts and those with small enrollments (fewer than 300 students) have relatively older facilities, in both real and functional terms.[6] (See Table 6.4.) The average real age of a rural school is 41 years, and its functional age is 16 years. In general, schools with small enrollments, which typify many rural communities, have a real age of 43 years and a functional age of 20 years.

Table 6.3. Percentage of Children Aged 5–17 in Families Below the Poverty Rate in Rural Areas, 1999

State	Percentage
Alabama	43.12
Alaska	22.63
Arizona	52.97
Arkansas	42.20
California	39.71
Colorado	16.51
Connecticut	9.66
Delaware	17.57
District of Columbia	0.00
Florida	48.63
Georgia	36.38
Hawaii	0.00
Idaho	27.78
Illinois	20.19
Indiana	17.23
Iowa	19.52
Kansas	19.82
Kentucky	44.80
Louisiana	50.96
Maine	22.02
Maryland	24.72
Massachusetts	14.12
Michigan	27.88
Minnesota	20.49
Mississippi	53.30
Missouri	34.60
Montana	33.81
Nebraska	17.18
Nevada	9.72
New Hampshire	11.24
New Jersey	6.08
New Mexico	66.59
New York	28.52
North Carolina	33.49

Table 6.3.   (cont.)

State	Percentage
North Dakota	28.74
Ohio	24.95
Oklahoma	41.21
Oregon	28.42
Pennsylvania	24.99
Rhode Island	15.02
South Carolina	57.59
South Dakota	36.80
Tennessee	36.13
Texas	46.16
Utah	11.51
Vermont	18.83
Virginia	28.11
Washington	27.54
West Virginia	31.95
Wisconsin	19.50
Wyoming	15.23
United States	31.24

Source: U.S. Bureau of the Census, http://www.census.gov.

Table 6.4.   Age of Public Schools by School Characteristics, 1999

School Characteristic	Years Since Construction	Years Since Most Recent Renovation	Functional Age of the School*
School enrollment size			
Less than 300	43	15	20
300 to 599	42	11	15
600 or more	35	9	14
Locale			
Central city	42	12	17
Urban fringe/large town	37	10	14
Rural/small town	41	12	16

* Functional age is defined as the age of the school based on the year of the most recent renovation or the year of construction of the main instructional building(s) if no renovation has occurred. Source: U.S. Department of Education, *Survey on the Condition of Public School Facilities, 1999* (Washington, DC: National Center for Education Statistics, Fast Response Survey System, 1999).

The functional age of rural and small enrollment schools may be further disaggregated, as shown in Table 6.5. Here the functional age of schools is divided into four categories: Less than five years old; 5–14 years old; 15–34 years old; and 35 or more years old. While 32% of rural schools are relatively new with a functional age under five years, 26% are 5–14 years old; 29% are 15–34 years old; and 13% have a functional age greater than 35 years. Twenty-five percent of schools with small enrollments have a functional age under five years while 21% are 5–14 years old. A little over one-third, or 35%, of these schools have a functional age of 15–34 years, and 20% are older than 35 years.

Table 6.5.   Percentage Distribution of Public Schools According to the Functional Age of the School, by School Characteristics, 1999

School Characteristic	*Functional Age of Schools and Percentage Distribution**			
	Less Than 5 Years Old	*5–14 Years Old*	*15–34 Years Old*	*35 or More Years Old*
School Enrollment Size				
Less than 300	25	21	35	20
300 to 599	32	32	23	13
600 or more	37	28	23	12
Locale				
Central city	30	27	26	17
Urban fringe/large town	34	31	23	12
Rural/small town	32	26	29	13

* Functional age is defined as the age of the school based on the year of the most recent renovation or the year of construction of the main instructional building(s) if no renovation has occurred.
Source: U.S. Department of Education, *Survey on the Condition of Public School Facilities, 1999* (Washington, DC: National Center for Education Statistics, Fast Response Survey System, 1999).

Given building age and lack of recent renovation, it is not surprising that a high percentage of school facilities in rural areas receive poor ratings with regard to environmental factors like lighting, heating, ventilation, indoor air quality, acoustics, and physical security (See Table 6.6). Almost half, or 47%, of rural schools have at least one of these environmental factors rated as unsatisfactory or very unsatisfactory, according to survey conducted by the U.S. Department of Education.[7] Similarly, 45% of small enrollment schools are rated in this manner.

Overall, the data presented in this section paint an alarming picture of the quality of school facilities available to rural children. Rural children are more likely to attend older schools that have not been renovated recently.

Table 6.6. Percent of Public Schools Rating the Condition of Environmental Factors as Unsatisfactory, by School Characteristics, 1999

School Characteristic	At Least One Environmental Factor in Unsatisfactory Condition	Lighting	Heating	Ventilation	Indoor Air Quality	Acoustics or Noise Control	Physical Security of Buildings
School Enrollment Size							
Less than 300	45	12	16	27	19	22	21
300 to 599	46	14	18	31	20	19	21
600 or more	39	10	16	21	16	12	18
Locale							
Central city	47	14	18	30	22	20	14
Urban fringe/ large town	37	11	16	20	13	13	17
Rural/small town	47	12	16	29	21	21	26

Note: Ratings of unsatisfactory include the ratings of unsatisfactory and very unsatisfactory.
Source: U.S. Department of Education, *Survey on the Condition of Public School Facilities, 1999* (Washington, D.C.: National Center for Education Statistics, Fast Response Survey System, 1999).

These building conditions translate into a substandard physical environment where factors like unsatisfactory lighting, acoustics, and ventilation hinder teaching and learning. Moreover, these conditions point to a backlog of deferred maintenance in rural schools and an inability to provide students and staff with up-to-date features, like new technology. Together, these place rural students at-risk of receiving a second-class education.

STATE AND LOCAL FUNDING OF RURAL SCHOOL INFRASTRUCTURE

A major hindrance to meeting the infrastructure funding needs of schools is the lack of the type of broad state financial assistance that is more readily available for school districts' general operational costs. Hence, most local communities bear primary responsibility for their infrastructure needs, leaving school districts in many areas of the nation dependent on deficit financing through the bond mechanism. In rural areas, particularly those serving very small student population bases, this difficulty is exacerbated by the fact that local tax bases may not be adequate to meet the debt service requirements inherent in utilizing bonding as the primary or sole infrastructure funding mechanism. To give the reader a sense of the scope of the problem, this section examines funding methods from a cross-section of states serving relatively high percentages of rural students in general, and rural students in poverty, more specifically. These states include: Idaho; Iowa; Kentucky; Mississippi; Montana; and South Dakota.

In Idaho, over half of the state's children live in rural areas. Approximately one-fourth of these children are considered poor. A review of Idaho statutes indicates that no statutory authority exists to provide state support for local school districts' infrastructure needs. Instead, infrastructure financing is authorized locally through general maintenance and operations, a school plant facilities fund,[8] or by authorization of the sale of general obligation bonds subject to approval of a supermajority of two-thirds in a general referendum.[9] The state of Iowa also counts over half of its enrollments as rural students, of which approximately one-fourth live in poverty. Like Idaho, Iowa provides no specific state aid mechanism to support local school districts in meeting infrastructure needs. Instead, local tax revenues are expected to support these needs, with the proceeds of bond issues being subject to a supermajority of 60% approval at referendum. In addition, maximum school district indebtedness is restricted to 5% of the district's assessed valuation.[10] Similarly, no state aid for school infrastructure exists in South Dakota,[11] a state where over two-thirds of students are rural, and approximately half live in poverty. The state of Montana, whose demographic profile is similar to that of South Dakota, does not provide aid for school infrastructure, but some state debt service support is statutorily authorized.[12]

In moderate contrast, state support for infrastructure funding is available in Kentucky and Mississippi. The state of Kentucky, with approximately half of its student population considered rural and poor, makes a specific appropriation through the state aid formula for school infrastructure and debt service. This change took place through reform of the state's financing system following the dramatic ruling in *Rose v. Council for Better Education*,[13] which mandated specific improvements in the physical environment of schools.[14] Mississippi, with over two-thirds of its students living in rural areas and more than one-third poor, provides funding for school infrastructure through legislative appropriation, state grants, and state level school bonds.[15] As an overriding principle, however, it should be noted that the availability of state infrastructure funding sources of any significance for local school districts, specifically in states serving heavily rural populations of students, is the exception rather than the rule.

THE CASE OF OKLAHOMA

To provide a better sense of the importance of mechanisms for funding rural school facilities, an analysis of school infrastructure funding in the state of Oklahoma is instructive. Primarily a rural state, Oklahoma maintains more than 540 school districts, most of which are heavily rural, and many of which include single campus clusters of school facilities. The state operates a multi-tiered, equity-based school finance distribution system for general fund purposes, with the bulk of funding derived from state sources. The Oklahoma school funding system has demonstrated a relatively high degree of fiscal equity when examined using nationally accepted standards of interdistrict fiscal equity.[16]

Yet, as with many states, Oklahoma provides no state support to local school districts to help defray school infrastructure costs. Instead, local revenues provide the sole source of funding via a five mill building fund levy, the proceeds from which are not included in the statewide equity formula. As with other states, local districts rely heavily on bonded indebtedness to financially support school infrastructure.[17] As a result, school districts relying on the bond mechanism are authorized to sell general obligation bonds subject to approval by 60% of voters in a special election. Concurrent with passage of a bond issue is the approval of a debt service levy to finance repayment of the issue. Though no specific millage limit is in place, districts may not exceed 10% of the total net assessed *ad valorem* valuation, with few exceptions.[18] Oklahoma, along with many other rural states, depends on a regressive debt financing system in which the local tax base becomes a critical factor in school districts' ability to support infrastructure needs. As readily demonstrated throughout the literature of school finance, inequities are inherent in any system that is primarily dependent upon local wealth to fiscally support educational opportunities for children.

The points made in the above paragraph are further demonstrated in the disparity in bonding capacity between rural and non-rural school districts in Oklahoma.[19] (See Table 6.7.) The average assessed valuation of real property in rural school districts is $1,176,418. In contrast, non-rural districts enjoy a mean assessed valuation almost eight times greater, at $9,288,002. As evidenced by the data in Table 6.7, rural school districts in Oklahoma are significantly disadvantaged in their ability fund infrastructure needs due to their small tax bases.

Table 6.7.   Bonding Capacity of Oklahoma School Districts by District Classification, 1999*

District Classification	N	Mean	Standard Deviation	Standard Error
Non-rural	81	$9,288,002	$21,144,767	$2,349,419
Rural	464	1,176,418	1,772,281	82,276

Independent samples test:
  t = −8.13592
  df = 543
  Significance (2-tailed) = .001

* Expressed as assessed valuation of real property.
Source: Data provided by the Oklahoma Department of Education and the U.S. Bureau of the Census, http:// www.census.gov.

Table 6.8 provides a snapshot of the magnitude of tax proceeds derived from successful bond issues in Oklahoma between Fiscal Years 1995 and 1999. Although two-thirds of school districts in the state are classified as rural and the number of bond issues in rural districts outweighed those in non-rural districts by more than two-to-one, non-rural school districts yielded the lion's share of dollars to support capital financing. Non-rural districts generated a total of 75% more revenue through the bond mechanism, while the mean non-rural single issue was approximately four times larger than the average rural bond issue. Clearly, school districts outside rural areas were in an advantageous position to secure funding to support debt service, a critical component of equal educational opportunity as defined by support for school infrastructure capacity.

Table 6.8.   Dollar Amount of Successful Bond Elections in Oklahoma by District Classification, 1995–1999

District Classification	Mean	Standard Deviation	Sum	N
Non-rural	$4,002,423	$7,858,209	$520,315,000	130
Rural	1,103,444	1,995,311	297,930,000	270
State	2,045,612	4,949,458	818,245,000	400

Source: James D. Beckham, "An Examination of the Influence of Technology Inclusion in Determining the Outcome of School Bond Issue Elections in Oklahoma" (Ph.D. diss., University of Oklahoma, 2001).

It is also informative to compare the number and rate of passage in bond issue elections between rural and non-rural school districts. Between 1995 and 1999, rural school districts placed 359 bond issues before their voters while non-rural districts placed 163, or less than half as many, on the ballot. (See Table 6.9.) This disparity may point to greater school infrastructure needs in rural districts as well as the difficulty of securing passage of bond issues, i.e., the same bond issue may need to be placed before rural voters multiple times before securing passage. However, rural school districts are somewhat more successful overall in gaining passage of bond issues. In rural districts, the passage rate is approximately 32% while in non-rural communities the passage rate is somewhat lower at 25%. Overall, passage rates are not encouraging as they indicate that 68% of rural school district bond issues and 75% of those in non-rural school districts fail.

Table 6.9.   Success of Bond Issue Elections in Oklahoma by District Classification, 1995–1999

District Classification	Fail	Pass	Total
Non-rural	33	130	163
Rural	89	270	359
Total	122	400	522

Chi-square Tests (Pearson Chi-square):
   Value = 1.29339755
   df = 1
Significance = 0.255422841

Source: James D. Beckham, "An Examination of the Influence of Technology Inclusion in Determining the Outcome of School Bond Issue Elections in Oklahoma" (Ph.D. diss., University of Oklahoma, 2001).

In sum, the data from Oklahoma typify the plight of rural school districts across the nation with regard to their inability to meet infrastructure funding needs. State aid to infrastructure is largely nonexistent. Local bonding capacity in rural districts is a fraction of that found in non-rural school districts. Bond issues must be passed by a supermajority of voters, a particular problem in rural districts where residents are often property-poor and reluctant to pay higher property taxes. These factors relegate rural students to school facilities that are not conducive to provision of a 21st century education.

CONCLUSION

This chapter has highlighted the plight of rural schools in funding school infrastructure needs. The research literature on the diseconomy of scale experienced by rural school districts with regard to operating costs serves as a basis to examine the challenges they face in funding school facilities. Nationally, rural school enrollments represent approximately 25% of total student population. When examined on a state-by-state basis, the concentration of rural students exceeds the national average in 34 states, ranging from 29.7% in Delaware to 83.4% in Vermont. In addition, it is important remember that a state like Texas, with only 20.9% of its student population classified as rural, educates over a quarter million rural students. The extent of poverty in rural communities also factors into school infrastructure funding needs since, across the board, students in poor communities often attend schools in the worst condition. Approximately 13% of students in the United States are considered poor. However, the poverty rate for rural students exceeds that in 33 states, ranging from 13.25% in Arizona to 58.2% in South Dakota.

Most states do not fund school infrastructure to any significant extent, and analysis of a cross-section of rural states confirms that many states with substantial rural student populations provide no funding at all, leaving school districts reliant upon local wealth as defined by real property values. The case study of Oklahoma reveals that rural districts are also property poor and at a significant disadvantage in passing bond issues to finance improvements in school infrastructure. Taken together, these data suggest a significant and growing crisis in infrastructure funding needs among rural school districts. While additional research on the diseconomy of scale faced by rural schools in financing infrastructure is clearly needed, it is incumbent upon states to create more adequate and equitable school infrastructure funding systems for all children, regardless of geographic location.

NOTES

1. Faith E. Crampton and David C. Thompson, "Introduction to the Special Issue: The Crisis in School Infrastructure Funding," *Journal of Education Finance* 27 (Fall 2001): 625–631; David S. Honeyman, "Finances and the Problems of America's School Buildings," *Clearinghouse* 68 (November-December 1994): 95–97; David S. Honeyman, "School Facilities and State Mechanisms that Support School Construction: A Report from the Fifty States," *Journal of Education Finance* 16 (Fall 1990): 247–272; David S. Honeyman, R. Craig Wood, David C. Thompson, and G. Kent Stewart, "The Fiscal Support of School Facilities in Rural and Small Schools," *Journal of Education Finance* 13 (Winter 1988): 227–239.

2. U.S. General Accounting Office, *School Facilities: Condition of America's Schools,* HEHS-95-61 (Washington, D.C.: February 1995), http://www.gao.gov; U.S. General Accounting Office, *School Facilities: Accessibility for the Disabled Still an Issue,* HEHS-96-73 (Washington, D.C.: December1995), http://www.gao.gov; U. S. General Accounting Office, *School Facilities: America's Schools Not Designed or Equipped for 21st Century,* HEHS-95-95 (Washington, D.C.: April 1995), http://www.gao.gov; U.S. General Accounting Office *School Facilities: States' Financial and Technical Support Varies,* HEHS-96-27 (Washington, D.C.:, November 1995), http://www.gao.gov.

3. U.S. General Accounting Office, *School Facilities: Condition of America's Schools.*

4. For a fuller discussion of the school infrastructure funding needs of urban school districts, see Chapter 5 of this volume, "Capital Needs and Spending in Urban Public School Systems: Policies, Problems, and Promises," by James G. Cibulka and Bruce S. Cooper.

5. See, for example, Henry M. Levin, "The Effect of Different Levels of Expenditure on Educational Output," in Roe L. Johns, Irving J. Goffman, Kern Alexander, and Dewey H. Stollar, eds., *Economic Factors Affecting the Financing of Education* (Gainesville, Florida: National Educational Finance Project, 1970); James W. Guthrie, "Organization Scale and School Success," *Educational Evaluation and Policy Analysis* 1 (Spring 1979): 17–27; Herbert Walberg and William J. Fowler, Jr., "Expenditures and Size Efficiencies of Public School Districts," *Educational Researcher* 16 (October 1987): 5–13; David S. Honeyman, David C. Thompson, and R. Craig Wood, *Financing Rural and Small Schools* (Charleston, West Virginia: ERIC Clearinghouse on Rural Education and Small Schools, 1989); Deborah A. Verstegen, "Efficiency and Economies of Scale Revisited," *Journal of Education Finance* 16 (Fall 1990): 180–191.

6. Real age represents the age of the school based upon years of construction, whereas functional age is defined as the age of the school based on the year of the most recent renovation or the year of construction of the main instructional building(s) if no renovation has occurred. See, U.S. Department of Education, *Survey on the Condition of Public School Facilities, 1999* (Washington, D.C.: National Center for Education Statistics, Fast Response Survey System, 1999).

7. Ibid.

8. Idaho Statutes, Title 33, Chapter 9.

9.   Idaho Statutes, Title 33, Chapter 11.

10. Iowa Code, Title VII, Subtitle 1, Chapter 257.

11. South Dakota Statutes, Title 13, Chapter 13.

12. Montana Statutes, Title 20, Chapter 9.

13. *Rose v. Council for Better Education,* 790 S.W.2d 186 (Ky. 1989).

14. Kentucky Revised Statutes, Title XIII, Chapter 157.

15. Mississippi Code, Title 37, Chapters 022, 037.

16. Pamela Dale Deering and Jeffrey Maiden, "The Fiscal Effects of State Mandated Class Size Requirements in Oklahoma." *Journal of Education Finance,* 25 (Fall 1999): 195–210; and Jeffrey Maiden, "A Examination of Fiscal Effects of Statewide Education Reform on Oklahoma School Districts," *The Journal of School Business Management* 10 (Fall 1998): 17–25.

17. Oklahoma Statutes, Chapter 70, Section 1.

18. Oklahoma Constitution, Article X, Section 26.

19. The U.S. Census classification system was utilized to define school districts as rural or non-rural, http://www.census.gov.

CHAPTER 7

INFRASTRUCTURE FUNDING CONSIDERATIONS AND STUDENTS WITH DISABILITIES

William T. Hartman
Pennsylvania State University

ABSTRACT

Much progress has been made in the last 25 years in providing accessible facilities for students with disabilities, and substantial funds have been invested in the school infrastructure for these students. However, much remains to be done to meet the needs of students with disabilities and comply with federal and state requirements, and greater future costs can be anticipated. Federal statutes and regulations establish most of the infrastructure requirements related to students with disabilities, but these federal requirements are an unfunded mandate. School remodeling and new construction costs are financed through local and state funds; no federal financial assistance is provided to meet the federal accessibility requirements. Special education represents a significant cost element of school districts' current operating budgets, and it also represents a significant element in their capital budgets. While at present these infrastructure costs cannot be aggregated to the state or national level with any certainty due to limited data, they certainly must be considered by school districts in planning facilities for the future.

Saving America's School Infrastructure, pages 147–162

INTRODUCTION

Students with disabilities are more vulnerable to their educational environment than their non-disabled peers. This is particularly true of the physical environment in which they receive their education. Without access to appropriate classrooms, they cannot be integrated into the least restrictive environment as required by IDEA. Special facilities are required to provide additional instructional programs and related services. Recreation areas need special treatment to make them safe and accessible for some students with disabilities. "The design and layout of the physical environment, which includes the building, interior finishes, outdoor spaces, room arrangement, and selection of equipment, has a profound effect on children's behavior."[1] In other words, the physical environment for these students is critical for their educational success.

Much progress has been made in the last 25 years in providing accessible facilities for students with disabilities, and substantial funds have been invested in the school infrastructure for these students. However, much remains to be done to meet the needs of students with disabilities and comply with federal and state requirements, and greater future costs can be anticipated. The purpose of this chapter is to identify the infrastructure considerations for students with disabilities and to link those with the cost implications for schools to meet these needs.

LAWS AND REGULATIONS[2]

Federal statutes and regulations establish most of the infrastructure requirements related to students with disabilities. Three primary laws guide this area: the Individuals with Disabilities Education Act (IDEA); Section 504 of Rehabilitation Act of 1973; and the Americans with Disabilities Act (ADA) of 1990. The three statutes are complementary and function together to require that schools provide a free and appropriate education for all students with disabilities in the least restrictive environment. Other relevant federal regulations that govern access to facilities include the Uniform Federal Accessibility Standards (UFAS) and the ADA Accessibility Guidelines (ADAAG).

IDEA[3]

The Individuals with Disabilities Education Act is the primary federal statute that governs the provision of educational programs and services to students with disabilities. Originally passed in 1975 as the landmark Education for All Handicapped Children Act (P.L. 94–142), the law established the educational rights of students with disabilities. Of particular importance for facility considerations were the provisions for the following:

- Individualized educational program (IEP) that specifies the necessary educational programs and services that are to be provided for a student with a disability, including placement in regular education programs.
- Appropriate education, which means that a variety of modifications to the regular education program, classroom, and other school facilities could be required in order to carry out the IEP.
- Least restrictive alternative, which means that to the maximum extent feasible disabled students are to be educated in the same setting as their non-disabled peers.
- Access to programs specified in the student's IEP is required.

The act was reauthorized and amended in 1990, and renamed as IDEA. The act was amended again in 1997. In both cases, the law reinforced the commitment to the original concepts of including students with disabilities in regular education programs and classrooms with accommodations to both curriculum and facilities if necessary.

Section 504[4]

Section 504 of the Rehabilitation Act of 1974 is "a civil rights law to prohibit discrimination on the basis of disability in programs and activities, public and private, that receive federal financial assistance."[5] The law further states:

In determining the site or location of a facility, an applicant for assistance or a recipient may not make selections (i) that have the effect of excluding handicapped persons from, denying them the benefits of, or otherwise subjecting them to discrimination under any program or activity that receives Federal financial assistance or (ii) that have the purpose or effect of defeating or substantially impairing the accomplishment of the objectives of the program or activity with respect to handicapped persons.[6]

Section 504 functions together with IDEA to guarantee access for students with disabilities to educational programs and related services offered by school districts. Following the mandates of IDEA will satisfy many of the requirements of Section 504 relating to eligibility, provision of a free appropriate public education, individual educational program, procedural safeguards, and evaluation and placement procedures. Circumstances, policies, or arrangements that cause discrimination against students with disabilities and prevent them from receiving a free appropriate education are expressly illegal. This includes facilities that are inaccessible or inappropriate and prevent students from participating in necessary educational programs. Thus, Section 504 and IDEA combine to establish the educational program guarantees for students with disabilities.

The requirement to provide program access is not confined to students with disabilities only. Section 504 (and Title II of the Americans with Disabilities Act) requires schools to provide access to programs to parents, guardians, or other members of the public with disabilities to activities and programs that are open to parents or members of the public who are not disabled. These would include activities such as parent-teacher organization meetings, athletic events, school plays, and graduation ceremonies.[7]

ADA[8]

Public Law 101-336, the Americans with Disabilities Act, was enacted in 1990. The ADA prohibits discrimination on the basis of disability. It extends the anti-discrimination provisions of Section 504 of the Rehabilitation Act to the activities of state and local governments, including those that do not receive federal financial assistance. It specifically ensures equal opportunity for persons with disabilities in employment, state and local government services, public accommodations, commercial facilities, and transportation. Consequently, all services, programs, and activities provided by schools are covered under Title II regulations of its provisions. The ADA was designed to be compatible with Section 504, and many of its sections are identical or very similar.

While the ADA is a broad and wide-ranging law, two particular areas are important for infrastructure considerations for schools: (1) program accessibility for existing facilities and for new construction and alterations; and (2) communications.

Existing facilities

For existing facilities, schools must ensure that individuals with disabilities are not excluded from services, programs, and activities because buildings are inaccessible. There are a number of approaches to achieve physical accessibility, but in choosing among them priority should be given to using the most integrated setting appropriate to the needs of individuals with disabilities. Contrary to some popular misconceptions, the ADA does not mandate schools to remove physical barriers, such as stairs, in all existing buildings, as long as they make their programs accessible to individuals who are unable to use an inaccessible existing facility. While in some cases removal of physical barriers may be necessary, in other instances, alternatives may be feasible, including relocating a service to an accessible facility, providing an aide or personal assistant, providing benefits or services at an individual's home, or at an alternative accessible site.[9]

The requirement for program accessibility is limited in that schools are not required to take any action that would result in a fundamental alteration in the nature of its service, program, or activity or would place undue financial and administrative burdens on them. This limitation does not relieve the school from its obligations to provide the benefits or services to individuals with disabilities, but requires it to implement alternative approaches to make them accessible. Thus, the program access requirement of Title II should enable individuals with disabilities to participate in and benefit from the services, programs, or activities of public entities in all but the most unusual cases.[10]

New construction and remodeling

The Act also covers new construction and major alterations to existing facilities. New school buildings, as well as remodeled facilities, must be readily accessible to and usable by individuals with disabilities. The requirements cover physical access to the facilities, rather than educational access to programs and services. Another difference with new construction is that there is no limitation relating to fundamental alteration or undue burden to achieving physical access. There are two standards for accessible new construction and alteration: Uniform Federal Accessibility Standards (UFAS) and the Americans with Disabilities Act Accessibility Guidelines for Buildings and Facilities (ADAAG).[11] In January 1998, the Architectural and Transportation Barriers Compliance Board (Access Board) published special guidelines for children (Barrier Elements Designed for Children's Use)[12] that established alternatives based on children's needs to the more general, earlier ADAAG guidelines. More recently, in October 2000, the Access Board has published rules that cover accessibility for children with disabilities to newly constructed or altered play areas, including those of schools. These guidelines include ground level and elevated components, accessible routes, ramps, and transfer systems, and ground surfaces and play structures.[13]

Communications[14]

Title II of the ADA establishes requirements for effective communications for schools. This means that communications with applicants, participants, and members of the public with disabilities must be as effective as communications with others. To carry out this provision, schools must furnish appropriate auxiliary aids and services when necessary to afford an individuals with visual, hearing, or speech disabilities an equal opportunity to participate in, and enjoy the benefits of, the school's services, programs, or activities. Individuals with disabilities may request the auxiliary aids and services of their choice, which must be honored unless the request would fundamentally alter the program or service or would result in undue financial and administrative burden on the school.[15] Examples of auxiliary aids or services for students with hearing impaired include sign language interpreter, notetakers or other transcription services, amplified or hearing-aid compatible telephones, assistive listening systems, open or closed captioning, text telephones or telecommunication devices, and flashing alarms. For students with visual impairments, possible aids and services include audiotape cassettes or computer diskettes, Braille or large print materials, readers, verbal descriptions of performances and presentations, and mobility guides.[16]

APPROACHES TO MEETING STUDENT NEEDS AND ACHIEVING COMPLIANCE

With the establishment of IDEA, Section 504, and particularly ADA, Title II, schools and education facility planners began to take the needs of disabled students into account when designing and remodeling classrooms and other school facilities. To achieve the accessibility requirements necessitates a broader look at the school's physical facilities than just classrooms, wheelchair ramps, and wider doorways. Physical access for students with disabilities to appropriate instructional programs, support services, as well as common areas in the school, remains at the heart of achieving the program accessibility required by law. To achieve accessible school facilities involves a variety of factors, not all of which are instructional. Many resources are available to aid school districts in planning accessible schools.[17] As an example, the Ministry of Education, Skills and Training of British Columbia has prepared a set of considerations to reference when planning accessible school facilities.[18] The range of items that they recommend to consider is shown in Table 7.1. It covers all areas of the school to which students with disabilities should have access.

Disability Design Focus

Initially, this often took the form of detailed design requirements for each of the separate disability categories.[19] A recent example of this approach was prepared by the North Carolina Department of Public Instruction.[20] Their *Exceptional Children Facilities Planner* is divided into two major sections—instructional services and support services. The instructional services section covers each major type of disability (autism; behav-

Table 7.1.   Considerations for Access for Schools

Areas for Planning	*Other Facilities Access Issues*
Parking	Room size and shape
Doors	Specialized rooms
Ramps	Sound features
Elevators	Health considerations
Washrooms	Records storage
Drinking fountains	Dimensions of children
Signage	
Room identification	
Children signals and alarms	
Staff areas and central office	
Workrooms	
Change rooms and gymnasiums	
Auditorium, lecture hall, theater	
Cafeteria, dining area, teaching kitchen	
Recreational spaces	

Source: Ministry of Education, Skills, and Training, *Accessible School Facilities: A Resource for Planning* (Province of British Columbia, Canada: 1999).

iorally-emotionally disabled; deaf-blind, multihandicapped, and severely/ profoundly handicapped; hearing impaired; mentally disabled; specific learning disabled; speech-language impaired; and visually impaired). For each disability grouping, the facilities planner document begins with a program description that provides the grade levels, purpose of the instructional services, suggested methods of instruction, examples of instructional activities, and a maximum recommended class size. It goes on to identify the space requirements for that disability group. These requirements include suggested square footages for classroom space (elementary and secondary separately) and associated office and storage space. Importantly, this topic also includes guidance on the location of the special classroom and its relationship with the rest of the school building. Examples of typical furniture and typical equipment appropriate for the instructional space are identified. Finally, special notes related the special facility needs and considerations tailor the guidelines for each specific disability group. The specifications range from extensive for deaf-blind, multihandicapped, and severely/profoundly handicapped to minimal for speech-language impaired. Table 7.2 provides an example for autism from the facilities planner document.

Table 7.2. Accessibility Guidelines for Autism

Program Description:

<u>Grade Levels</u>: K–5 (Elementary); 6–12 (Middle/Secondary)

<u>Purpose</u>: To provide supplemental support and services that can enable the student with autism to achieve full educational potential.

<u>Suggested Methods of Instruction</u>: Individual, small-group, and independent learning; demonstration; computer-assisted instruction.

<u>Typical Activities</u>: Laboratory activities; hands-on individual and group activities; simulated work setting activities; learning center activities; computer learning activities.

<u>Maximum Recommended Class Size</u>: Six students with one teacher and one assistant.

Space Requirements:

<u>Relationships</u>: To facilitate inclusion of the student with autism in the regular school program, the classroom for autistic students should be centrally located within the school, with easy access to support areas such as the media center, cafeteria, computer lab, multipurpose room or gymnasium, toilet, and health room.

<u>Square Footages</u>:

K–5 classroom: 1,400–1,600 (Additional 125–200 for office and storage)

6–12 classroom: 1,600–1,800 (Additional 125–200 for office and storage)

Furnishings and Equipment:

<u>Typical furniture</u>:

- Age-appropriate individual and group student tables with stacking chairs
- Heavy-duty work tables (benches) for vocational training activities
- Computer stations
- Storage units ("cubbies" or plastic storage bins on shelves) for student materials
- Low portable bookcases and low built-in bookshelves

<u>Typical equipment</u>:

- Networked computers (4–6)
- Printers (one per three computers)
- Wall-mounted TV monitor with built-in VCR
- Dry marker and tack boards
- Telephone
- Clock
- File cabinets (lockable) (4)
- Individual work carrels

Special notes:

1. Toilets (handicapped accessible) with showers, contiguous to the classroom, should be provided. Doors should swing outward.
2. Handicapped accessible countertop with sink (hot and cold water) should be provided.
3. A family skills training area contiguous to the classroom should contain a washer, dryer, range with oven, microwave oven, refrigerator-freezer with icemaker, dishwasher,

Table 7.2.   (cont.)

handicapped-accessible sink with hot and cold supply, and kitchen-type cabinetry and countertop.

4. Sinks and lavatories should have lever-type handles.
5. Laundry, family skills, and toilet areas should have resilient tile floor covering; other areas should use short, tight-loop carpet.
6. Storage units, partition walls, and bookcases should be portable to facilitate the creation and reconfiguration of learning centers and specific activity areas.
7. Computer stations should be networked to the LAN and WAN and to the Internet.
8. Electrical receptacles should be located at six feet on center on perimeter walls and may be required at strategic locations in the floor to accommodate assistive technology.
9. A two-way intercom system with administrative and security offices should be provided.
10. A fenced playground off the K–5 classroom(s) should be provided.
11. Outside storage should be provided for portable playground equipment and toys.
12. A covered outside play area oriented to capture the winter sun should be provided.
13. A greenhouse (6–12) should be considered.
14. Acoustic isolation is required.
15. Classroom windows should not front areas that pose potential distractions from outside windows.
16. Floor treatments may be used to define specific areas of the room, with flush transitions between spaces and flooring materials.
17. Wall surfaces should be sturdy and easily cleaned. Rough-texture surfaces (such as unfinished concrete blocks) or those vulnerable to easy penetration (such as sheetrock) should be avoided.
18. Avoid sharp corners on walls, furniture, and cabinetwork.
19. Electronic ballasts should be used on fluorescent fixtures.

Source: Division of School Support, School Planning, *Exceptional Children Facilities Planner: Sample Plans, Accessibility Guidelines* (Raleigh, North Carolina: North Carolina Department of Public Instruction, 1998), 5–6.

A similar approach is followed for support services, but the orientation is on the type of service provided rather than the disability condition. The support services for which guidelines are provided include: adapted physical education; occupational therapy; physical therapy; and school psychological services. The facilities requirements range from minimally different from regular education (adapted physical education) to specialized furnishings and equipment and private space in which to provide the service (physical therapy and school psychological services).

However, the focus on disability and the creation of specific instructional spaces with specialized requirements for square footage, furniture, equipment, and room arrangement for each type of disability has proved limiting and inflexible.[21] The emphasis has shifted to flexibility and modification of physical facilities as students with disabilities and their needs change. The change is derived from a change in the philosophy and approach to special education instruction and programming. Instructional strategies, such as inclusion, call for more integration of students with disabilities into the regular classroom and programs and less of an exclusionary approach. This has led to a more generalized approach to facilities planning to be compatible with more inclusive instructional strategies.

Universal Design

Universal design is an architectural concept that incorporates adaptations into the initial design of a school (or other facility) so that it not only provides access for students with disabilities, but also improves ease and efficiency of use by all students. It is defined as: "The design of products and environments to be useable by all people, to the greatest extent possible, without the need for adaptation or specialized design."[22]

As noted in the definition, it attempts to build in the necessary access features to the original facility, rather than adding them as a later feature. This approach to facilities design is now the preferred approach. While the emphasis is on initial design, the concept can also be applied to modifications of existing facilities. The Center for Universal Design has developed seven principles to evaluate existing designs and to guide and improve new design. Each of the principles has guidelines that provide further assistance for effective implementation:

1. *Equitable use.* The design is useful and marketable to people with diverse abilities.
2. *Flexibility in use.* The design accommodates a wide range of individual preferences and abilities.
3. *Simple and intuitive.* Use of the design is easy to understand, regardless of the user's experience, knowledge, language skills, or current concentration level.
4. *Perceptible information.* The design communicates necessary information effectively to the user, regardless of ambient conditions or the user's sensory abilities.
5. *Tolerance for error.* The design minimizes hazards and the adverse consequences of accidental or unintended actions.
6. *Low physical effort.* The design can be used efficiently and comfortably and with a minimum of fatigue.
7. *Size and space for approach and use.* Appropriate size and space is provided for approach, reach, manipulation, and use regardless of user's body size, posture, or mobility.[23]

Implementation of Design Principles

The principles of universal design provide general direction to designing new school facilities and for remodeling or renovating existing ones. However, to be effective, more specific applications to schools are necessary. These can range from strategies for use of classroom space to complementing instruction and curriculum approaches to minimizing segregation of students with disabilities in the school.[24]

Versatile classroom space

Rather than a generic-type classroom, a more useful approach could be to design and construct multiple spaces within a single classroom containing a larger common area, an alcove area, and a small adjacent room that can be acoustically isolated. With varying ceiling heights to define the spaces, a wide variety of students and instructional approaches can be accommodated in educationally appropriate ways. Further, the uses of the spaces can change from year to year to serve students with different types of disabilities. Modular furniture can enhance the versatility of the space as well.

Travel distances

Centralized locations for common instructional programs, such as music, art, and physical education, central office, and food services make it more convenient for all students, including those with disabilities. Easy access to elevators for multi-story buildings is essential along with consideration of multiple elevators in larger school buildings.

Program integration

Facilities should encourage integration of special education and regular education programs. Segregation of special education classrooms and special facilities should be minimized. The same is true of administrative, planning, and lounge areas for teachers and other staff. Common facilities for special education and regular education personnel should be a part of the building design. In this way, physical facilities encourage and support curricular integration.

Parental involvement

Participation by parents of students with disabilities in the planning and delivery of their children's special education program is mandated by IDEA. To encourage their taking part in these activities, a special room is helpful. Other considerations include convenient parking, storage space for personal belongings, and computer and printer access. Communication from parents outside of school is also important. So easy access by telephone and email to teachers and administrators needs to be available in instructional, support, and administrative areas.

Student dignity

Facilities should not segregate students with disabilities from their non-disabled peers in instructional or common school areas. Rather than accentuating their condition, facilities should integrate these students into the regular flow of school life. Areas of concern are: laboratory stations that are usable for all students to permit individual and group activities; and seating in auditoriums, lecture halls, and sports facilities for equivalent viewing of and participation in the events. On the other hand, there are instances where the privacy of students with disabilities must be respected, particularly in health areas and services.

Outdoor recreation areas

Federal guidelines have also been established by the Access Board to provide accessibility to play areas for students with disabilities in accordance with ADA. The guidelines cover both new construction and alterations in such areas as ground level and elevated play components, accessible routes, ramps and transfer systems, ground surfaces, and soft contained play structures.[25]

Classroom acoustics

A substantial number of students with hearing impairments spend the majority of their instructional time in regular classrooms. Further, other students experience short-term hearing loss due to illness and seasonal allergies. The forthcoming development of a national acoustic standard for classrooms has significant implications for facilities design, including heating, ventilating, and air conditioning systems, wall and floor treatments, and windows.

Building security

For some students with disabilities (e.g., emotional disabilities) the concern is keeping them from leaving the building, rather than the traditional concerns of preventing unauthorized individuals from entering the building. Proper placement and control of entry points is important to curtail student flight. Within the building, areas that present health and safety hazards—equipment rooms, chemical storage—need to be secured and protected against student entry.

As an example of a universal design approach, basic features incorporated into the general planning and design of a building for efficient and accessible traffic flow and maneuverability of all students throughout the building could include: providing adequate curb drop-off areas and close accessible entryways, avoiding bottlenecks in the circulation pattern, clearly defining space utilization, using graphics to orient users, including color schemes to assist students with visual impairments, eliminating sharp projections from walls, and providing connecting doors with adequate width to accommodate traffic flow, including students with disabilities.[26]

FISCAL IMPLICATIONS

It is obvious that all of the requirements imposed on school districts to have their existing facilities and their new and remodeled facilities comply with IDEA, Section 504, and ADA, Title II, have significant cost implications. Meeting the principles of universal design and their implications for instructional, support, and administrative spaces are and will be costly. However, these federal requirements are an unfunded mandate. School remodeling and new construction costs are financed through local and state funds; no federal financial assistance is provided to meet the federal accessibility requirements. While limited anecdotal descriptions are available,[27] there is little information on what the costs implications of improving and updating the infrastructure for special education are and will be in the future. According to the U.S. General Accounting Office (GAO):

> The requirement that programs and activities of schools receiving federal financial assistance be accessible to the disabled has been in force for two decades. Yet no comprehensive nationwide study has been done or is currently planned to evaluate schools' accessibility to the disabled. Meanwhile, the passage of the Americans With Disabilities Act of 1990 (ADA)—although not changing the accessibility requirements for schools from the earlier law—has highlighted the need to improve accessibility.[28]

The most recent national data are from this 1995 GAO report which surveyed a nationally representative sample of 10,000 schools in 5,000 school districts.[29] They asked for information about spending on accessibility requirements for remodeling or retrofitting existing facilities. The survey results showed wide variability among schools, districts, and states in reported expenditures for both the prior and future three years. As a result, expenditure estimates were not considered particularly reliable. From 1992 through 1995, the national average expenditure per school was estimated at $40,000, but about 20% of schools reported that spending for accessibility was not needed. Based on those districts that reported spending, it was estimated that a total of $1.5 billion was spent to improve accessibility. GAO's assessment for the future was that a substantial increase in spending for accessibility was needed; a national average expenditure per school of $124,000 was estimated, which aggregated to an additional $5.2

billion for accessibility in the next three years (1996–1999). Several aspects of the reporting districts indicate that these estimates should be approached cautiously. Over a quarter of the schools reported that additional spending to achieve accessibility was not needed, and more than three-quarters of the total estimated spending came from the above average spending districts, which were only 21% of all schools. The characteristics of those schools that were most likely to report above average spending in the future are indicated in Table 7.3.

Table 7.3.   Characteristics of Schools Most Likely to Report Above Average Spending to Improve Accessibility in the Next Three Years

Characteristics (mutually exclusive)	*Characteristics of Schools Most Likely to Report Above Average Spending*
Location	
Community type	Central city/urban
Geographic region	Northeast
School characteristics	
Size	Large
Level	Secondary
Student characteristics	
Proportion of students approved for free or reduced-price lunch	No notable difference among schools
Proportion of minority students	50.5% or more

Source: U.S. General Accounting Office, *School Facilities: Accessibility for the Disabled Still an Issue*, GAO/HEHS-96-73 (Washington, D.C.: December 1995), 10.

Costs for new school buildings that are related to the infrastructure to support special education and to achieve federal requirements are due to changes in architectural design, space needs, and specialized equipment. These come from architectural cost standards for new construction and will vary considerably by type of building, type of construction, and region of the country.

CONCLUSIONS

With very limited data available, the most that can be concluded is that a national estimate of the costs of providing an adequate and statutorily required infrastructure for students with disabilities is substantial, but largely unknown. Special education represents a significant cost element of school districts' current operating budgets, and it also represents a significant element in their capital budgets. The costs will arise in remodeling existing facilities and in new construction. The costs of accessibility will be part of any proper design and will be incorporated into the overall costs of a construction project. While they cannot be aggregated to the state or national level with any certainty, they certainly must be considered by school districts in planning facilities for the future.

NOTES

1. Vicki Stoecklin, *Designing for All Children* (Kansas City, Missouri: White Hutchinson Leisure & Learning Group, 1999), 1.

2. For a comprehensive review of the relevant statutes and regulations, see James Ansley, *Creating Accessible Schools* (Washington, D.C.: National Clearinghouse for Educational Facilities, 2000).

3. The law became P.L. 105-17 when it was reauthorized in 1997. It is known as IDEA '97. The full text of the law can be found on the Web site of the Office of Special Education and Rehabilitative Services, http://www.ed.gov/offices/OSERS/Policy/IDEA/the_law.html. Another Web site that provides more information on the law and regulations for IDEA is http://www.ideapractices.org/lawandregs.htm.

4. The relevant regulations for Section 504, Part 104—Nondiscrimination on the Basis of Handicap in Programs or Activities Receiving Federal Financial Assistance—are found in *Federal Register,* November 13, 2000 (65 *Fed. Reg.* 68050). They are also located at http://www.ed.gov/offices/OCR/regs/34cfr104.html.

5. ERIC Clearinghouse on Disabilities and Gifted Education, *An Overview of ADA, IDEA, and Section 504: Update 2001,* ERIC EC Digest E606 (2001).

6. Section 504, Part 104.4 (5).

7. Office for Civil Rights, *Compliance with the Americans with Disabilities Act: A Self Guide for Public Elementary and Secondary Schools* (Washington, D.C.: U.S. Department of Education), 156, http://www.edlaw.net/service/guidcont.html.

8. For a review of the regulations for ADA, Title II, see http://www.usdoj.gov/crt/ada/reg2.html. This discussion draws on that material.

9. Title II Highlights downloaded from the Web site of Disability Rights Section, Civil Rights Division, U.S. Department of Justice at http://www.usdoj.gov/crt/ada/t2hlt95.htm.

10. §35.150, Title II, ADA.

11. §35.151(c), Title II, ADA.

12. *Federal Register,* 36CFR Part 1191. [Docket No. 94-2], RIN 3014 AA17 (January 13, 1998).

13. *Federal Register,* Architectural and Transportation Barriers Compliance Board, Part IV. Americans with Disabilities Act (ADA) Accessibility Guidelines for Buildings and Facilities (Wednesday, October 18, 2000; amended November 20, 2000); Play Areas, Final rule, 36 CFR Part 1191, http://www.access-board.gov/play/finalrule.htm.

14.   This discussion is based on *A Self Guide for Public Elementary and Secondary Schools*, Chapter 7, http://www.edlaw.net/service/guidcont.html.

15.   §35.160, Title II, ADA.

16.   *A Self Guide for Public Elementary and Secondary Schools*, 226.

17.   The National Clearinghouse for Educational Facilities maintains a resource list specifically devoted to accessibility that provides a current listing of useful sources at http://www.edfacilities.org/rl/accessibility.cfm.

18.   Ministry of Education, Skills, and Training, *Accessible School Facilities: A Resource for Planning* (Province of British Columbia, Canada: 1999).

19.   An early example of this approach is provided in Allen Abend, Michael Bednar, Vira Froehlinger, and Yale Stenzler, *Facilities for Special Education Services: A Guide for Planning New and Renovated Schools* (Annapolis, Maryland: Maryland Department of Education, 1979).

20.   Division of School Support, School Planning, *Exceptional Children Facilities Planner: Sample Plans, Accessibility Guidelines* (Raleigh, North Carolina: North Carolina Department of Public Instruction, 1998), http://dpi.state.nc.us/clearinghouse.

21.   James E. Rydeen, "Universal Design," *American School and University* 71 (July 1999): 56, 58, 60, 62.

22.   Betty Connell, Mike Jones, Ron Mace, James Mueller, Abir Mullick, Elaine Ostroff, Jon Sanford, Edward Steinfeld, Molly Story, and Gregg Vanderheiden, *What Is Universal Design?* (Raleigh, North Carolina: The Center for Universal Design, North Carolina State University, 1997), http://www.design.ncsu.edu/cud/univ_design/princ_overview.htm.

23.   Ibid.

24.   These considerations come from Allen Abend, *Planning and Designing for Students with Disabilities* (Washington, D.C.: National Clearinghouse for Educational Facilities, 2001), http://www.edfacilities.org.

25.   U.S. Architectural and Transportation Barriers Compliance Board, Architectural and Transportation Barriers Compliance Board, Part IV; Americans with Disabilities Act (ADA) Accessibility Guidelines for Buildings and Facilities; Play Areas; Final Rule, 36-CFR-Part-1191, (Washington, D.C.: 2000), http://www.access-board.gov/news/playrule.htm.

26.   Rydeen, "Universal Design."

27.   Mike Kennedy, "Gaining Access," *American School and University* 73 (December 2000); 14,16–18.

28.   U.S. General Accounting Office, *School Facilities: Accessibility for the Disabled Still an Issue*, GAO/HEHS-96-73 (Washington, D.C.: December 1995), 3, http://frwebgate.access.gpo.gov.

29.   Ibid.

CHAPTER 8

SCHOOL FINANCE LITIGATION

One Strategy to Address Inequities in School Infrastructure Funding

David C. Thompson
Kansas State University

Faith E. Crampton
**University of Wisconsin
Milwaukee**

ABSTRACT

The overall lesson of this chapter is that school finance litigation has been an effective strategy for addressing inequities—a strategy that promises additional success when steadily and longitudinally applied to school infrastructure funding. At the same time, litigation is an incomplete strategy and should never be relied upon exclusively because society and its courts are not yet leading on this issue, even though significant progress has occurred and the signs of establishment of a permanent change in social acceptance of this issue is increasingly visible. Although the physical environment in schools would be much worse without the existing legislative mechanisms that provide infrastructure aid to education in many states, the magnitude of unmet funding need leaves little hope for fully redressing schools' needs under entirely amicable conditions. As a result, the force of adversarial litigation takes on even more attractiveness to those who perceive the true depth of the nation's extant dilemma.

Saving America's School Infrastructure, pages 163–190
Copyright © 2003 by Information Age Publishing

INTRODUCTION

The complexities of funding school infrastructure at all levels of education are well chronicled in this book. The context of educational capacity as a critical issue spells deep-seated troubles for education, and the problems seen throughout this book for both urban and rural schools seem to defy resolution by any amicable means. Infrastructure funding deficits apparently have no finite or even predictable limits, as horizons are constantly being redefined or even newly invented in ways that were unforeseeable only a few years ago. If, for example, general infrastructure issues are already deep and expensive, the ever-widening landscape related to special needs populations further and continuously frustrates any permanent progress toward solution by embracing new definitions of infrastructure needs, and in the same vein, the overwhelming demands of technology seen in this book are clear evidence that solving today's understanding of a problem merely guarantees a good decision will be woefully obsolete a short while later.

Searching for legislative solutions to these complex issues is naturally the first expected order of events, a fundamental principle of both progress and courtesy in a civilized society. Legislatures rightly have been charged with responsibility for funding public education at all levels, and great progress has been made toward understanding the linkages between infrastructure and equal educational opportunity.[1] But the speed of all such civilized progress has been slowed by certain inevitabilities, some of which are nearly unique to the school infrastructure dilemma. One such inevitability is that broad scale linkages between educational opportunity and infrastructure are quite nascent—although this chapter will suggest that while a level of awareness is longstanding, action is only relatively recent so that as a consequence fairness in infrastructure funding is still in its infant stages and very rudimentary when compared to the sophistication that generally characterizes other areas of educational funding equity. Another inevitability is that federal and state legislatures are responsible for many heavy burdens on behalf of society, so that every available dollar in a finite resource environment is fiercely coveted by a wide array of constituent groups, each crying foul when another interest group such as education seems to gain some ground in capturing available resources. Equally inevitable is that legislative representation nurtures protectionism by deliberate design, as individual legislators find it hard to vote against their particular constituencies' selfish interests and are likewise expected to vote for anything that particularly advantages their electoral base. Finally, school infrastructure funding faces the inevitability that its needs are of breathtaking size, generally outside the scope of federal government and far beyond the capacity of most state governments to effectively address. And the situation is compounded by a final inevitability in that state legislatures and local communities alike have long been reluctant to depart from a historical tradition that has made bricks and mortar a local responsibility. The interaction of all these events has caused many local communities to be unable to satisfy their school infrastructure needs, and the current state of disrepair in schools, combined with ever-expanding horizons, has virtually ensured only mediocre progress even when legislatures are ready and willing to accept an aggressive partnership in funding infrastructure.

Although the physical environment in schools would be much worse without the existing legislative mechanisms that provide infrastructure aid to education in many states, these depressing observations leave little hope for fully redressing schools' needs under entirely amicable conditions. As a consequence, litigation has been seen as another avenue to help alleviate infrastructure problems. At once an old and a new path in relation to finding infrastructure solutions, litigation in the larger general school aid context has provided an analog that may offer some additional hope because general school aid formulas have managed to progress to a point through litigation that would never have been reached solely by relying on persuasion and legislative volunteerism. The force of law, therefore, has benefited general school aid through adversarial interpretation and application of constitutional responsibility, and litigation is now understood to coexist simultaneously with legislative solutions to produce a greater gain in the end. Because the force of law is likely to factor into any eventual resolution of schools' capital needs, this chapter explores the extant record of infrastructure funding litigation at both federal and state levels with the intent of making a realistic assessment of available solutions to the nation's deep and worsening school infrastructure dilemma.

LITIGATION AS A TOOL
FOR BROAD SCHOOL FUNDING REFORM[2]

The history of litigation as a tool for reform in public school funding is widely documented in the professional literature. Aimed at increasing the amount of fiscal resources to public schools in the belief that more money provides more equal opportunities for children to learn, lawsuits have steadily hammered at wealth-based variations in educational opportunities for more than 100 years. Plaintiffs have followed a predictable strategy in first attacking through the federal court system by focusing on interpreting the U.S. Constitution in such a way that would establish a guaranteed right to education. Still other litigation has focused on individual states' courts, seeking a favorable interpretation of states' unique constitutional and statutory requirements apart from any federal protections. In this way, failure at one level would not necessarily lead to failure at the other level; i.e., forcing states to comply with higher authority if successful at the federal level, while creating a fallback position if federal protections were lacking. Necessarily adversarial by virtue of the nature of litigation itself, the pursuit of fairness in school funding has been nerve-wracking as both federal and state constitutional interpretation can be significantly affected by the times and evolving attitudes of courts—a reality that has caused neither strategy to have a guarantee of success. But the aims of school funding litigation have been consistent in all instances, as litigants on both sides of the argument have asked federal and state courts to determine the meaning and limits of equal educational opportunity.

Although school funding litigation is often regarded as highly and even uniquely state-specific, the federal case led the way. Plaintiffs first sought equal funding for school children by seeking a favorable U.S. Supreme Court ruling as the law of the land, under the logic that states would have to conform to federal demands. Bringing a federal lawsuit was a reasonable act, as equality had long been of great legal significance ever since the nation's earliest struggles to free itself from British rule and to establish a new democratic order. Equality was at the heart of the Bill of Rights when it was adopted into law in 1791, and the Fourteenth Amendment to the U.S. Constitution, ratified in 1868, promised equality to everyone in America. The Fourteenth Amendment was critically important to school finance litigation because its provisions were binding on the individual states, as it held that, "…no State shall make or enforce any law which shall abridge the privileges or immunities of citizens of the United States; nor shall any State…deny to any person within its jurisdiction the equal protection of the laws"[3]—a principle of pivotal importance in securing the rights of minorities and other protected classes against unlawful discrimination. Conjointly, a set of earlier court cases involving issues such as voting rights had established that certain rights were so constitutionally protected that these rights were fundamental to individuals and that denial could only occur under the most extreme circumstances. On these two grounds, a two-pronged attack for fiscal fairness in schools was laid. One prong hoped to show that fiscal resource variability was illegally related to race or to social class in schools, while the other prong hoped to show that fiscal resource variability resulted in violation of some other fundamental right: i.e., school resource variability would hopefully be found to impermissibly violate the U.S. Constitution's Fourteenth Amendment equal protection clause and simultaneously establish a fundamental right to full and equal educational opportunity. In essence, the strategy was to ask the federal judiciary whether unequal money in schools is a kind of inequality under law.

The search for a favorable federal posture on school funding was based in part on the U.S. Supreme Court's historic ruling in *Brown v. Board of Education* in 1954 when it overturned "separate but equal" provisions relating to racial segregation.[4] *Brown* had held that "...education is perhaps the most important function of state and local governments...In these days, it is doubtful that any child may reasonably be expected to succeed in life if he is denied the opportunity of an education. Such an opportunity...is a right which must be made available to all on equal terms."[5] With such encouraging and explicit words, school finance reformers believed that *Brown* could apply to school funding since money and educational opportunity can easily be shown to vary widely based on residence in school districts of unequal tax base.

Although enthusiasm for a federal victory relating to school funding was high, actual experience was more sobering as the principles of equity so strongly supported in relation to race fell short when applied to equality in money. A series of federal school funding equity cases failed badly, usually viewed as beginning with the district court case styled as *Burruss v. Wilkerson*[6] in Virginia in 1969 and effectively ending poorly for plaintiffs at the U.S. Supreme Court in *San Antonio Independent School District v. Rodriguez*[7] in Texas in 1973. The response by the courts throughout the federal assault echoed the same constant thread in ruling that, unlike immutable characteristics such as race that make a clearly identifiable class of victims who endure inescapable discrimination, a constitutionally protected class could not be found in wealth-related data on school funding, largely because school districts' boundaries do not correlate closely enough with individual wealth. The federal courts also could not find a convincing connection between education and access to other fundamental rights, thereby denying the necessary nexus sought by plaintiffs. As a result, federal courts effectively told plaintiffs in classic school finance litigation to file their claims in state courts, where state constitutional provisions might give greater protections than are available at the federal level.

The state case for school fiscal resource equalization has paralleled the federal case in many ways. In fact, lawsuits were often brought simultaneously in state and federal courts in the early days of funding reform, and in some instances the practice still holds today, although the reasoning has changed. For example, both *Burruss* and *Rodriguez* were federal court filings in the 1960s, but *Serrano v. Priest*[8] which contained both federal and state claims had already made its way entirely through the California state supreme court by 1971—fully two years before the U.S. Supreme Court turned away the federal claim in *Rodriguez* in 1973. The dual-front strategy was based in multiple reasons, but the primary goal was to enhance the likelihood of success by attacking on two fronts with both similar and different legal claims—a strategy that succeeded more readily because state litigation experienced significantly better results for plaintiffs.

Beginning with *Serrano* in 1971 when the California state supreme court triggered a national school finance reform movement by finding education to be a fundamental right under that state's constitution and deserving of full fiscal equalization, the state case developed rapidly. The reform side of the state fiscal equalization case was epitomized by *Serrano,* as the state supreme court's ruling for plaintiffs struck at exactly the right moment to launch a frenzy of copycat state school finance litigation across the nation. Plaintiffs in *Serrano* had sought a ruling on issues of a fundamental right to education, wealth as a suspect class, and federal and state equal protections—claims simultaneously raised under both federal and state constitutions. Plaintiffs had charged that the state aid plan for schools actually created fiscal disparity and that these differences meaningfully impacted the quality of education. The net sum was to make the quality of a child's education dependent on differences in local taxable property wealth. The state's high court agreed, harshly declaring:

> We have determined that this funding scheme invidiously discriminates against the poor because it makes the quality of a child's education a function of the wealth of his parents and neighbors. Recognizing as we must that the right to an education in our public schools is a fundamental interest which cannot be conditional on wealth, we can discern no compelling state purpose necessitating the present method of financing.[9]

That the federal claim was later overturned in *Rodriguez* did not detract from the practical and political effects of *Serrano* at the state level, either in California or in the reform movement that swept the rest of the nation. *Serrano* illustrated the value of the two-pronged attack and showed that state courts would not always adopt the same posture as their federal counterparts, and it encouraged plaintiffs to believe that state constitutions might be vulnerable despite apparent federal indifference to educational inequality as defined by resource accessibility. Equally important was the psychological effect of *Serrano* on the fifty state legislatures, as many state lawmakers understood *Serrano* to be a sign of the future. As a result, a simultaneous explosion of litigation and voluntary legislative reform of school funding laws followed across the nation, essentially producing the significantly more equalized funding systems that exist today.

In the overall picture, school funding reform over the past four decades has produced enormous gains favoring equalization, regardless of whether reform has been legislatively volunteered or whether it has been compelled by force of law. But reform has had a very checkered history, with false starts and clearly imperfect results. The long view maintains that school finance litigation is still high stakes gambling for plaintiffs, with no sure strategy for success.[10] At times, court decisions have seemed to coincide with a highly variable political climate, and winning a case has not necessarily ended the fighting, as compliance litigation has been a recurring struggle to enforce court rulings. Likewise, the scope of plaintiffs' claims has tended to grow over time, and at the same time the various courts have vacillated quite unpredictably in their willingness to fully embrace plaintiffs' views on exactly what should be equalized. Equally constraining has been the variability in legislative resistance to court orders, and the impact of economic conditions in states has at times had a severe dampening effect both on lawmakers' desire and ability to fund existing aid programs or to willingly expand existing definitions of equalization. With the full spate of general state aid programs, special needs mandates, and other targeted federal aid to schools that drove revenues in 1998–99 to a combined total of more than $347 billion in the fifty states,[11] it is not surprising that legislators have not rushed to adopt full funding for school infrastructure—despite powerful evidence of need approximated at more than $266 billion in 1999.[12]

SCHOOL INFRASTRUCTURE FUNDING LITIGATION IN FEDERAL COURTS

Widespread awareness regarding the struggle for equity in school funding largely has been restricted to general fund state aid plans, all but obscuring other areas with the notable exception of special education funding which is oftentimes viewed as a distinct niche. But the battles over fiscal fairness have not ignored the high cost of school infrastructure, and the struggle has been significantly greater than perhaps appreciated to this point. Litigation addressing the adequacy and equality of school infrastructure is actually longstanding and deeply intertwined with other areas of educational equity litigation, making it necessary to define the landscape of such litigation in terms of focus and situs.

Although the professional literature periodically has shown significant interest in the infrastructure needs of public schools,[13] there has been no extended analysis of either the extent or impact of capital needs litigation. Yet a systematic search across all courts for all available time periods shows a protracted struggle, both in direct applicability of the question of infrastructure funding equity and by the inevitable implication of related concerns to this costly and important school funding arena. As seen in Table 8.1, infrastructure funding litigation has occupied significant time and space in federal courts, reaching to the highest judicial levels in much the same context as general fund litigation.

Table 8.1.   Federal Cases Involving School Facilities

Location	Number of Cases	Percent of Total	Claim
U.S. Supreme Court	18	36	Desegregation
	13	26	Parochial
	7	14	Equal access/speech
	12	24	Wide-ranging
Other Federal Courts	2	8	Desegregation
	8	31	Higher ed access
	4	15	Special populations
	12	46	Wide-ranging
Total	76		

Table 8.1 is instructive not only for the court docket activity it identifies, but further for its implications about the past and future. While federal courts have not taken a case strictly on the merits of broad school facility equalization, federal courts nonetheless have been intensely engaged in the relationship between facilities and related topics that ultimately end up with federal courts making meaningful statements about the impact of infrastructure on equal educational opportunity. The most directly affected area in which federal courts have become engaged rests in the issue of desegregation, where a very long and bitter struggle has unfolded as plaintiffs have attempted to end discrimination in resources, both fiscal and material, with enormous implications and direct references involving both quality and equality of school facilities. Largely due to race, over a third of facility-related cases heard at the U.S. Supreme Court level have had direct infrastructure implications. First coming to a full-blown head in *Brown v. Board of Education* in 1954, the Supreme Court held that all unfounded discrimination was inherently unconstitutional, and striking down the "separate but equal" provisions in states which attempted to claim that educational programs and facilities separately maintained for racial minorities were permissible. Although *Brown* has never been widely recognized as a school funding case, from the outset its broad ramifications engaged massive sums of money with pervasive and wide-ranging impacts, and the Court was unequivocally clear in stating the interrelationships between educational opportunity, programs, and facilities as it overturned the separatist doctrine in *Plessy v. Ferguson*.[14] In sharp contrast to its historical posture, the Court in *Brown* clearly indicated an interest in equality in all areas of schooling and further pointed up that the argument about equality, including overtones relating to infrastructure, was actually a longstanding concern, excerpted in part to say:

...Where a State has undertaken to provide an opportunity for an education in its public schools, such an opportunity is a right which must be made available to all on equal terms...Does segregation of children in public schools solely on the basis of race deprive children of the minority group of equal educational opportunities, even though the physical facilities and other 'tangible' factors may be equal? We believe it does.[15]

Although first enunciated in the context of separatism, these budding themes of equality and equal provision dominated desegregation litigation for many years beyond *Brown* and drove the expenditures of countless dollars to meet the Court's demand or, alternatively, massive expenditures aimed at avoiding the spirit of the Court's words. Yet like all court mandates, opinion has wavered and even shifted, as in *San Antonio Independent School District v. Rodriguez*[16] in 1973, as the Court this time held against plaintiffs for strict equalization of educational funding while at the same time commenting, "...[w]hile all would agree that there is a correlation up to the point of providing the recognized essentials in facilities and academic opportunities, the issues of greatest disagreement include the effect on the quality of education of pupil-teacher ratios and of higher teacher salary schedules...."[17] Yet the breadth of defining equal opportunity was revealed in the sharply divided Court, as illustrated in a dissenting opinion by Justice White, joined by Douglas and Brennan, as he noted:

It is an inescapable fact that if one district has more funds available per pupil than another district, the former will have greater choice in educational planning than will the latter. In this regard...the question of discrimination in educational quality must be deemed to be an objective one that looks to what the State provides its children, not to what the children are able to do with what they receive. That a child forced to attend an underfunded school with poorer physical facilities, less experienced teachers, larger classes, and a narrower range of courses than a school with substantially more funds—and thus with greater choice in educational planning—may nevertheless excel is to the credit of the child, not the State. Indeed, who can ever measure for such a child the opportunities lost and the talents wasted for want of a broader, more enriched education? Discrimination in the opportunity to learn that is afforded a child must be our standard.[18]

The Court's same interest in interrelationships impacting equal educational opportunity was repeated most recently in *Missouri v. Jenkins*[19] in 1995, as the Court held that the improvement of school facilities remains an important factor in desegregation litigation. The case stemmed from a 1985 ruling by the district court that the state was obligated to erase discrimination in facilities and programs at a cost that had reached more than $540 million by the time the case reached the U.S. Supreme Court. In reaching its ruling, the Court cited its own past actions in the form of *Board of Education of Oklahoma City Public Schools v. Dowell*[20] and *Green v. School Board of New Kent County,*[21] reiterating in *Jenkins* that it had "...identified "student assignments, faculty, staff, transportation, extracurricular activities and facilities as the most important indicia of a racially segregated school system."[22] Although the Court finally held in *Jenkins* that the state had done enough to equalize educational opportunities, its continued interest in infrastructure indicated that children cannot learn well in poor facilities and that the state has an obligation to provide children with adequate facilities under at least a minimal and substantially equal definition.

The entire federal litigation scene at the highest level has been a lengthy struggle for genuine equality. Lower federal court cases have also occasionally involved school facilities, and in most instances these courts also have taken the position that facilities are important to equal educational opportunity. Yet caution must dominate when considering the implications of this discussion because although these cases seemingly suggest an aggressive desire among federal courts to equalize school infrastructure and to consider it an integral part of equal educational opportunity, such interpretation must be severely tempered by recognition of the claims where infrastructure seems to carry the greatest influence. A careful reading of all federal cases largely fences out the broader equity claim envisioned by school finance reformers, as the struggles have not really been about general infrastructure equity (although implicated), but rather focused on how unequalized school infrastructure frustrates equal educational opportunity in the context of racial discrimination. Significance should also be attached to the fact that the remainder of cases across the federal level have not been discussed here, a manifestation of the fact that the balance of federal cases has involved narrowly drawn localized disputes over such issues as taxing authority, parochiaid/equal access concerns, or issues irrelevant to the larger question in which this chapter takes interest. But ironically, a significant amount of time in federal courts also has been devoted to disputes over unsafe physical conditions in schools, a major detractor to equal educational opportunity—i.e., no broad equity claim is found in the one area of significant activity which does not include racial overtones as the driving force. Yet a broad constitutional right to an equal physical learning environment (apart from racial segregation or handicapping condition) has not been overwhelmingly evident in federal court—in part because the question either has not ripened sufficiently or simply goes unasked.

SCHOOL INFRASTRUCTURE FUNDING LITIGATION IN STATE COURTS

By comparison to the relatively small amount of federal litigation involving education's physical infrastructure, Table 8.2 illustrates a much larger body of legal disputes over funding school facilities. In contrast to the 20 desegregation cases (accompanied by no broad federal equalization litigation) at the federal level, activity in the 50 states has produced 1,913 cases covering a wide range of issues, although still with only 77 cases involving in some manner the broader equity claim of equal provision in school infrastructure funding. As with the federal case, numerous narrowly drawn lawsuits have dominated the majority of these disputes. An analysis of the universe of court decisions finds innumerable small cases that dispute provision of adequate and equal facilities, but for the most part these cases are tied to very parochial concerns such as school consolidation or annexation on the basis of inadequate facilities in the receiving district,[23] to small disputes over the interpretation of what a state means when it says school districts should provide adequate facilities,[24] or unique conditions related to school growth and developer fees[25] or conversely related to sparse population and difficult geography.[26] As a consequence, only about 4% of state cases involving school facilities are relevant to the purpose of this chapter, permitting a few leading cases to illustrate the issues in order to assist in drawing conclusions about the value of litigation as a strategy to address school infrastructure funding inequities. Table 8.3 identifies a small set of representative state-level court cases that have directly approached the larger school infrastructure equity question as framed in this chapter. Of these representative decisions, the states of West Virginia, New Jersey, Arizona, Texas, Ohio, and Wyoming are among the most interesting and illustrative of the potential for litigation as a tool for school infrastructure funding reform.

As a preface to examining these states, the history of infrastructure litigation at the state level involving broader equity issues should be recognized as dating from at least 1837, with a distinct line of thought to be drawn between the earliest days and the present time. Cases prior to the modern spate of school finance litigation that began in the 1960s largely dealt with highly localized arguments about whether local communities must provide educational facilities, disputes over the power of government to tax for school construction and maintenance, and whether existing facilities were adequate to meet minimum educational needs. For example, Table 8.3 shows the state of Iowa with 58 cases involving school facilities between the years 1872–1997, standing as a good illustration of the early struggle as local communities refused to build schools and were required by courts to provide "adequate" school facilities for children,[27] and as courts ordered local units of government to levy school taxes over protest.[28] As a consequence, cases truly involving the broader equity question are of more recent origin, coinciding with general school funding equity debates throughout the nation.

Table 8.2.   State Cases Involving School Facilities

State	Number of Cases Involving School Facilities	Number of Cases in Broad Equity Claim—Includes Appeals
Alabama	21	8
Alaska	9	1
Arizona	21	5
Arkansas	31	4
California	141	3
Colorado	17	1
Connecticut	51	1
Delaware	13	1
District of Columbia	6	1
Florida	57	2
Georgia	29	0
Hawaii	4	0
Idaho	18	0
Illinois	106	1
Indiana	38	1
Iowa	58	0
Kansas	42	2
Kentucky	36	2
Louisiana	36	2
Maine	13	0
Maryland	37	0
Massachusetts	24	0
Michigan	27	0
Minnesota	30	0
Mississippi	48	1
Missouri	75	1
Montana	17	0
Nebraska	35	0
Nevada	6	0
New Hampshire	9	0

Table 8.2.   (cont.)

State	Number of Cases Involving School Facilities	Number of Cases in Broad Equity Claim—Includes Appeals
New Jersey	100	10
New Mexico	9	0
New York	114	1
North Carolina	70	4
North Dakota	26	1
Ohio	65	2
Oklahoma	36	1
Oregon	25	0
Pennsylvania	125	1
Rhode Island	16	1
South Carolina	26	1
South Dakota	17	2
Tennessee	30	2
Texas	62	2
Utah	15	2
Vermont	8	0
Virginia	21	0
Washington	39	1
West Virginia	18	8
Wisconsin	24	0
Wyoming	12	1
Total	1,913	77

West Virginia

Apart from equal provision issues in the context of school desegregation seen earlier in federal litigation, the broad infrastructure equalization question did not really blossom until the 1970s in state-level litigation, first finding its potential in 1979 in the pioneering case of *Pauley v. Kelly*[29] in West Virginia. In a ground-breaking analysis of equal educational opportunity in the classic vein, the trial judge held that equal opportunity under the West Virginia constitution required a thorough and efficient education for every child without exception, held that the mandatory requirements of a thorough and efficient system of free public schools made education a fundamental constitutional right in that state, and enumerated the specific

Table 8.3.   Representative Leading Cases Involving Broader School Infrastructure Claims

State	Case	Holding
Arizona	*Roosevelt Elementary School District No. 66 v. Bishop* (1994)	Held that the statutory financing scheme for public education was the cause of gross disparities in school facilities and that such a system failed to comply with the "general and uniform" requirement of state constitution.
Idaho	*Idaho Schools for Equal Educational Opportunity v. State* (1999)	Held that that the legislature has the duty to provide a means for school districts to fund facilities that offer a safe environment conducive to learning and that the state itself had set up explicit rules regarding facilities that oblige the state to honor its own definition of facilities as a critical factor in carrying out educational programs.
Kentucky	*Rose v. Council for Better Education* (1989)	Citing extensively from *Pauley v. Kelly* (W.Va.), held the entire educational system in Kentucky violated the state's 'efficient' constitutional requirement. Held that the constitution demands a substantially uniform system and equal school facilities.
New Jersey	*Abbott v. Burke* (1989)	Held the entire educational system violative of the state's requirement for a "thorough and efficient" (T&E) system of education. Infrastructure deficits were harshly criticized, with the state required to pick up all costs associated with parity for "*Abbott*" schools. Effectively, the state was required to assume total responsibility for past and present conditions and to guarantee full parity for disadvantaged children.
New York	*Campaign for Fiscal Equity v. State* (1995)	Reinstated plaintiffs' cause of action. Focused on "minimum provision" in the state constitution, i.e., that children are entitled to minimally adequate physical facilities and classrooms that provide enough light, space, heat, and air to permit children to learn. Children must have minimally adequate tools such as desks, chairs, pencils, and reasonably current textbooks. Children are entitled to minimally adequate teaching of basic curricula such as reading, writing, mathematics, science, and social studies, by personnel adequately trained to teach those subject areas. However, fundamentality is denied under both state and federal constitutions, and no equal protection claim exists in this case since no intentional discrimination can be shown.

Table 8.3. (cont.)

State	Case	Holding
Ohio	*DeRolph v. State* (1997)	Held the entire school funding system unconstitutional on the thorough and efficient constitutional requirement, finding facilities integral to equal opportunity and specifically finding the state's Classroom Facilities Act unconstitutional to the extent that it is underfunded.
Texas	*Edgewood Independent School District v. Meno* (1995)	Reviewed *Edgewood I* which held the state's school funding system violative of the state constitution's efficiency clause, including a duty to provide school facilities. In *Meno,* the sole issue was whether the state was meeting its obligation to facilities, with the court holding that no instance of failure was present, but emphasizing the court's aggressive interest and vigilance on this matter.
W. Virginia	*Pauley v. Kelly* (1979)	Held entire educational system violative of the state's requirement for a "thorough and efficient" (T&E) system of education. Infrastructure deficits were harshly noted and specific requirements laid down by the court, including creation of a master plan denoting size, contents, and quality of individual classrooms.
Wyoming	*State v. Campbell County School District* (2001)	Continued to hold unconstitutional the state's entire school aid scheme as found earlier in *Washakie* (1980), and holding facilities implicit to all definitions of equal opportunity and establishing a court-ordered timetable for compliance with full parity statewide.

and detailed requirements that would form a mandated master plan for educational improvement in all schools in West Virginia. The court-ordered Master Plan included sweeping school facilities mandates and specified in detail that every individual school must provide adequate space and quality for each area of the curriculum: for example, the court ordered that each elementary school must have an art room for each 350–500 pupils with at least 50 square feet per child, and that every secondary school of 500 students would need at least one art room with a minimum 65 square feet per pupil. Even storage areas were detailed. Similar minute specifications were provided for each academic and activity function of elementary, middle, and secondary levels. In subsequent judicial review, the state supreme court effectively endorsed this conceptualization of infrastructure as a vital element of educational opportunity, tightly defining a thorough and efficient system of schools as one which:

> ...[D]evelops, as best the state of education expertise allows, the minds, bodies and social morality of its charges to prepare them for useful and happy occupations, recreation and citizenship, and does so economically. Legally recognized elements in this definition are development in every child to his or her capacity of: (1) literacy; (2) ability to add, subtract, multiply and divide numbers; (3) knowledge of government to the extent that the child will be equipped as a citizen to make informed choices among persons and issues that affect his own governance; (4) self-knowledge and knowledge of his or her total environment to allow the child to intelligently choose life work—to know his or her options; (5) work-training and advanced academic training as the child may intelligently choose; (6) recreational pursuits; (7) interests in all creative arts, such as music, theatre, literature, and the visual arts; (8) social ethics, both behavioral and abstract, to facilitate compatibility with others in this society. Implicit are supportive services: (1) good physical facilities, instructional materials and personnel; (2) careful state and local supervision to prevent waste and to monitor pupil, teacher and administrative competency...We recognize that many facets of public education are being examined by...critics...However, there are undeniable legal bases for all our conclusions, including the elements specifically distilled from the debates and cases that are the specifications of what a thorough and efficient school system should have, and should do.[30]

The ruling in *Pauley* led to massive educational changes in West Virginia under the court-ordered Master Plan, both in the political climate and in the organization and operation of schools themselves. The ruling applied not only to infrastructure,[31] but also to reforming the wider educational system's equal opportunity assurances. The state supreme court's words left little doubt that it took strict compliance with its views seriously, as it stated that the basic test would become whether funds provided by the state under existing and subsequent changes to the state's aid scheme would be allocated in a manner providing essential physical facilities to meet the thorough and efficient standard—so much so that education in each individual school district would be held up to the test. As with other school finance lawsuits, however, *Pauley* has returned to court for compliance litigation,[32] including disputes over whether the state's School Building Authority, created in 1988 partly in response to the lawsuit and charged with the duty to "facilitate and provide state funds for the construction and maintenance of school facilities so as to meet the educational needs of the people in an efficient and economical manner" is being met.

New Jersey

While it is inaccurate to say that *Pauley* launched a *Serrano*-like revolution among state courts in relation to equal educational opportunity as expressed in school infrastructure funding, other state courts have also expressed similar strong interest in the relationship between physical environment and educational opportunity. One of the longest running battles over general school funding rests in the New Jersey case of *Abbott v. Burke*[33] which has exhibited great interest in equality as expressed in expenditures on bricks and mortar.

The struggle for fair funding in New Jersey as expressed in *Abbott* actually goes back to 1973 when the state supreme court in *Robinson v. Cahill*[34] held that the state's general school funding scheme violated the thorough and efficient education clause of that state's constitution. The court held that a thorough and efficient education requires equality for all children and must prepare each child to be a citizen and to compete in the labor market and that the state must ensure delivery of the constitutionally mandated educational programs and facilities. In a long series of new and compliance-related issues consumed under judicial monitoring styled first as iterations of *Robinson* and later as *Abbott*, the state supreme court consistently measured progress toward the stated goals of high quality education throughout the entire state, identifying those districts in greatest need as "*Abbott*" districts and specifying strict details on improvements that must be made to bring educational and fiscal parity to all children. In particular, the court's vigilant monitoring resulted in new legislative appropriations for a wide array of improvements to schools, including capital construction and repair in *Abbott* districts, with a total price tag for the state of approximately $3 billion.[35] At times eloquent in justifying the ruling in subsequent reviews, the court found that its own directives required the state to fund all costs of necessary facilities remediation and construction in the *Abbott* districts, specifically ordering that the state must secure funds to cover the costs of remediating life-cycle and infrastructure deficiencies in *Abbott* schools, to fund the costs of temporary facilities, and to initiate effective managerial responsibility over school construction.[36]

The struggles in New Jersey, while extraordinary in depth of need and quite atypical of judicial monitoring across the history of school finance litigation, are nonetheless meaningful in understanding that courts may particularly see the relationship between infrastructure and equality when the disparity becomes unconscionable. Similarly, the ability of a court to rule for plaintiffs using a "lesser" standard (i.e., succeeding on the thorough and efficient claim compared to the failed fundamentality test in New Jersey) indicates that some degree of conceptual readiness in the expansion of definitions of equal opportunity comes into play over time. While many states will never approach the sheer depth of need found in New Jersey and consequently are unlikely to encounter the shocking disparities that aided plaintiffs in *Robinson* and *Abbott*, trends are sometimes born and incrementally established from extraordinary circumstances because it can be easily shown that while few states share many of New Jersey's educational problems, many states' rulings on general fund financing readily turned to the original *Robinson* language when considering the constitutionality of their own parochial circumstance—a trend that could once again follow from the infrastructure emphasis found in New Jersey's school finance wars.

Arizona

The emerging struggle for infrastructure funding fairness took a surprising turn in 1994 in the Arizona case of *Roosevelt Elementary School District v. Bishop*.[37] The only state case to have been brought solely on school infrastructure inequity, a trial court originally dismissed claims by plaintiffs that the quality of school facilities were highly variable among districts and that many plaintiff schools were unsafe, unhealthy, in violation of building and safety codes, and that other plaintiff schools lacked libraries, laboratories, computer rooms, fine arts programs, gymnasiums, and auditoriums.[38] On appeal, the state supreme court took great interest in contrasting these poorer districts to their wealthier counterparts, noting schools with indoor swimming pools, covered athletic stadiums, television studios, and state-of-the-art computer systems. The court squarely laid the blame for such disparity on differences in assessed valuation, noting a taxable valuation of $5.8 million per pupil in one district housing a nuclear power plant, while another district could only access $749 in taxable wealth per pupil.

The Arizona high court, in reaching an obvious conclusion about such differences, then went beyond the scope of the initial claim to consider the entire meaning of the state's "general and uniform" clause in its constitution and its meaningful application to both the general fund financing scheme and the capital needs of school districts. The court first held that "general and uniform" did not mean that each school system had to exhibit identical programs or funding—instead, the court noted that sound evidence showing sufficient funds to educate children on substantially equal terms would be enough to meet the general and uniform requirement, but it went on to rule that state funding schemes which themselves create and further gross disparities cannot by definition be general and uniform in their operation. The court further ruled on the traditional argument offered by states in such cases that disparities are the result of local choices under a system of legitimate local control, holding that disparities caused by local control are not necessarily violative of the state constitution, but that no local choice really exists given such disparities in wealth that prevent effective local decisionmaking. In this way, the entire school funding system in Arizona was implicated and thereby invalidated, inasmuch as the court held the funding system to be insufficient to meet the needs of children, saying that it is "...intuitive that there is a relationship between the adequacy of education and the adequacy of capital facilities...[so that]...even if every student in every district were getting an adequate education, gross facility disparities caused by the state's chosen financing scheme would violate the uniformity clause."[39] The court finally went on to say that the circumstances of the case were particularly unusual in that the state had not disputed—indeed, had conceded—the existence of both substantial disparities and a causal relationship to the statutory scheme. In its sweeping condemnation of the system by which Arizona funds its schools, the state's high court moved the only case to have been brought on facility inadequacy to an overthrow of an entire system of funding schools.

Texas

The struggle for equity in school infrastructure funding is further well illustrated in the state of Texas, which has also been the site of one of the longest running battles in the United States over general school finance. Beginning with the failed federal case of *Rodriguez* in 1973, the wars over school funding in Texas have extended to the present time, with a dramatically different outcome favoring plaintiffs in the 1989 state-level case of *Edgewood Independent School District v. Kirby,*[40] with subsequent compliance litigation due to the considerable legislative turmoil that followed the initial court ruling for plaintiffs. In *Edgewood I,* the state supreme court had held that the state's school funding scheme violated the state constitution's efficiency clause, striking down a 700:1 ratio in taxable wealth per pupil and further faulting that differential as the source of many unconstitutional disparities in educational opportunity for children. The Texas supreme court held, in part:

> The amount of money spent on a student's education has a real and meaningful impact on the educational opportunity offered that student. High-wealth districts are able to provide for their students broader educational experiences including more extensive curricula, more up-to-date technological equipment, better libraries and library personnel, teacher aides, counseling services, lower student-teacher ratios, better facilities, parental involvement programs, and drop-out prevention programs. They are also better able to attract and retain experienced teachers and administrators.[41] [The court also emphasized, having earlier stated in the same vein, that] …Most importantly, there are no Foundation School Program allotments for school facilities or for debt service.[42]

Lawmakers' response was to enact new legislation in the form of Senate Bill 7, which was quickly challenged by widely diverse constituent groups. Senate Bill 7 was subsequently found constitutional at the district court level, but it was held that the legislature had not adequately met its obligation to fund educational infrastructure deficits. On appeal in *Edgewood Independent School District v. Meno*,[43] the state supreme court clearly restated its earlier position, saying that an efficient system of public education requires both instruction *and* classrooms and that the components of an efficient educational system—both direct instruction and facilities—are inseparable. The court went on to say, however, that its search of the extant record could not find any instance of plaintiffs' inability of provide the required facilities under the state's new funding law, and that on final analysis the court was obliged to affirm the constitutionality of the public school finance scheme. However, the court emphasized strongly that the challenge based on inadequate facilities had failed only because plaintiffs had failed to provide sufficient evidence and that the court's judgment "…should not be interpreted as a signal that the school finance crisis in Texas has ended."[44]

The issue in Texas is clearly illustrative of how public and judicial opinions and attitudes can shift over time. As a leading example of the contentiousness of school funding and the necessity of requiring the adversarial force of litigation in some instances, the history in Texas from *Rodriguez* forward through *Edgewood* points up the progress that can be made via litigation when legislation is not willingly forthcoming.

Ohio

As a further leading illustration, the case of *DeRolph v. State*[45] in Ohio also provides some useful instruction on the benefits of litigation and legislation in tandem when faced with formidable school infrastructure deficits. At the time of trial, Ohio's infrastructure problems were well-documented and largely undisputed by the state, reaching more than $10 billion across the state's various school districts. In finding the system in violation of the state constitution's thorough and efficient requirement, the state supreme court held that the state legislature must entirely rewrite the state's school funding laws and that a thorough and efficient system of common schools necessarily includes facilities along with the supplies, materials, and funds to meet all local, federal, and state mandates. The court particularly held that the Classroom Facilities Act was unconstitutional to the extent that it was underfunded and that the legislature must demonstrate significant progress in addressing all deficient aspects of public education.

As in other states, compliance litigation followed, in part to define the parameters of state responsibility and to test the speed at which progress must occur. In *DeRolph II*,[46] the court recognized the complexity of school funding, giving more time to meet requirements and further defining the meaning of an efficient system of schools. In particular, the court noted that "...a thorough system means that each and every school district has enough funds to operate...[and is one]...in which each and every school district in the state has an ample number of teachers, sound buildings that are in compliance with state building and fire codes, and equipment sufficient for all students to be afforded an educational opportunity."[47] By 2001, however, the court had satisfied itself on these conditions as the case returned for yet another review,[48] with the court holding that based on evidence regarding progress showing that the Facilities Commission had provided funding to 34 school districts and that the Commission was administering projects for over 300 new buildings in the year 2001, there was no longer reason to retain jurisdiction in the case, although the court warned that remedies are readily available to plaintiffs if compliance lags— a significant level of confidence from a court that had earlier stated that substandard facilities are a sure formula for failure.[49]

Wyoming

Although Table 8.2 and Table 8.3 suggest that a wide range of cases could be discussed for their implications, recent school funding litigation in Wyoming provides a final example for purposes of this chapter in the form of *State v. Campbell County School District*.[50] A long-term struggle in

Wyoming over school finance dates from the early 1970s,[51] with a dramatic ruling in *Washakie County School District Number One v. Herschler*[52] in 1980 which held that the entire school funding system was unconstitutional inasmuch as education is a fundamental right in that state and that equality of opportunity can never be achieved until equality of funding is also realized. The court in *Washakie* gave the state legislature until July 1, 1997 to enact the necessary changes.

Washakie, as is the case after many plaintiff victories, gave rise to new legislation in an effort to meet the court's stern mandate. As is also the case after such legislative changes, the state's school finance formula returned to court in 1995 in *Campbell County School District v. State*,[53] with subsequent litigation in 2001 styled as *State of Wyoming v. Campbell County School District*.[54] The court, while noting that Washakie had concerned itself primarily with the fairness of current operations funding, vowed that the ruling was meant to be equally applicable to capital construction and maintenance. The court held that although it had long stated that deficient physical facilities deny equal educational opportunity, the state had yet to enact an acceptable funding scheme for aiding infrastructure. The court harshly characterized the existing aid formula under review in *Campbell*, calling it fundamentally unchanged, unconstitutionally wealth-based, and inadequate. The court further noted that since *Campbell*, the legislature had identified over $565 million in school infrastructure needs, with over $303 million in deferred maintenance alone, all in the face of lapsed time and "…devoid of evidence that it has funded or intends to fund the undisputed deficiencies any time soon."[55] At the same time, only $30 million had actually been appropriated for capital needs at the legislative level. The court went on to say that the constitutional mandate for a fair, complete, and equal education had not been met and that to meet the court's litmus test, the state must: (1) adequately determine the cost of maintenance and operations, including utility costs; (2) fund the required facilities needed to deliver a "full basket" of educational services to all students in the state either through statewide taxes or other revenue plan equally imposed on all taxpayers; and (3) adhere to a court-established timetable for remedying all deficient facilities within a six year period.

While elements of the Wyoming court's opinion drew on prior cases in sister states for both substance and influence, the court in *Washakie* and *Campbell* signaled the parameters of emerging thought regarding equality of infrastructure opportunity,[56] particularly in the context where a state's constitution has granted both fundamentality and full equal protection. More specifically, the Wyoming court could see no reason to separate facilities from general fund financing or any other educational program, saying that "…it [infrastructure] is a part of the total educational package and tarred with the same brush of disparate tax resources…The point is that statewide availability from total state resources for building construction or contribution to school buildings on a parity for all school districts is required just as for other elements of the educational process."[57]

CONCLUSION

The broader history of school finance litigation outlined early in this chapter is instructive in its potential application to funding school infrastructure deficits because the path, both historically and prospectively, involves fundamentally the same milestones. As with other areas of life, lessons in success and failure are best learned by living long enough to witness the outcome of actual experience, and in the school finance litigation arena it is clear that individual battles come and go while the war never ends. Another way of stating that same view of school finance litigation is that progress (as defined by plaintiff causes) is usually incremental, seldom cataclysmic, and sometimes nearly imperceptible. But the history of school finance litigation says that change does occur, and from the evidence presented in this chapter—indeed, by all of history itself—there is reason to expect that litigation does offer one strategy (among others) for addressing the very large inequities that exist in school infrastructure funding.

The lessons offered in this analysis are numerous and enumerate broadly:

School infrastructure litigation, like general fund equity, has its best opportunity for success under two specific sets of circumstances. One opportunity rests in attaching to desegregation claims, while the other opportunity significantly turns on strength of states' constitutional language. More specifically, desegregation claims are never fully satisfied, are ever expansive and fluid in definition, and automatically offer the highest level of federal scrutiny, while the state judicial standard heightens nearly in direct proportion to the strength of constitutional language that can be mustered. While the latter issue is characterized by ebb and flow and seems significantly affected by external forces apart from strict application of law, the sum of state-level school finance litigation and current state-of-the-art school funding formulas bears strong witness to the likelihood of progress under these circumstances.

All school funding litigation is an endurance race that may span generations and is rooted in a reshaping of societal readiness that, when considering issues that truly reshape social foundations, occurs nearly imperceptibly. Seldom are there revolutions of the *Serrano* sort; more often there are the "technicalities" of the *Robinson* sort by which plaintiff causes succeed, eventually creeping into a society's unquestioned concept of fairness. While capital needs litigation has been slow to even enter into the realm of fairness and has far to go before it is as unquestioningly accepted as general fund equity, the cases in this chapter clearly illustrate the subtle and pervasive spread of such language in court rulings, entering even in some cases where the state's constitutional language is only moderately strong.

The courts, while subject to their own rules and interpretation and at times to their particular political bent, are generally reflective of the larger society, at times leading the way to new conceptualizations and at other times being led into the future. One of the struggles of democracy is the rule of law versus the rule of majority opinion, and courts are not completely impervious to this eternal whipsaw. It might be argued that an imperious court in *Serrano* dragged an unwilling society (elected representative legislatures) to a new concept of educational equity, but it could be equally argued that other federal and state rulings on the threshold on the new millennium are attempting to drag society back to an earlier time which this nation has already left behind. The lesson to be learned is that whipsawing is a natural manifestation of democracy in action, and that courts eventually must resolve any significant dissonance between themselves and society, usually with the outcome that progress occurs more slowly than reformers desire, but at a speed that society eventually manages to tolerate and even internalize. Again, witness the pervasive spread of general fund equalization formulas over the last 40 years, even into states with sparse or no supporting constitutional provisions—while not fully accepted yet, equalization seems more normal through the interaction of time and waiting for society's readiness. In the particular case of school infrastructure funding equity, courts are increasingly articulating the seamlessness of a funding system that includes bricks and mortar—a position that, given enough time, is nearly certain to spread universally.

As states rush eagerly toward ever-tightening school performance accountability standards, seeking to capture control of schools and to command rigorous outputs, these same laws are likely to simultaneously increase states' obligation to fund schools equally and to redress inequality in infrastructure. This observation has already begun to take deep root, as states have busied themselves with physical inventories, assessments of infrastructure deficits, and exhortatory language in statutes bemoaning the deferred maintenance backlog. Nearly every state has engaged in one or more of these activities, and many states have implicitly or explicitly written into statute a level of obligation that cannot be easily escaped. Several cases examined at some length in this chapter bear witness to courts quoting state legislatures, whose words have frequently identified school infrastructure as one of the "critical" components in carrying out good educational programs. In sum, the lesson may be that a third strategy is being developed which will be used concurrently with political persuasion and litigation: i.e., performance-driven standards at the state level are providing the strength of language that is often lacking to ensure a victory in court.

The ultimate lesson undoubtedly rests in more fully developing the imperfect knowledge base relating to the complex interaction of variables in the learning equation. Courts have recognized that children learn best under the best circumstances, and those same courts have often begun including the physical environment among those variables that contribute meaningfully to a constitutionally acceptable educational setting. Gradually, the "minimal provision" words that characterized many of the nearly 2,000 court cases examined in this study have disappeared from use as time has gone by, and virtually none of the leading cases any longer even contemplates their validity. Instead, there is a growing recognition that the physical infrastructure is not a tag-on to equal educational opportunity—rather, it is part and parcel of an equation that is both complex and elusive in quantification—but nonetheless real to the extent that deficits are deleterious to equal opportunity. The lesson, then, is that development of more and better knowledge about the true effects of infrastructure on student achievement is likely to hasten a desirable—indeed, inevitable—outcome.

In the end analysis, the overall lesson of this chapter is that school finance litigation has been an effective strategy for addressing inequities—a strategy that promises additional success when steadily and longitudinally applied to school infrastructure funding. At the same time, litigation is an incomplete strategy and should never be relied upon exclusively because society and its courts are not yet leading on this issue, even though significant progress has occurred and the signs of establishment of a permanent change in social acceptance of this issue is increasingly visible. Success in infrastructure funding equity has been long-suffering thus far, and future success depends on more patience and unyielding perseverance. Reformers must recognize that such profound change takes place over generations of social thought, hastened only by wisely joining litigation with the art of wise policymaking in the legislative arena. Unfortunately, however, the infrastructure deficit in America will not proceed at the same measured pace, if for no other reason than the desperate depth of the billions in unmet need. As a result, the force of adversarial litigation takes on even more attractiveness to those who perceive the true depth of the nation's extant dilemma.

NOTES

1. For a discussion of the growing body of research into infrastructure effects on student achievement and equal educational opportunity, see Chapter 1 of this volume, "Unmet School Infrastructure Funding Need as a Critical Educational Capacity Issue: Setting the Context," by Faith E. Crampton.

2. This section on the roots of litigation as a reform tool is based on portions of Chapter 3 in David C. Thompson and R. Craig Wood, *Money and Schools,* 2d ed. (New York: Eye on Education, 2001). See also, R. Craig Wood, David C. Thompson, Lawrence O. Picus, and Donald I. Tharpe, *Principles of School Business Management,* 2d ed. (Reston, Virginia: ASBO International, 1995). See also, David C. Thompson, R. Craig Wood, and David Honeyman. *Fiscal Leadership for Schools: Concepts and Practices* (New York: Longman,1994). See also, R. Craig Wood and David C. Thompson, *Education Finance Law: Constitutional Challenges to State Aid Plans,* 2d ed. (Topeka, Kansas: Education Law Association, 1996).

3. U.S. Constitution, Amendment XIV.

4. The Supreme Court had earlier upheld "separate but equal" provisions in *Plessy v. Ferguson,* 163 U.S. 537 (1896).

5. *Brown v. Board of Education,* 347 U.S. 483, 493 (1954).

6. *Burruss v. Wilkerson,* 310 F.Supp. 572 (1969).

7. *San Antonio Independent School District v. Rodriguez,* 411 U.S. 1 (1973).

8. *Serrano v. Priest, 487 P.2d 1241 (1971).*

9. Ibid.

10. For full development of this concept, see David C. Thompson, *School Finance Litigation: Does It Make A Difference? A Review of Literature and Analysis of Selected Data in Four States* (Washington, D. C: The National Education Association, in press); see also, David C. Thompson and Faith E. Crampton, "The Impact of School Finance Litigation: A Long View," *Journal of Education Finance* 27 (Winter 2001): 783–816.

11. U.S. Department of Education, *Digest of Education Statistics, 2001* (Washington, D.C: National Center for Education Statistics, 2001).

12. *Modernizing Our Schools: How Much Will It Cost?* (Washington, D.C.: National Education Association, 2000).

13. See special issue on infrastructure funding in the *Journal of Education Finance,* 27 (Fall 2001), David C. Thompson and Faith E. Crampton, eds.; see also, two special issues of the *Journal of Education Finance* on the status of state and local funding of capital outlay, David S. Honeyman, R. Craig Wood, and David C. Thompson, eds., 27 (Winter 1988 and Spring 1988); see also, Thompson et al., *Fiscal Leadership;* see also, Chapter 1 of this volume, "Unmet School Infrastructure Funding Need as a Critical Educational Capacity Issue: Setting the Context," by Faith E. Crampton.

14. *Plessy v. Ferguson,* 163 U.S. 537 (1896).

15. *Brown v. Board of Education,* 347 U.S. 483, 493–495 (1954).

16. *San Antonio Independent School District v. Rodriguez* 411 U.S. 1 (1973).

17. Id., 47.

18. Id., 83.

19. *Missouri v. Jenkins* 515 U.S. 70 (1995).

20. *Board of Education of Oklahoma City Public Schools* v. *Dowell*, 498 U.S. 237 (1991).

21. *Green* v. *School Board of New Kent County*, 391 U.S. 430, 88 (1968).

22. *Missouri v. Jenkins*, 515 U.S. 70 (1995), quoting *Green* v. *School Board of New Kent County*, 391 U.S. 430, 88 (1968).

23. See, for example, *Carver v. Bond/Fayette/Effingham Regional Board of School Trustees*, 586 N.E.2d 1273 (Ill. 1992).

24. See, for example, *Wright v. Board of Public Instruction*, 48 So.2d 912 (Fla. 1950).

25. See, for example, *Sinclair Paint Co. v. State Board of Equalization*, P.2d 130 (Cal. 1997).

26. See, for example, *Hootch v. Alaska State-Operated School System*, 536 P.2d 793 (Alaska 1975).

27. See, for example, *Hancock v. District Township of Perry*, 78 Iowa 550 (1889).

28. See, for example, *District Township of Union v. Independent District of Greene*, 41 Iowa 30 (1875).

29. *Pauley v. Kelly*, 255 S.E.2d 859 (W.Va. 1979); later *Pauley v. Bailey*, 324 S.E.2d 128 (W.Va. 1982); *Pauley v. Gainer*, 353 S.E.2d 318 (W.Va. 1986).

30. *Pauley v. Kelly*, 255 S.E.2d 859, 877 (W.Va. 1979).

31. See, for example, David C. Thompson, *Preliminary Analysis and Recommendations Regarding the Closing of Select Rural Schools in West Virginia: Consultant's Report to Attorneys* (Manhattan, Kansas: UCEA Center for Education Finance, 1990).

32. *State ex rel. School Building Authority v. Marockie*, 481 S.E.2d 730 (W.Va. 1996).

33. *Abbott v. Burke*, 495 A.2d 376 (NJ. 1985). Subsequent litigation through *Abbott v. Burke*, 798 A.2d 602 (NJ. 2002) and actually predated by multiple iterations of *Robinson v. Cahill*, 303 A.2d 27 (NJ. 1973).

34. *Robinson v. Cahill*, 303 A.2d 27 (NJ. 1973). Known as *Robinson I*, later citations omitted.

35. *Abbott v. Burke*, No. A-63, 575 A.2d 359 (NJ. 1989).

36. *Abbott v. Burke*, 751 A.2d 1032 (NJ. 2000); see also *Abbott by Abbott v. Burke*, 710 A.2d 450 (NJ. 1998).

37. *Roosevelt Elementary School District No. 66 v. Bishop*, 877 P.2d 806 (Ariz. 1994).

38. See, for example, David C. Thompson and R. Craig Wood, *Analysis for Plaintiffs: Roosevelt Elementary School District et al v. C. Diane Bishop et al.* (Manhattan, KS: UCEA Center for Education Finance, 1992).

39. *Roosevelt Elementary School District No. 66 v. Bishop*, 877 P.2d 806, 814 (Ariz. 1994).

40. *Edgewood Independent School District v. Kirby*, 777 S.W.2d 391 (Tex. 1989) (*Edgewood I*).

41. Id., 391, 393.

42. Id., 392.

43. *Edgewood Independent School District v. Meno*, 893 S.W.2d 450 (Tex. 1995).

44. Id., 450, 459.

45. *DeRolph v. State*, 677 N.E.2d 733 (Ohio 1997).

46.   *DeRolph v. State,* 728 N.E.2d 993 (Ohio 2000).

47.   Id., 1001.

48.   *DeRolph v. State,* 754 N.E.2d 1184 (Ohio 2001).

49.   *DeRolph v. State,* 728 N.E.2d 993 (Ohio 2000).

50.   *State of Wyoming v. Campbell County School District,* 19 P.3d 518 (Wyo. 2001).

51.   *Sweetwater County Planning Committee for Organization of School Districts v. Hinkle,* 491 P.2d 1234 (Wyo. 1971).

52.   *Washakie County School District Number One v. Herschler,* 606 P.2d 310 (Wyo. 1980).

53.   *Campbell County School District v. State,* 907 P.2d 1238 (Wyo. 1995).

54.   *State of Wyoming v. Campbell County School District,* 19 P.3d 518 (Wyo. 2001).

55.   Id., 559.

56.   This prospective analog to the future is best illustrated by the present time, as the Wyoming court in the year 2001 in *State v. Campbell* said, in rejecting the defense's argument that the state's constitutional duty is limited to merely ensuring no *deficient* facilities: "Although elimination of facilities deemed deficient according to state standards would go a long way toward meeting the constitutional mandate, equality of opportunity ultimately requires a rough measure of equality of facilities over time...Any system ultimately adopted must be capable of providing essentially equal facilities to all Wyoming's school children over the long term..." (quoting from *State v. Campbell,* 19 P.3d 518, 561 [2001]), and further noting the court's earlier statement that: "[The constitution] clearly allows a school district to build facilities considered innovative or world-class with money raised locally by property taxes...[but] then leaves it to the legislature to ensure that type of local enhancement does not ultimately create a disparity in equal educational opportunity," (quoting at p. 560).

57.   *State of Wyoming v. Campbell County School District,* 19 P.3d 518, 528 (2001), citing itself from *Washakie County School District Number One v. Herschler,* 606 P.2d 310, 337 (1980).

CHAPTER 9

FUNDING EDUCATION TECHNOLOGY VERSUS BRICKS AND MORTAR

Can We Have It All?

Faith E. Crampton
*University of Wisconsin
Milwaukee*

Janis M. Hagey
*National Education
Association*

Kathleen C. Westbrook
The deerStar Group

ABSTRACT

Unlike many other categories of educational expenditure, little systematic data exist for unmet funding needs in education technology. Yet education technology, along with the physical environment of schools, represents a critical area of school modernization necessary so that children may learn in safe, healthy schools with access to the resources that will maximize their success. This chapter explores the potential competition between school infrastructure and education technology for limited educational resources at a time when there are increasing demands being placed upon public education. Given that both education technology and school infrastructure suffer from underfunding, competition and duplication are serious issues.

Saving America's School Infrastructure, pages 191–214

INTRODUCTION

Although the focus of this volume is the funding of school infrastructure, it would be, at best, naive not to acknowledge that there is fierce competition for every education dollar at all policy levels—local, state, and federal—in part, because of the many societal demands placed upon elementary and secondary education in this country. For example, given the labor-intensive nature of education, personnel costs for school districts represent their largest single budget item, and hence are often the strongest competitor for education funding. Now in an era of heightened accountability and high stakes testing, the need for competitive salaries to attract and retain quality teachers who will be effective in improving student achievement places even greater demands upon existing and new education revenues. National teacher shortages in core academic areas, such as mathematics and science, raise teacher compensation to an even higher priority. At the same time, education reforms, such as class size reduction, require additional staffing, both teaching and supervisory. Another potentially costly education reform is the introduction of computers and other forms of education technology into the classroom, both to enhance learning and to prepare students for the labor markets of the 21st century. As a fiscal issue, education technology is unique in that it spans both operating and capital budgets, with its claim to capital funding making it a potential competitor with school infrastructure needs.

At a time when deferred maintenance for schools alone is estimated at over \$100 billion,[1] and total unmet funding need for all types of school infrastructure, inclusive of new construction and renovation, has reached over \$260 billion,[2] policymakers must carefully weigh funding priorities. Setting funding priorities where education technology and school infrastructure needs are being considered may be further complicated by perceptions of their relative worth. Admittedly, the image of engaged students working on state-of-the-art computers that open to them limitless worlds of new information may be more compelling to many education stakeholders than a mundane capital item, such as the repair or replacement of a leaky school roof, even though a roof in good condition is critical to keeping students safe from the elements and protecting the district's investment in education technology equipment. Like school infrastructure, education technology does not come cheaply. While the cost of most school infrastructure projects requires long-term or multi-year fiscal investments by school districts, the costs for education technology are also ongoing, but for different reasons. Because current technologies rapidly become obsolete, schools are faced not just with initial investments, but also with ongoing investments that stretch far into the future.

The central purpose of this chapter is to explore, as fully as possible, the potential competition between education technology and school infrastructure in the educational funding arena. To anchor the discussion, the chapter opens with a comprehensive definition of education technology. The second section presents 50-state data on state funding levels for education technology, as well as the mechanisms states use to allocate these funds. In the descriptions of state funding mechanisms, the potential for competition between education technology and school infrastructure begins to be revealed. In the third section, 50-state estimates of unmet funding need for education technology are contrasted with funding needs for school infrastructure. The chapter concludes with policy recommendations for the equitable and adequate funding of both education technology and school infrastructure.

COMPREHENSIVE DEFINITION OF EDUCATION TECHNOLOGY

It is important to situate the discussion of the potential competition of education technology and school infrastructure for the same pool of education resources in a comprehensive definition of education technology, as was done in the discussion of unmet funding need for school infrastructure.[3] As part of a national study of unmet education technology funding needs, the authors developed a comprehensive definition comprised of the following nine components:[4]

- Multimedia computers
- Peripherals
- Operating, applications, and educational software
- Connectivity
- Networks
- Technology infrastructure
- Distance education
- Maintenance and repair of technology equipment
- Professional development and support

Multimedia computers are generally newer, faster, and more powerful computers with sound capability and high-resolution graphics. Usually they have an internal CD-ROM and modem, the latter for Internet access. Peripherals represent a category of computer hardware that includes equipment such as printers, assistive/adaptive devices,[5] digital cameras, scanners, and computer projection units. Also included are various pieces of equipment such as CD-ROMS, zip drives, and modems that, although internally installed on many newer computers, are sometimes added externally to older computers. Operating software refers to computer programs, such as DOS and Windows, that provide the foundation for utilizing applications and educational software. Applications software includes computer programs such as word-processing and spreadsheets while educational software represents computer programs that are specifically designed for student learning. Connectivity refers to Internet access, video conferencing, and video phones. Networks found within a school or district include LANs (Local Area Networks) and WANs (Wide Area Networks). Technology infrastructure includes wiring and cables to, within, and between schools. For example, to accommodate computers and peripherals, electrical upgrades may be needed in order for the school facility to support more electrical outlets; or the school may require more phone lines or fiber optic cables to support connectivity to the Internet. Distance education makes use of a number of components listed above to allow courses to be taught at remote sites. Maintenance and repair of technology equipment includes maintenance contracts and repair costs to keep computers and peripherals functioning properly over the life of the equipment. Professional development and support is necessary so that teachers and other educational professionals make effective use of technology to enhance student learning.

The description above makes evident that education technology needs draw from both the operating and capital budgets of school districts. With regard to operating budgets, investments in education technology carry personnel costs for professional development and support; maintenance and repair costs for equipment; and the cost of several categories of equipment, which in some cases are categorized as part of the school district's operating budget and, in others, part of the capital budget, depending upon individual state classifications of equipment purchases for the purposes of budgeting, bonding, and accounting. Technology infrastructure represents a direct overlap with the broader category of school infrastructure and hence draws upon capital resources available to the district. In the next section, specific examples of overlap as well as direct competition are presented as part of the description of state funding levels and mechanisms for education technology.

CURRENT FUNDING LEVELS AND MECHANISMS
FOR EDUCATION TECHNOLOGY

In 1995–1996, only 21 states provided $451.6 million for education technology, ranging from $100,000 in Montana to $117 million in Florida.[6] On average, states provided $21.5 million. By contrast, in 1998–1999, the most recent time period for which 50-state data are available, 31 states provided

$847.8 million to local school districts for education technology funding.[7] (See Appendix for state-by-state information on technology funding programs.) Funding levels ranged from $600,000 in Delaware to $191.4 million in California. On average, states provided $27.3 million while, on a per-pupil basis, the average state expenditure for education technology was a modest $27.[8] However, these numbers tell only a small part of the funding story. In general, education technology is funded through a wide range of mechanisms at the state level.

Even a brief look at the summary table in the appendix reveals a dizzying array of funding mechanisms. In some states, such as Alabama and Tennessee, funding for education technology is part of the state's basic aid allocation to school districts. However, use of funds for education technology may be restricted to particular expenditure categories. If education technology funding is allocated through the state basic aid formula, there is a reasonable assurance that it is equalized, as most basic aid formulas are designed to provide greater assistance to property and/or income poor school districts.[9] A number of states use one or more forms of categorical aid. For example, Minnesota funds education technology through seven categorical programs and New York, four. Unlike education technology funding that is allocated through a state's basic aid program, funds distributed through categorical programs may or may not be equalized. Pennsylvania and South Carolina provide examples of equalized categorical funding programs. Other states, like Arkansas and California, may require school districts to submit a grant application to access education technology funds, a potential barrier for those districts without the personnel and expertise to write them. Four states—Connecticut, Idaho, Illinois, Washington—distribute a portion of state funding for education technology through a competitive grant process, a process that disadvantages districts lacking well-honed grantwriting skills. At least one state, Kansas, requires the local school district to match state funding for education technology and to have completed a state-approved education technology plan to be eligible for funding. To further complicate the funding picture, a few states use a combination of the funding mechanisms described here.

In nine states, the funding mechanisms for education technology compete or overlap with those that have traditionally been considered the province of capital outlay or school infrastructure. They include the following states: Arizona; Connecticut; Minnesota; Missouri; Nebraska; New Jersey; Pennsylvania; Rhode Island; and Texas. In Arizona, the new school capital finance system includes education technology as well as school infrastructure. As such, there is no separate state appropriation for education technology. Like Arizona, Minnesota funds education technology from capital resources, more specifically, the component of the general education revenue formula which is also used to finance school facilities needs. In Arizona and Minnesota, education technology competes directly with school infrastructure for the same pool of resources. The education technology funding mechanisms of the remaining seven states represent potential overlaps in funding between education technology infrastructure and broader funding mechanisms for school infrastructure; or when education technology infrastructure is funded as a stand-alone program, a potential overlap exists as well with school infrastructure funding programs. For example, Missouri's education technology funding program includes the funding of technology infrastructure. In Nebraska, funding for education technology is targeted toward training and technology infrastructure. Connecticut's funding for education technology is limited to the wiring of schools, an infrastructure item, to make them technology compatible. Texas also limits education technology funding to infrastructure issues, in particular providing connectivity; however, the funding program is broader than elementary and secondary education in that it includes institutions of higher education, libraries, and hospitals. New Jersey restricts education technology funding to the Distance Learning Network which includes costs associated with professional development, purchase of software, and maintenance, as well as education technology infrastructure. In Pennsylvania, the "Link to Learn" program provides school districts with education technology funding that includes the infrastructure component of cabling for LANs and WANs. Like Pennsylvania, Rhode Island's funding for education technology includes infrastructure.

Since most states allow education technology infrastructure to be funded through broader capital outlay or school infrastructure funding mechanisms that generally permit school districts to incur long-term debt, education technology infrastructure costs may potentially be supported through capital budgets. At the same time, education technology funding mechanisms generally target funds as operating expenditures. Hence in states with funding programs for both school infrastructure and education technology, technology infrastructure funding may be duplicative if it is also eligible for education technology funding. At the state policy level, this configuration raises issues of cost-effectiveness on two fronts. First it represents duplication of funding effort for education technology infrastructure, and secondly it raises concerns about the appropriate financing of technology infrastructure. Unlike other components of education technology, technology infrastructure, (e.g., wiring, cabling, retrofitting), represent long-term investments that may be financed more appropriately in a similar manner to other school infrastructure projects, such as the construction or renovation of school facilities, through longer-term debt instruments. Delineating the funding of education technology infrastructure as a capital investment in turn would free up additional resources in existing education technology funding mechanisms for operating expenditures, such as professional development and support. In the next section, the extent of unmet funding need for education technology is explored, with special attention to cost estimates for education technology infrastructure.

UNMET FUNDING NEED FOR EDUCATION TECHNOLOGY

Unlike many other categories of educational expenditure, little systematic data exist with regard to unmet funding need for education technology. Yet education technology, along with the physical environment of schools, represents a critical area of school modernization necessary so that children may learn in safe, healthy schools with access to the resources that will maximize their success at present, in the classroom, and in the future, in the labor force. In order to calculate an estimate of unmet funding need, the authors looked to existing statewide education technology plans, as earlier research has indicated that these are the best single source for systematic data on education technology funding needs.[10] In 1999, 38 states had statewide education technology plans in place, of which 26 had been developed in the prior five years.[11,12] (See Table 9.1.) Of these, only ten had developed cost estimates. A closer analysis of the cost estimates revealed that only three of the ten states—California,[13] Connecticut,[14] Delaware[15]—had developed cost estimates inclusive of all of the elements of a comprehensive definition of education technology needs. California's education technology plan was the most costly, calling for an investment of $10.9 billion, or $1,969 per pupil. In contrast, the Connecticut plan estimated unmet funding need at $555.2 million, or $579 per pupil. Finally, Delaware's education technology plan called for $120 million in new state dollars, or $1,072 per pupil. For the purposes of estimating total unmet funding need for education technology across states, Delaware was selected as the benchmark, as it represented the median. Using 1999 student enrollments,[16] state-by-state estimates of unmet funding need for education technology were calculated. (See Table 9.2.) Unmet funding need for education technology ranged from $103.5 million in Wyoming to $10.9 billion in California, for a total of $53.7 billion.

The unmet funding need for school infrastructure, estimated at $266.1 billion, is substantial as well. While it was not possible to partition out the portion of education technology plan cost estimates for education technology infrastructure with precision, education technology plans for Illinois[17] and New Mexico[18] may provide some insight as their cost estimates were limited to education technology infrastructure. Illinois projected costs for education technology infrastructure to be $787 million or $399 per pupil, while New Mexico projected $75.1 million or $237 per pupil. When compared to total estimates for unmet funding need, education technology

Table 9.1.   State Education Technology Plans

State	Technology Plan	Year	Cost Estimate	Notes
Alabama	X	1995		
Alaska				
Arizona				
Arkansas				
California	X	1995	X	
Colorado				
Connecticut	X	1995		
Delaware	X	1999	X	
Florida				
Georgia	X	1997		
Hawaii				
Idaho				
Illinois	X	1996	X	Technology infrastructure only.
Indiana	X	1998		
Iowa				
Kansas				
Kentucky				
Louisiana	X	1997	X	
Maine				
Maryland	X	1998	X	
Massachusetts	X	1998		
Michigan	X	1997		
Minnesota				
Mississippi	X	1995		
Missouri				
Montana				
Nebraska	X	(in press)		
Nevada	X	1998	X	
New Hampshire	X	1998		
New Jersey				
New Mexico	X	1999	X	Technology infrastructure only.
New York				
North Carolina				
North Dakota				
Ohio				

Table 9.1.   (cont.)

State	Technology Plan	Year	Cost Estimate	Notes
Oklahoma	X	(in press)		
Oregon	X	draft		
Pennsylvania				
Rhode Island	X	1996		
South Carolina	X	1998		
South Dakota				
Tennessee	X	1999	X	Computer hardware and software only.
Texas	X	1998		
Utah				
Vermont	X	1999		
Virginia	X	1996		
Washington	X	1998		
West Virginia				
Wisconsin				
Wyoming	X	1997	X	

Table 9.2.   Total Funding Need for School Modernization

State	Infrastructure	Technology	Total
Alabama	$1,519,210,061	$791,643,056	$2,310,853,117
Alaska	727,014,291	141,780,576	868,794,867
Arizona	4,748,568,494	920,959,488	5,669,527,982
Arkansas	1,761,701,495	494,704,416	2,256,405,911
California	22,000,000,000	10,901,183,414	32,901,183,414
Colorado	3,805,239,627	738,005,536	4,543,245,163
Connecticut	5,000,000,000	555,226,320	5,555,226,320
Delaware	1,046,354,648	120,021,120	1,166,375,768
Florida	3,300,000,000	2,187,697,936	5,487,697,936
Georgia	7,061,967,931	1,474,984,096	8,536,952,027
Hawaii	752,533,936	202,909,232	955,443,168
Idaho	699,469,537	268,321,600	967,791,137
Illinois	9,213,000,000	2,115,098,880	11,328,098,880
Indiana	2,477,797,613	1,059,940,000	3,537,737,613
Iowa	3,359,129,953	539,794,880	3,898,924,833

Table 9.2.   (cont.)

State	Infrastructure	Technology	Total
Kansas	1,793,241,845	503,561,280	2,296,803,125
Kentucky	2,441,607,196	685,628,688	3,127,235,884
Louisiana	3,104,098,619	836,972,576	3,941,071,195
Maine	452,064,540	232,710,832	684,775,372
Maryland	3,891,926,876	893,500,208	4,785,427,084
Massachusetts	8,919,014,500	1,023,047,120	9,942,061,620
Michigan	8,071,127,040	1,852,952,000	9,924,079,040
Minnesota	4,517,232,516	906,590,400	5,423,822,916
Mississippi	1,038,890,864	541,354,640	1,580,245,504
Missouri	3,475,160,989	975,861,968	4,451,022,957
Montana	901,492,663	175,806,928	1,077,299,591
Nebraska	1,608,849,896	313,754,032	1,922,603,928
Nevada	5,256,000,000	317,977,712	5,573,977,712
New Hampshire	409,511,478	210,805,584	620,317,062
New Jersey	20,709,650,065	1,319,695,248	22,029,345,313
New Mexico	1,410,624,747	339,560,288	1,750,185,035
New York	47,640,000,000	3,035,796,800	50,675,796,800
North Carolina	6,210,938,727	1,314,586,096	7,525,524,823
North Dakota	420,000,000	125,223,536	545,223,536
Ohio	20,900,000,000	1,977,840,000	22,877,840,000
Oklahoma	2,204,070,041	670,011,792	2,874,081,833
Oregon	2,407,425,974	579,506,048	2,986,932,022
Pennsylvania	8,465,134,387	1,943,407,360	10,408,541,747
Rhode Island	1,420,952,603	162,989,024	1,583,941,627
South Carolina	2,574,018,400	694,044,960	3,268,063,360
South Dakota	498,604,766	151,570,080	650,174,846
Tennessee	2,273,702,904	971,081,920	3,244,784,824
Texas	9,467,620,774	4,186,434,432	13,654,055,206
Utah	8,490,336,757	513,648,800	9,003,985,557
Vermont	220,090,007	113,296,464	333,386,471
Virginia	5,701,313,528	1,190,793,680	6,892,107,208
Washington	5,478,902,777	1,062,603,920	6,541,506,697
West Virginia	1,000,000,000	322,390,064	1,322,390,064
Wisconsin	4,762,337,059	955,782,336	5,718,119,395
Wyoming	530,888,665	103,532,688	634,421,353
Total	$266,138,818,788	$53,716,590,054	$319,855,408,842

infrastructure represented 37% and 22% of total unmet funding need for education technology in Illinois and New Mexico, respectively. As noted in the previous section, state funding mechanisms for education technology may overlap with funding available under broader capital outlay or school infrastructure funding programs. However, the evidence presented in this section is not conclusive; these areas of potential overlap, duplication, and competition warrant further research.

CONCLUSIONS AND POLICY RECOMMENDATIONS

The purpose of this chapter was to explore the potential competition between school infrastructure and education technology for limited educational resources at a time when there are increasing demands being placed upon public education for both higher student achievement and greater cost-effectiveness. An important first step was to define education technology funding needs comprehensively in order to contrast them with those of school infrastructure. In doing so, it became apparent that there is a direct overlap between the component of education technology infrastructure and the broader category of school infrastructure. An analysis of current state funding mechanisms revealed an eclectic approach to funding of education technology through basic and categorical aid programs, as well as the use of selective grants requiring school district application and eligibility criteria. Even so, nine state funding systems have some overlap between education technology infrastructure which has traditionally been viewed as capital outlay or school infrastructure. In a few cases, education technology is being funded through a capital funding system, even though a number of components of education technology would generally be considered operating costs. This configuration leads to direct competition between education technology and school infrastructure for the same pool of resources. In other cases, education technology infrastructure, such as wiring and cabling, appears to be eligible for funding under a state's education technology funding program as well as its infrastructure funding provisions. In this instance, the policy issue is overlap, potential duplication, and the resulting potential for ineffective use of resources.

Given that both education technology and school infrastructure suffer from underfunding at the state level, competition and duplication are serious issues. As a first step, policymakers must insure that current education technology and school infrastructure funding is equalized. At the same time, it is imperative that policymakers think of a state education funding system as an integrated whole so that various funding components do not have the unintended effect of working against one another. Yet because aspects of education technology and school infrastructure funding can be quite technical, it may be more challenging at the policy level to discern the potential for overlap and competition. The development of comprehensive long-range plans for both education technology and school infrastructure needs with accurate cost estimates that delineate clearly between operating and capital needs can serve as the foundation for state funding mechanisms and assist state policymakers in setting funding priorities to insure that existing resources are used cost-effectively. The ultimate answer, however, is more complex because of the magnitude of unmet need in both of these areas, totaling over $300 billion. While states constitutionally bear the responsibility for funding education, the present unmet need is so vast that substantial federal involvement should be considered to backfill the immense funding gap that has developed over a number of years. However, in order to determine the appropriate federal and state roles, better data are needed on the current level of local school district investment in education technology. At that point, a realistic local/state/federal partnership can be forged to address the pressing need for the funding of education technology and school infrastructure that affects millions of school children in every state of the nation.

NOTES

1. U.S. General Accounting Office, *School Facilities: The Condition of America's Schools* (Washington, D.C., February 1995).

2. For a description of unmet funding need for school infrastructure, see Chapter 1 of this volume, "Unmet School Infrastructure Funding Need as a Critical Educational Capacity Issue: Setting The Context," by Faith E. Crampton.

3. For a comprehensive definition of school infrastructure funding needs, see Chapter 1 of this volume, "Unmet School Infrastructure Funding Need as a Critical Educational Capacity Issue: Setting The Context," by Faith E. Crampton.

4. See, National Education Association, *Modernizing Our Schools: How Much Will It Cost?* (Washington, D.C.: 2000). Faith E. Crampton and Janis M. Hagey served as co-principal investigators, and Kathleen C. Westbrook served as a technical consultant for the education technology portion of the study.

5. Assistive/adaptive devices refer to peripherals that enable individuals with physical disabilities or limitations to utilize technology.

6. See, Faith E. Crampton, "The Coming Crisis in Student Access to Education Technology: Revisioning the State and Federal Roles in Funding," in *Technology and the Educational Workplace: Understanding Fiscal Impacts*, Kathleen C. Westbrook, ed., Eighteenth Annual Yearbook of the American Education Finance Association (Thousand Oaks, California: Corwin Press, Inc., 1997), 79–83.

7. Calculated from data in state chapters, in Catherine C. Sielke, John Dayton, C. Thomas Holmes, and Anne Jefferson, eds., *Public School Finance Programs of the United States and Canada, 1998–1999*, Publication #NCES 2001-309 (Washington, D.C.: U. S. Department of Education, National Center for

Education Statistics, 2001), http://www.nces.ed.gov/edfin/state_finance/statefinancing.asp.

8. Given the nature of the 1995–1996 data, it was not possible to compute a per-pupil expenditure figure.

9. For a description of basic aid formulas, see David C. Thompson and R. Craig Wood, *Money & Schools*, 2d. ed. (Larchmont, New York: Eye on Education, 2001), 73–100.

10. Crampton, "The Coming Crisis in Student Access to Educational Technology."

11. Copies of education technology plans and related documents were collected via a 50-state questionnaire to NEA state affiliates and searches of state department of education Web sites. For a complete list of state education technology plans and related documents, see National Education Association, 49–53.

12. In order to insure that the education technology plans were relatively up-to-date with current technology, the study included only those plans developed in the prior five years. Plans without identifying dates were not included.

13. "California Department of Education's Education Technology Office Home Page" http://www.cde.ca.gov/edtech/.

14. Connecticut State Board of Education, *Connecticut Statewide Educational Technology Plan*, Final Report (Marlborough, Massachusetts: Center for Educational Leadership and Technology, December 1995); Connecticut State Department of Education, *Guidelines for Technology Infrastructure in Connecticut Schools*, An Implementation Guide for the *Connecticut Statewide Educational Technology Plan*, in cooperation with the Center for Educational Leadership and Technology (Marlborough, Massachusetts: December 1995).

15. Delaware Education Network, *Delaware Center for Educational Technology. Strategic Plan FY1999–FY2001* (Delaware Center for Educational Technology: September 1998); and Delaware Center for Educational Technology, *Action Plan FY2000* (April 1999).

16. Source for 1999 student enrollments: Debra E. Gerald and William J. Hussar, *Projections of Education Statistics to 2009* (Washington, D.C.: National Center for Education Statistics, U.S. Department of Education, September 1999).

17. Illinois State Board of Education, *K–12 Information Technology Plan* (Springfield, Illinois: State of Illinois, 1996).

18. New Mexico State Department of Education, *New Mexico's Educational Technology Plan: A Road Map to Student Success* (Santa Fe, New Mexico: January 1999).

APPENDIX

State Technology Funding Programs, 1998–1999

State	Funding ($ millions)	Description of State Funding Program
Alabama	3.5	General state aid to local boards of education for technology began with the 1995 foundation program. In the calculation of cost factors in the 1995 foundation program, one of the components of the "Classroom Instruction Support Factor" is funding for technology. This shall be a uniform amount for each teacher unit and is recommended annually by the state board of education. This amount for Fiscal Year 1998–1999 is $75.00 per teacher unit. This allocation may be expended by school or by the school system as a whole. In addition, allocations from state bond issues are allowed to purchase technology equipment.
Alaska	0	Funding for the state educational technology program was eliminated in 1998.
Arizona	0	Technology is included in the new "Students FIRST" school capital finance system established in Fiscal Year 1998–1999. There is no separate state appropriation for technology, nor is any amount earmarked in the Students FIRST program for technology. The School Facilities Board, which is responsible for implementing the Students FIRST program, has not yet made any decisions related to technology standards, nor has it distributed any money for technology.
Arkansas	2.2	An agency called IMPAC, funded separately from the state school fund, provides computer hardware to school districts. The aid is based upon grant applications, and poorer districts are favored.
California	191.4	The "Digital High School Program" provides grants to high schools to purchase hardware, software, and infrastructure, and to train staff in its use. Schools that apply to the program are selected on the basis of a random draw each year. The educational technology program coordinates all of the technology efforts of the California Department of Education: $136.0 million for the Digital High School Program, and $55.4 million for educational technology.
Colorado	0	No state aid provided.
Connecticut	10.0	Now in its fourth year, this program provides funding for the wiring of schools to make them technology compatible. One million dollars is earmarked for the state's largest four urban districts, and the balance is distributed on a competitive basis to other school districts. Local area networks, wide area networks, and Internet access have been among the major areas of emphasis for this funding. It should be noted that the school construction grant program also allows wiring to be included in the scope of new construction and building renovations with the state participating in 20% to 80% of eligible costs. Within the limits of the grant awards, the technology grant has provided up to 100% of the cost of wiring a school that has been successful in competing for an award.

State Technology Funding Programs, 1998–1999 (cont.)

State	Funding ($ millions)	Description of State Funding Program
Delaware	0.6	The state recently established the Delaware Center for Educational Technology that receives funding from federal, private, as well as state appropriations. For 1998–99, the state appropriated $614,000 for the center. The center's mission is to assist schools and districts in adopting and adapting to new technologies. Other technology funding falls under Division II (material and supply), while many districts elect to use some of their Division II or III funding towards technology-related purchases.[a]
Florida	80.1	Funds are allocated based on each district's share of the state total unweighted student enrollment. This funding includes $1,000,000 for library automation grants. Public school technology funds may be used to purchase both hardware and software; however, priority is given to students and programs with the highest need and with the oldest equipment.
Georgia	26.8	Technology funding is supported in Georgia by the lottery. Originally, lottery funds could only be used to purchase hardware. A 1996 amendment to the law added training for teachers in the use of technology and repairs and maintenance of technology as additional eligible uses for lottery funds.
Hawaii	0	na[b]
Idaho	10.4	A continuation of funding both on a competitive grant process as well as direct distribution to districts based on a district's percent of the general school income fund.
Illinois	30.8	The state board of education awards grants on a competitive basis to school districts for the purpose of implementing the use of computer technology in the classroom. $500,000 has been appropriated from the School Technology Revolving Fund for the purpose of funding the statewide educational network.

[a] In Delaware, Division I is the primary component that is determined by enrollment through a unit (primarily the equivalent of the number of students per staff) funding system. It drives the allocation of personnel (weighted units based on average daily membership) that eventually determines the primary component of funding depending on a state salaries and benefits scale. In 1998–1999, this fund provided nearly 76% of total state appropriations to districts, which pays roughly 70% of all districts' personnel expenditures, ranging from teaching to administrative to support staff. The second component of the formula, Division II, funds all other school costs (excluding transportation and debt service), such as material, supplies, and energy costs. Those funds are flat grants based on units of enrollment. The third component, Division III, is an equalizing factor used to compensate for funding disparities between property rich and poor districts.

[b] Not applicable (na).

State Technology Funding Programs, 1998–1999 (cont.)

State	Funding ($ millions)	Description of State Funding Program
Indiana	15.0	The general assembly provides annual funding to the Indiana Department of Education's Technology Grant Program that is to be distributed to all school corporations [districts] within a six-year cycle. The total grant to a qualifying school corporation is not to exceed $200 per student.
Iowa	30.0	Beginning in 1996–97, the legislature appropriated $30 million for a school improvement technology program. Each district is allocated an equal amount per pupil; however, the minimum amount a district receives is $15,000. The legislation calls for this program to be funded for five years. Funds may be expended for equipment acquisition, installation, maintenance, and software associated with instructional technology. Funds may also be expended for staff development; however, the legislature prohibited the hiring of additional staff with these funds.
Kansas	10.0	There is no provision specifically for technology; however, in 1998–99, the legislature allocated $10 million of windfall tax dollars to K–12 education for technology. The money was used as a matching grant that each school district was eligible for as long as the district had a state-approved technology plan. The money was split among all 304 school districts as a flat $12,500 per district plus $13.70 per student.
Kentucky	15.0	The "Master Plan for Education Technology" establishes the criteria for funding and access to computer technology. Funds for technology are distributed on a per-pupil basis, and purchases for equipment and software are negotiated for all so that pricing, payment schedules, and all other contracts are the same for each school. All schools have the same access to state-provided support services and networks. Minimum computer-to-student ratios are defined. The state pays 100% of the cost of the district administrative (support services and network) costs. The state and local school districts share, on an equal basis, funding for operational costs, equipment replacement, and upgrades.
Louisiana	25.0	The 1998 legislature once again allocated monies for the Classroom-Based Technology Fund. This $25 million statutorily dedicated allocation is being used to continue efforts to carry out the state's educational technology goal: "All educators and learners will have access to technologies that are effective in improving student achievement." Funds are being used to purchase additional classroom computers, connect more classrooms to the Internet, purchase software to support curriculum, and provide additional technology tools needed implement district and school technology plans. The funds are distributed to local school districts, special schools, and non-public schools. The Classroom-Based Technology Fund is supported solely by the state. Over the past three years, funding was provided annually from non-recurring sources.

State Technology Funding Programs, 1998–1999 (cont.)

State	Funding ($ millions)	Description of State Funding Program
Maine	0	Maine's "Computers for Schools and Libraries Program" is a program where surplus computers are donated by businesses and other organizations, refurbished by prison inmates, and distributed to schools and libraries. The distribution criteria are designed to offer refurbished computers to those schools determined to be least able to purchase new computers. The guidelines for the dispersal of computers related to schools are: (1) a goal of one computer for every six students; and (2) the basis for selection of schools is the school's E-rate percentage. Computers provided are "Internet-ready." The program is self-supporting: parts and supplies for refurbishing the computers are funded by a charge of $150 per computer to schools.
Massachusetts	nr[c]	In 1996, the Education Technology Bill authorized a $30 million matching grant program for school districts, with the intent of improving classroom connections to the Internet. By 1998, 90% of districts and charter schools had received grant awards. MassEd.Net provides state-subsidized unlimited Internet access service for Massachusetts teachers and administrators. The cost is $25 per year, which may be paid on behalf of their employees by local school districts. The Massachusetts Department of Education's Information Management System is currently in the late design phase. When fully implemented, it will provide enrollment, fiscal, testing, and other information from all school districts.
Michigan	0	No state aid provided.
Minnesota	28.0	The operating capital component of the general education revenue formula provides funding which can be used for technology or other equipment and facility needs. School districts are also permitted to use unrestricted general education revenue for technology. Categorical funding for technology is described below: (1) Interactive television (ITV) revenue ($6 million) may be used for the construction, maintenance, and lease costs of an interactive television system for instructional purposes. A district that has completed the construction of its ITV system may also purchase computer hardware and software used primarily for instructional purposes and access to the Internet, provided that its total approved expenditures must not exceed its ITV revenue for Fiscal Year 1998. All school districts located outside of the Minneapolis–St.Paul metropolitan area are eligible to participate. The maximum revenue is the greater of $25,000 or 0.5% of the district's adjusted net tax capacity (ANTC). Beginning in 1999–2000, the ITV revenue will be phased out over a four-year period. The state aid is the difference between the ITV revenue and the ITV levy. A district's ITV levy equals the ITV revenue times the lesser of one or the ratio of the district's ANTC per weighted average daily membership

[c] Not reported (nr).

State Technology Funding Programs, 1998–1999 (cont.)

State	Funding ($ millions)	Description of State Funding Program
		(WADM) to $10,000; (2) Technology grants ($22 million) provide one-time funding for several technology programs; (3) Telecommunications access grants ($12.4 million) provide funding for telecommunications services to provide Internet access, data transmission, and interactive television capability to school districts and libraries; (4) Electronic curriculum grants ($1.6 million) provide funding for development of curriculum and an electronic curriculum repository to be available as a teacher resource; (5) Technology transformation grants ($1.2 million) fund projects that demonstrate the use of technology in support of graduation standards record-keeping and information management; (6) Computer refurbishment ($4.5 million) funds partnerships with business and nonprofit organizations to refurbish computers for distribution to schools with the goal of increasing student access to technology; (7) Site-based technology grants ($2.3 million) fund technology projects in support of learning that increases community ties.
Mississippi	nr	These funds were distributed to local school districts for computer hardware, equipment, and computer-based instructional programs based on grant proposals written at the local school district level.
Missouri	20.6	This funding is to implement computer network infrastructure for Missouri's public schools, provide computer access to the Department of Elementary and Secondary Education and to improve the use of classroom technology.
Montana	0	The state provides funding to school districts for technology acquisition and the associated technical training for school district personnel. The source of the state funding is revenue from the sale of timber from state school trust lands. The revenue from any timber sales in excess of 18 million board feet are dedicated to schools for technology. Schools did not receive any monies from this funding source in the 1998–1999 school year due to an over-distribution of monies in the 1997–1998 school year. In general, the revenue source is projected to generate $9 per student annually for a school district.
Nebraska	0	The 1999 unicameral legislature passed Legislative Bill 386 that appropriates $3 million during 1999–2000 fiscal year and $3.075 million for 2000–2001 fiscal year for the use of technology in schools. Training and infrastructure support are targeted area for the dollars.
Nevada	28.7	Funding in 1998–1999 was $4.4 million (state and local combined). Funding for technology is provided for the following: updating library databases and licensing for publication; updating of school software and licenses; funding for satellite down links; and bringing all Nevada schools to Level I technology use (i.e., a network capable computer in each classroom or its equivalent in computer laboratory stations). In addition, $28.7 million was appropriated for education technology on a one-time basis in 1998–1999.

State Technology Funding Programs, 1998–1999 (cont.)

State	Funding ($ millions)	Description of State Funding Program
New Hampshire	0	No state aid provided.
New Jersey	52.3	Distance learning network aid is a restricted aid program to support the acquisition and installation of technology with aid allocated on the basis of the number of pupils enrolled in the district multiplied by the cost factor of $41 per pupil in 1998–1999. Such aid may be used for equipment, wiring, access fees, software and supplies, professional development, staffing, maintenance, and other uses that may be necessary for the establishment of effective distance learning networks. The eight county special service school districts (disabled pupils only) receive $120,000 of this aid.
New Mexico	7.0	The 1998 legislature provided funding for 1998–99 of $14.02 per student with a total appropriation of $4.4 million. Districts budgeted a total of $3.2 (0.5% of total capital outlay revenues) in Technology for Education Act revenues for 1998–99.
New York	43.5	New York state aids school technology through the following programs: (1) Computer hardware and technology equipment aid ($17.1 million): All districts are eligible for aid to purchase or lease computer and technology equipment for instructional purposes. Schools may use up to 20% of this aid for the repair of hardware and equipment or for staff development; (2) Computer software aid ($14.1 million): All districts are eligible for computer software aid to purchase instructional software; (3) Aid for instructional computer technology ($9.0 million): This aid supports approved instructional computer technology expenses (those that are not eligible for building aid or are not claimed for any other technology aid); (4) Learning technology grants ($3.3 million). The state aids learning technology programs, including services benefiting nonpublic school students.
North Carolina	nr	The state of North Carolina began special funding for technology in 1995–1996. As of 1998–1999, $111.5 million have been dedicated to technology equipment and programs. Local school systems are required to write a technology plan which must be approved by the local board of education and submitted to the state board of education for final approval before money can be received. Plans must be reviewed annually.
North Dakota	0	No state aid. School districts could, with voter approval, levy up to five mills for distance learning technology.
Ohio	32.5	Significant investment in technology is made outside the basic aid and categorical aid to schools programs. For example, the Education Management Information System (EMIS) and Ohio Educational Computer Network (OECN) are used to provide administrative and instructional information technology and computer services for schools across the state. As well, the SchoolNet Plus program contains provisions for assistance in funding technology purchases.

State Technology Funding Programs, 1998–1999 (cont.)

State	Funding ($ millions)	Description of State Funding Program
Oklahoma	16.4	$16.4 million was distributed for common education classroom technology. Of that, $8.2 million went to help school districts obtain technology access (Internet capabilities, etc.), and another $8.2 million to purchase computer hardware.
Oregon	1.0	The state has no statewide technology plan. The Department of Administrative Services is devising a Technology Enterprise Network for all state agencies, including schools and higher education to begin in the 1999–2001 biennium. Through 1998–1999, all agencies and schools have developed their own plans for implementation. For the past five years the Education Service Districts have pooled resources with local districts and created a K–12 technology network that serves all school in the state. Through this Oregon Public Education Network (OPEN), schools gain technology connectivity and access.
Pennsylvania	36.3	1998–1999 was the third year of the three-year Link-to-Learn program. Its purpose is to improve the basic technology infrastructure and capabilities of public elementary and secondary schools. Funding is provided for school districts and area vocational technical schools to assist them to: invest in the acquisition of new, or replacement of obsolete, personal computers for use in classrooms; purchase cabling and equipment needed to install local area networks and wide area networks to position schools for eventual connection to the Pennsylvania Education Network; and train teachers to integrate technology effectively into course curricula. The amount of the Link-to-Learn grant is based on the average daily membership and market value/personal income aid ratio of the school district or area vocational technical school.
Rhode Island	3.4	The student technology investment fund is designed to provide schools and teaching staff with up-to-date educational technology and training to help students meet the demands of the 21st century. The program distributes an annual state allocation determined as part of the state budget process based on each district's average daily membership in grades pre-K to 12. Only 35% of the annual allocation can go to support ongoing activities, i.e., 65% of the allocation must support new technology activities. Funds may be used for curriculum development, professional development, and infrastructure requirements such as equipment, instructional materials, software and networking of systems. Each district must have (under a separate requirement) a technology plan, and use of these funds must be consistent with that plan. There is a legislative technology task force in place, which also must review plans for the use of these funds. Finally, the statute again states that the funds must focus on closing student performance gaps. The department of education issues guidelines for and monitors the use of the fund.

State Technology Funding Programs, 1998–1999 (cont.)

State	Funding ($ millions)	Description of State Funding Program
South Carolina	28.4	State funding supports local implementation of the South Carolina Educational Technology Plan and district strategic and school renewal plans. Purchases consider issues projected in long-range plans, such as the application of technology for teaching and learning. Funds may not be expended for personnel positions but may be used for contractual services. School technology funds are divided among all districts using the ratio of the district free/reduced lunch count for grades 1–3 to the statewide free/reduced lunch count for grades 1–3 of the second preceding year. Purchases must adhere to the following guidelines: (1) Provide for any lacking hardware, software or training needed to ensure extended connectivity to and usage of the dedicated telecommunications lines of the state network; (2) Focus on resources that facilitate integrated curriculum-based use of technology with correlation to curriculum frameworks and academic standards; (3) Supplement, but not supplant, the existing or projected school technology budgets; (4) Serve as seed money to stimulate technology innovation for Act 135; (5) Be supplemented or matched at the local level by entering into partnerships and arrangements with such groups as businesses and parent organizations and by using vehicle license plate sales, etc.; (6) Reflect equitable distribution of funds throughout the district; (7) Be planned for by a broadly representative committee within the district; and (8) Match technologies to the local need, considering the fact that all technologies, video, computers, telecommunications routers, DSUs, hubs, wiring, etc. are appropriate uses for these funds. Technology Professional Development Initiative: Expenditures made with these funds must have an emphasis on curriculum applications that support the South Carolina Educational Technology Plan and must have a technology focus. Funds earmarked for technology professional development are divided among all school districts based on average daily membership (ADM). These funds must be used for graduate course contracts with South Carolina colleges and universities, instructor stipends for re-certification courses offered by districts, mini-course modules and professional development conference and workshop registration fees. This funding source may also be used to purchase instructional materials to support the courses and workshops offered in districts They must center on weaving technology resources into daily instruction and on using them to support curriculum standards.
South Dakota	0	No state aid is provided.
Tennessee	20.0	Technology is one of the components of the Basic Education Program (BEP) cost formula. The districts are allowed to use the funds for any item considered "technology." The BEP provides 75% of the technology appropriation as provided in the formula based on $22.39 per average daily membership (ADM) until the fund is depleted.

State Technology Funding Programs, 1998–1999 (cont.)

State	Funding ($ millions)	Description of State Funding Program
Texas	nr	Beginning in 1992–1993, the foundation school program (FSP) included a technology allotment of $30 per average daily attendance (ADA). The technology allotment provides for the purchase of electronic textbooks or technology equipment for instruction, and it pays for training instructional personnel in the appropriate use of technology equipment and electronic textbooks. An "electronic textbook" means computer software, interactive videodiscs, CD-ROM, computer courseware, on-line services. The state also funds other technology initiatives such as the Texas Center for Educational Technology (TCET) located at the University of North Texas, the preview centers and training programs at the regional education service centers, the T-STAR telecommunications system, and the Texas Educational Telecommunications Network (TETN) that provides interactive video conferences, facsimile transmission, and two-way transmission of data. The Telecommunications Infrastructure Fund (TIF) was established in 1995 with the Public Utility Regulation Act. The act was intended to generate $150 million each year to provide telecommunications access to schools, hospitals, libraries, and institutions of higher education. A TIF board is charged with disbursing the funds. The mission of the TIF board is to help Texas deploy an advanced telecommunications infrastructure by stimulating universal connectivity. In addition, the TIF board funds training programs. During the 1996–1997 biennium, the TIF board awarded $52 million to help schools implement Internet connections. In 1998–1999, the Texas Education Agency received $14.6 million in TIF funds for various technology projects. Although the TIF was structured to collect $150 million a year over ten years, lower assessments on commercial mobile telecommunications lowered anticipated collections by $25 million per year. Legislation passed in 1997 removed the ten-year limit on deposits to the fund and placed a $1.5 billion cap on the fund, excluding interest and loan repayments. Half of the revenue is dedicated to public school projects, and the remaining half is available for other qualifying projects.
Utah	8.5	Utah's Educational Technology Initiative is intended to expand the use of computer-based technologies within schools and classrooms for administrative and instructional use. The goal is to enhance the teaching/learning process and to empower students to become productive members of a technology-oriented society. Funds may be used to maintain existing programs and for inservice programs required to implement the technology. Allocations are made to all districts based on total average daily membership for grades K–12.
Vermont	na	State law requires access to current technology, and funding is subsumed in the general state support grant and in the guaranteed yield. There was no state categorical appropriation in Fiscal Year 1999. In addition, Vermont interactive television sites allow for statewide teleconferencing for business, education, and other general purposes. The appropriation for this freestanding agency was $763,933. Most high-schools are equipped for satellite reception of lessons with telephone feedback loops. These facilities were funded in an earlier fiscal year with one-time grants.

State Technology Funding Programs, 1998–1999 (cont.)

State	Funding ($ millions)	Description of State Funding Program
Virginia	1.0	The Electronic Classroom Program (also known as the Virginia Satellite Educational Network) created a satellite delivery network offering high school and middle school students credit courses that are not widely available, particularly in small or rural schools. Advanced placement courses in English, calculus, statistics, U.S. history, and government are offered in addition to three years each of Latin and Japanese. A number of staff development programs supporting Virginia's Standards of Learning are also offered to teachers.
Washington	na	Currently, there is no state K–12 general fund category specifically earmarked for technology. Instead, the Washington State Department of Information Services is responsible for coordinating the development of the state's K–20 Network. This is a high-speed, high-bandwidth network that connects Internet, videoconferencing, and satellite-delivered video programs. The effort is a collaboration of public and private K–12 schools, higher education, state government, and the private sector which builds on an existing state-run telecommunications infrastructure. Since 1996, the state has appropriated $62.3 million to construct the network. Phase one was completed in September 1997 at a cost of $23.2 million. Phase one connected the main campuses of the state's higher education system and the nine regional education service districts. Phase two began in July 1998 and will connect the state's K–12 school districts, with an anticipated completion date in the year 2000. Subsequent phases will add public libraries, state and local governments, and community resource centers to the network. In addition to the K–20 network, the Superintendent of Public Instruction sponsors a number of competitive grant awards for innovative uses and technology, and also assists districts in developing the local technology plans required for districts in order to qualify for the federally-sponsored E-Rates. State share is 100% of allocation for the K–20 network. Beginning in 1999–2001, a general fund category for the costs of the K–12 portion of the K–20 network will be added.
West Virginia	22.0	The Basic Skills/Computer Education program is an on-going initiative, providing hardware and software for every K–6 classroom in the state. Currently, 29,000 student workstations are in use, and 21,000 teachers have received training. The program was initiated in 1989 when the West Virginia legislature requested that computer hardware, software, and training for grades K–6 be implemented to improve basic skills.

State Technology Funding Programs, 1998–1999 (cont.)

State	Funding ($ millions)	Description of State Funding Program
Wisconsin	47.4	Public school districts are eligible to receive technology block grants administered by the Technology for Educational Achievement in Wisconsin (TEACH) board. The grants may be used for any purpose related to technology use in the education or training of any person or in the administration of a school and related telecommunications services, except for the funding of salaries or benefits of any school district employee. Of the total, $30 million of the funding is distributed based on a formula that uses equalized value per member. Each eligible school district receives $5,000 from the amount appropriated. The balance of the $30 million is distributed in proportion to a weighted membership of each district. The remaining $5 million is distributed based on the number of persons residing in the district between the ages of 4 and 20.
Wyoming	nr	Technology is considered to hold promise for improved student knowledge, especially in Wyoming's small remote schools. In addition to including a school finance model component providing per student equipment funding within the total block grant amount, the legislature has provided incentive payments for the foundation program account for programs involving distance learning technology, as well as significant funding, $11 million over a two year period, for implementation of the Wyoming Education Technology Plan. The plan provides a structure for implementing and integrating technology into educational programs, with data connectivity between all schools to be accomplished as of July 1, 1999, and interactive two-way video capability within all high schools by July 1, 2001. Funding is phased-in over time to accomplish these goals. Technology is also addressed through a technology readiness factor included within the statewide assessment of school building and facility needs used in prioritizing statewide capital construction needs. The readiness component assesses the existence of required building and facility infrastructure to support informational technology and associated equipment.

Source: Compiled from Catherine C. Sielke, John Dayton, C. Thomas Holmes, and Anne Jefferson, *Public School Finance Programs of the United States and Canada, 1998–1999*, Publication #NCES 2001-309 (Washington, D.C.: U. S. Department of Education, National Center for Education Statistics, 2001) http://www.nces.ed.gov/edfin/state_finance/statefinancing.asp.

CHAPTER 10

SHOULD PRINCIPALS BE INVOLVED IN SCHOOL RENOVATIONS?

Brian O. Brent
University of Rochester

Marie Cianca
Rochester City School District

ABSTRACT

In the year 2000, public school districts in the United States spent $21.2 billion on school construction and renovations, marking the end of a decade in which expenditures grew by nearly 40%. Yet, little is known about the role of school principals in this activity. Because principals are managing the environments in which renovations take place, it is reasonable to believe that they play some role in this process, particularly with the increasing emphasis on site-based management. This chapter establishes the importance of understanding the nature and efficacy of principals' involvement in the school renovation process in New York. The study found that two-thirds of principals surveyed participated in such renovations, and although they recognized that activities associated with renovations took time away from other responsibilities, such as instructional leadership, they believed the benefits outweighed the costs. The implications of these findings are far-reaching and include the need to give greater attention to preparing principals to manage such projects effectively.

Saving America's School Infrastructure, pages 215–231

215

INTRODUCTION

Previous chapters in this volume have offered ample evidence that school infrastructure will be a pressing issue for some time. While progress toward documenting the unmet funding need is encouraging, further information is necessary and desirable for policymaking purposes. What is notable about the need to renovate and update school facilities is that principals are managing the environments in which these changes take place. Further, it is reasonable to believe that principals will play some role in this process. If so, they will necessarily have less time to devote to educational duties, such as instructional leadership and promotion of better ways for teachers to teach and students to learn.

Given that the renovation and updating of school facilities might augment principals' duties, it is surprising that little systematic research exists in the principalship literature. Most efforts to document the nature of principals' involvement are anecdotal and tend to report positive experiences only, potentially overstating the efficacy of principals' participation in this process.[1] Moreover, the limited empirical data available offers only highly aggregated measures of principals' commitment to managing school facilities, including in these measures such diverse tasks as maintenance, budgeting, and course scheduling.

The purpose of this chapter is to establish the importance of understanding the nature and efficacy of principals' involvement in the school renovation process and to report on a study that informs this discussion. The goal here is not to champion any specific approach to managing school renovations, as a number of thoughtful handbooks perform this task.[2] Instead, the central task of this chapter is to reveal how school renovations currently affect principal practice and, accordingly, schools and students. A diverse set of factors has fostered the need to improve many of America's schools. Earlier chapters in this volume have documented the costs to upgrade and expand school infrastructure, and so the issue is not revisited here. Rather, this discussion serves to demonstrate the complexity and varied nature of school renovation projects and the circumstances to which principals must respond.

The first section of the chapter explores the varied nature of school renovations. Next, the study that frames this chapter is described. This section leads to a series of analyses that offer new insight into the effect of school renovations on principals and schools. First, the extent and level of principals' commitment to the renovation process is examined, and the number of hours that principals devote to renovations when they occur is reported. Most efforts to determine the cost of school renovations consider capital expenditures only. The findings of this study make it evident that the real cost of school renovations includes the imputed value of principals' time as well as capital resources.

Simple time metrics offers a useful first account of how principals support school renovations. The second analysis extends this understanding by detailing-the specific roles that principals play in the renovation process. School renovations require that principals perform a remarkably diverse set of duties, ranging from project design to mediating disputes among staff and construction workers. Many of these tasks require that principals possess skills not typically associated with school leadership, and this issue is considered here. A third analysis examines the efficacy of principals' involvement in school renovations. Some argue that principals should spend more time on instructional duties and less time on administrative tasks, such as managing facilities.[3] The findings of this study challenge this notion and offer evidence that involving principals in renovations benefits schools in a number of important ways.

The fourth and final analysis probes the type of training, if any, that principals need to manage renovation projects effectively. Recently, a number of scholars have questioned the efficacy of graduate administrative training.[4] Underlying the concerns raised by these critics is the belief that such programs often lack connection to the realities of the workplace.

What underlies these analyses is the belief that policymakers should expand debates about the costs of school renovations to include discussions of how these activities affect principals' roles and responsibilities. The point is not that personnel costs exceed capital costs. However, it is surprising that, given the growing level of infrastructure needs and the likelihood that principals will participate in school-level improvements, the efficacy of principals involvement in school renovations is unstudied. It is hoped that this chapter will provoke greater interest in the issue.

THE VARIED NATURE OF SCHOOL RENOVATIONS

There are many terms used to describe the process of improving an existing school facility, including "renovating," "modernizing," "retrofitting," and "remodeling."[5] Renovating, for example, commonly refers to the complete overhaul of a building, while remodeling is limited to one area, such as the science laboratories. Retrofitting, alternatively, applies to efforts to improve energy conservation or technology readiness. All of these terms refer to some type of school facilities improvement.

Regardless of the term used, many factors might contribute to a district's decision to improve an existing building. Perhaps, most obvious is the need to add classroom space because of increasing enrollments or class-size reduction initiatives. Consider that California's recent effort to reduce K–3 classes to 20 students will require as many as 20,000 new classrooms.[6]

Another factor serving to alter the physical structure of a building is taxpayer expectation that schools will satisfy multiple community needs, including provision of space for civic meetings, local sports clubs, and adult and youth programs. Added space, parking, access, and security are examples of changes that might be required when facilities house more than the regular school program.[7]

The high and increasing cost of energy also has prompted many districts to modify their facilities in ways that attempt to save energy. Before the management of energy emerged as an important issue, schools were commonly constructed with high ceilings, single pane-windows, and little insulation—even in cold-weather regions.[8] Measures that attempt to redress these and other energy inefficiencies include changes in building design and materials, and the replacement of selected parts of the heating, cooling, ventilation, and electrical systems.[9]

The safety of students and school personnel has also become a prime concern of district officials and policymakers. Safety hazards in schools might be due to antiquated building design; air, water, or ground pollution; and other environmental dangers, such as radon and asbestos. In recent years, a number of tragic and well-publicized incidents have also prompted many districts to alter their school facilities in an attempt reduce student violence and crime. For example, some school officials have made efforts to eliminate hidden or hard-to-see areas in their buildings by adding or altering windows, walkways, stairways, doors and lighting.[10] Others have added sophisticated security devices, such as surveillance cameras and metal detectors.[11]

Closely related to safety issues is the need for buildings to comply with federal regulations regarding individuals with disabilities. For example, the Rehabilitation Act of 1973 (P.L. 93-112) dealt with the elimination of architectural barriers in public school facilities (Section 502) and mandated accessibility to educational programs (Section 504). Although this act did not require that existing facilities be made completely barrier-free, as is the case with new construction, it required that officials strive to make schools physically accessible to disabled persons. This might require the modification of classrooms to accommodate special equipment, or the installation of walkways and elevators.[12]

Facility renovations are often spurred by environmental considerations, such as those described above, but they also may be generated by efforts to improve the instructional program.[13] Indeed, buildings can become educationally obsolete before they become physically unsound. For example, most of the schools-without-walls that were built in the 1970s soon erected walls to limit noise and distraction.[14] More recently, educators have turned to advanced telecommunications technology to support various teaching strategies and programs. Many schools now have distance learning class-rooms, computer labs, media centers, and Internet capabilities; and there is a national effort to those equip those schools that do not (NCES, 1995).[15] Similarly, school officials are seeking to take advantage of technol-ogy in the areas of communication, budgeting, scheduling, and atten-dance. Each effort to integrate technology into an existing building implicates a number of functional areas, including space as well as electri-cal, telecommunication, security, ventilation, and cooling systems.

The renovations described here provide only a few examples of the ways in which districts might improve their school facilities. Nevertheless, the exam-ples illustrate two points. First, because principals are the persons in the dis-trict who are responsible for the operation and maintenance of schools, they are likely to be affected in some way by renovations. Second, the varied nature of renovations suggests that the skills developed in managing one type of ren-ovation, say, adding a stairwell, might not be wholly transferable to other types of projects, such as equipping a building for the Internet.

THE STUDY

To learn more about the effects of renovations on schools, a sample of principals in New York state was surveyed and asked about their experi-ences with these activities.[16] New York was chosen for analysis because it ranks first among states with nearly $48 billion in school infrastructure needs.[17] Moreover, roughly 70% of New York's school construction dollars are currently spent renovating existing buildings.[18]

Renovations were defined as any project that expands or modernizes an existing school facility. This definition includes the construction of addi-tions needed to relieve overcrowding or to meet government mandates, as well as projects intended to make an existing facility ready for technology, improve energy efficiency, or address health or safety concerns. It also includes major improvements to school grounds, such as landscaping and paving. This definition, however, does not include the construction of new school buildings or activities related to routine maintenance.

Data were collected for the study from principal surveys. To determine whether district size influenced principals' involvement in the renovation process, a proportionate, stratified sampling procedure was used. First, all regular elementary, middle, and secondary schools (n=4,226) were grouped according to district size (i.e., large city, small city, large central, and small central).[19] Then, equal proportions of schools from each of the four groups were randomly selected, resulting in a sample of 505 schools. The survey elicited data on four topics: (1) level of principals' involvement in school renovations; (2) types of renovation-related activities performed by principals; (3) benefits and concerns of principals with their involvement in renovations; and (4) training of principals for involvement in school renovations. Respondents from 280 schools returned the surveys, a response rate of 55%.

LEVEL OF INVOLVEMENT

The general strategy for the analyses was to begin by examining the extent of principals' involvement in the renovation process and then to move toward more refined indicators of the nature of this involvement. First, the percentage of principals involved in renovations during the five-year period, 1995–2000, was determined. Table 10.1 reports on the results of this analysis and reveals that 73% of the respondents participated in school renovations. This is a substantial figure and suggests that most principals will be involved with renovations when they occur.

Table 10.1.   Percentage of Principals Involved in School Renovations by Type of School District

Involvement in Renovations	All Schools (n=280)	Large City (n=60)	Small City (n=31)	Large Central (n=122)	Small Central (n=67)
Involved in Renovations	73	73	61	76	70
Reason Involved in Renovations:					
District policy or practice	77	63	77	79	85
Choose to be involved, not district policy	23	37	23	21	15
Not Involved in Renovations	27	27	39	24	30
Reason Not Involved in Renovations:					
No renovations	66	60	50	72	70
District office oversees renovations	17	7	25	21	17
Construction manager oversees renovations	12	13	25	7	12
Other reason	5	20	—	—	1

Next, the study sought to determine why some principals were involved and others were not. Chi-square analyses revealed that there was no statistically significant association between principals' involvement in renovations and the following variables: district size (X^2 = 3.01, p > .05); building-level (X^2 = 3.19, p > .05); building age (X^2 = 2.81, p > .05); years of administrative experience of the principal (X^1 = 0.08, p > .05); and gender of the principal (X^2 = 0.50, p > .05). These findings were surprising given that one might reasonably anticipate that larger districts would likely have centralized administrative support teams to manage renovations. In addition, gender appears to play no role in whether principals will be included in renovation-related activities.

Instead, two factors explained principals' participation in the renovation process: (1) district policy or practice required that they be involved; or (2) they chose to be involved. As Table 10.1 indicates, most respondents reported that district policy dictated that they participate in the process. A relatively small percentage of principals participated because of their own volition, particularly those in small central schools. These findings might reflect the move toward decentralized decision-making that has characterized school governance structures recently, a management approach that many believe will lead to school improvement.[20] Nevertheless, this finding substantiates the view that district-level officials continue to mete out a growing number of responsibilities to building principals.

Of the respondents, 27% were not involved in renovations. Most respondents reported that they simply had no renovations during the period examined. Given the earlier finding, one could argue that about 70% of these principals would have been involved in renovations if they had taken place. Indeed, relatively few principals reported that district oversight or the use of an external construction manager was the reason they were not involved. Taken together, these findings offer the possibility that the proportion of principals involved in renovations will increase as more districts renovate and expand their buildings.

The data reported in Table 10.1 provide background for understanding the scope of principals' involvement in school renovations. Next, the amount of time principals devoted to this task when projects were underway was examined. During the regular school year, respondents spent, on average, 5.4 hours each week managing renovations. This figure increased to 7.6 hours during the summer months of July and August. Undoubtedly, the complexity and duration of renovation projects varied, but, on average, principals spent five to eight hours each week when involved in such efforts. This is not a trivial claim. If one assumes a 50-hour work week, the findings indicate that principals spent about 10% to 15% of their time on renovations. This represents a substantial amount of time given principals' many and increasing responsibilities.

NATURE OF INVOLVEMENT

Although every renovation is unique, there are several activities that are common to most projects, including:

- Needs assessment
- Design
- Securing funds
- Bidding and contracting
- Architect and contractor consultation
- Inspections and project approval
- Troubleshooting

To better understand the nature of principals' involvement in the renovation process, principals were asked to report how they divided their time among these and other renovation-related activities (See Table 10.2).

Table 10.2.   Percentage of Total Time Spent by Principals on Renovations Devoted to Specific Activities

Activity	All Schools (n=203)	Large City (n=44)	Small City (n=19)	Large Central (n=93)	Small Central (n=47)
Needs assessment	20	11	22	23	20
Design	15	5	21	18	18
Securing funds	2	2	0.5	3	2
Bidding and contracting	1	3	0.5	1	2
Architect consultations	16	14	19	18	13
Contractor consultations	14	27	6	9	13
Inspections and approval	10	12	13	9	10
Troubleshooting	18	22	14	14	19
Other	4	4	4	5	3

Needs Assessment

Principals typically spent 20% of their renovation-related time conducting needs assessments, the first phase in the renovation process. Put simply, needs assessments determine the status of the educational facility and specify the actions required if educational, administrative, or operational objectives are to be realized. Some needs are readily apparent, as would be the case with a damaged, leaking roof. In other instances, facility needs might not be obvious without undertaking a systematic, formal review. In many districts, principals conduct annual surveys to assess facility needs. District officials then review the surveys and determine which projects to undertake.[21]

Design

The design phase of the renovation process translates facility needs into construction plans. It is during the design phase that school officials identify and select architects, project managers, and engineers. Because many of these professionals are not educators, principals often take an active role in this process. Principals spent, on average, 15% of their time performing this activity.

Securing Funds

The third phase of the renovation process is making sure that adequate funds are available. Funds for school construction and renovation can derive from a number of sources, including federal, state, and local governments. Principals most often become involved in the funding process when districts seek funds from local sources. For example, if a renovation project is presented to voters in the form of a bond referendum, district officials, including principals, must garner public support. However, securing funds accounts for only a small percentage of principals' time. On average, they spend only 2% of their time on this activity. Nevertheless, one might reasonably argue that it should be a more important responsibility with regard to renovations. After all, renovations can occur only after the district secures funding.

Bidding and Contracting

Most states mandate that school districts use some form of competitive bid process when contracting for renovations. Although specific rules vary, in general, bidding requires that districts publicly advertise capital projects and award the contract to the lowest "responsible" bidder. The purpose of this process is to provide all vendors with an equal opportunity to secure the contract and to increase the likelihood that the district will receive the best possible price for the goods and services desired. Once district officials identify the lowest responsible bidder, the school board awards the contract. Principals generally dedicate little time to this phase of the renovation process. Because bidding and contracting implicate legal issues and board policies, district-level officials typically guide these activities.[22] Principals in the study reported spending only 1% of their time with such activities.

Architect and Contractor Consultations

Principals spent 16% of their time consulting with the architects and 14% with contractors. According to Earthman, principals conduct weekly meetings to discuss the progress of the project in most large renovations.[23] During the course of these meetings, the contractor details the work performed in the previous week and specifies the timing and areas of the building in which the coming week's work will take place. The parties then develop and agree upon a work schedule that minimizes disruptions to the educational program. This process often requires compromises between the principal and contractor so that the school can operate effectively and, at the same time, allow the contractor to meet contract deadlines.

Inspections and Project Approval

Principals spent 10% of their time inspecting renovations. Although construction contracts stipulate the work to be completed, good management practice dictates that school officials regularly inspect the quality of the work and the materials used by the contractor.[24] If officials inspect the project only upon completion, it is often difficult and costly to make necessary changes.

Troubleshooting

Principals spent 18% of their time troubleshooting problems that arise throughout the renovation process. This finding suggests that few renovations proceed to completion without difficulty. Such difficulties include conflicts between school staff and construction workers and students and construction workers. In these instances, principals must act quickly to resolve the issue. Sometimes the problem can be addressed with a warning to the staff member, student, or construction worker. More serious altercations, however, might require formal investigations and hearings.[25]

In addition, problems can arise from unanticipated conditions that affect the original renovation plans. For example, a contractor might open a wall and find asbestos, a material that had not been listed on the original architectural drawings. In these instances, school officials need to determine an appropriate remedy and amend the construction contract accordingly.[26]

BENEFITS AND CONCERNS OF INVOLVEMENT

In sum, renovations require that principals perform a wide range of duties and interact with diverse groups. Despite this useful insight, the analysis tends to obscure an important question: *Should* principals be involved in the renovation process? Principals' participation in the process is a necessary, but not sufficient, condition that will benefit schools. To explore this issue, principals were asked to provide Likert-type responses to a series of statements, each embodying a supposed benefit or concern of their involvement. Table 10.3 reports their responses and reveals several noteworthy findings.

Table 10.3.   Benefits and Concerns of Principals' Involvement in Renovations

Benefits and Concerns	Strongly Agree (%)	Agree (%)	Neither Agree nor Disagree (%)	Disagree (%)	Strongly Disagree (%)
My involvement in the renovation process...					
Helps me gain community support for the project.	34	44	17	4	1
Allows me to make decisions about projects.	15	46	17	15	7
Is valued by architects and contractors.	8	25	25	24	18
Helps ensure project quality.	37	49	10	3	1
Helps minimize instructional disruptions.	54	37	5	3	1
Allows me to make the project a learning experience for students.	11	25	39	19	6
Hinders my ability to be an instructional leader.	31	45	11	11	2
Causes me to work holidays, evenings, and weekends.	15	37	13	25	10
Overall, benefits the school.	51	45	3	1	—

Most principals reported that their involvement helped them generate community support for renovations. This is a valuable insight. In many states, districts require voter approval to fund renovations, and it would be unwise for school officials to rely solely on fate to determine whether a referendum will pass.

The analysis also indicates that most principals felt that they were able to influence decisions about renovations, but they were less certain that architects and contractors valued their input. This finding suggests that some renovation professionals may not have been enthusiastic about sharing decision-making authority with principals. Despite this concern, 86% of principals believed that their involvement in the process helped ensure project quality. This finding is important. Schools will invest billions of dollars in renovations in the next few years, and an increasingly vigilant public will hold educators accountable for spending those dollars wisely.

Most principals also thought that their involvement in the renovation process helped minimize instructional disruptions. Relatively few principals, however, were able to make these projects a learning experience for students, a disappointing finding given that some view renovations as an opportunity to explore the construction process with children.[27] In addition, nearly all principals reported that their involvement with renovations hindered their ability to be instructional leaders. It is important to remember that principals reported spending between five to seven hours each week attending to renovations. Simply put, the time that principals spent on renovations could not be spent on other duties, such as supervising teachers, evaluating programs, and designing curriculum.

In addition, most principals believed that their involvement with renovations caused them to work holidays, weekends, and evenings. This finding is not surprising given that some districts require that contractors work during these times. Such arrangements allow workers greater freedom in doing their job and, at the same time, minimize instructional disruptions and the likelihood of conflicts between workers and students and staff.[28]

The survey also offered respondents the opportunity to list other benefits and concerns about their involvement in renovations. Again, there were some noteworthy results. For example, some principals reported that renovations offered them an opportunity to improve school climate by engaging teachers in the project. Others reported that their involvement allowed them to prepare staff for the inconveniences that accompany renovations and to keep them regularly informed as the work progressed.

Principals also reported a number of additional concerns, mostly regarding their dealings with contractors and their crews. For example, many principals noted that their concern for students' safety and well-being caused them to continually monitor projects, performing such tasks as closing doors, removing sharp objects, and discouraging crews from smoking, using foul language, and engaging in other inappropriate behaviors. Several principals also found themselves resolving conflicts between contractors and custodians over cleaning responsibilities.

The data presented above invite serious debate about whether principals should be involved in the renovation process. On one hand, their involvement might improve project quality. On the other hand, their involvement might hinder their ability to be an instructional leader. To gain some insight into the overall efficacy of principals' participation in renovations, principals were asked whether they believed that the benefits of their involvement outweighed their related concerns. Nearly all principals agreed that their involvement yielded net benefits.

TRAINING NEEDS

If principals' involvement in renovations can benefit schools, then it is important to consider the training that they need to perform these duties effectively. This issue is the focus of the final analysis. Table 10.4 reports the types of training that principals actually received regarding how to manage renovations. It is interesting to find that only 12% of the respondents had taken graduate coursework, and only 11% had attended workshops on renovations. Together. these findings suggest that principals had few formal opportunities to learn how to manage renovations. Instead, principals learned how to manage renovations by consulting with facilities experts (88%) and experienced principals (52%) or learning on the job (92%).

Next, principals were asked to indicate the type of training that they believed would help them manage renovations more effectively. As Table 10.5 reports, most principals agreed that they would benefit from consultations with experienced principals (85%) or facilities experts (82%). Sixty-two percent of principals agreed that the use of interactive Web sites to facilitate consultations with persons familiar with the renovation process would be beneficial. However, Table 10.5 also suggests that principals believe that these informal support system should serve as supplements to more structured learning experiences. For example, 75% of the respondents believed that they would benefit from workshops on renovations. Similarly, 51% of the respondents supported graduate coursework on the topic. These findings should serve as a signal to administrative programs and professional development groups everywhere that principals welcome additional opportunities to learn how to manage renovations.

Table 10.4. Types of Renovation Training Received by Principals

Types of Preparation Received	All Schools (n=280)	Large City (n=60)	Small City (n=31)	Large Central (n=122)	Small Central (n=67)
Graduate coursework	12%	14%	23%	12%	7%
Professional workshops	11	10	10	16	3
Consultations with facilities experts	88	81	87	87	88
Consultations with experienced principals	52	71	58	50	36
On-the-job training	92	78	94	95	97

Table 10.5.   Principals' Preferred Type of Renovation Training

Type of Training	Strongly Agree (%)	Agree (%)	Neither Agree nor Disagree (%)	Disagree	Strongly Disagree (%)
I would benefit from the following type of renovation training…					
Graduate coursework	15	36	22	19	8
Professional workshops	23	52	15	8	2
Consultation with facilities experts	29	53	11	5	2
Consultation with experienced principals	26	59	11	2	2
Consultation via interactive Web site	12	50	27	7	4
Professional publications	6	36	40	13	5

CONCLUSION

In the year 2000, public school districts in the United States spent $21.2 billion on school construction and renovations, marking the end of a decade in which expenditures grew by nearly 40%.[29] Yet, despite this considerable capital investment, policymakers continue to know very little about how these improvements affect schools and students. The purpose of this chapter was to report on a study that examined one aspect of this important issue, the effect of school renovations on principals.

The research presented in this chapter yielded five major findings. First, district policy requires that most principals participate in the renovation process. Second, principals typically spend five to eight hours per week managing renovations when they occur. Third, renovations require that principals perform a number of diverse tasks. Fourth, despite several concerns, principals believe that their participation in the process benefits schools. Fifth and finally, principals believe that they would manage renovations more effectively if more training opportunities were available.

The authors make no claim that this study describes completely the effects of renovations on principals. The difficulties of doing research on this issue are numerous. For example, the analyses rely solely on the perceptions of principals. While principals are in a position to make judgments about the effectiveness of their involvement, they are certainly not the only judges. Absent a thorough cost-effectiveness analysis, there is no definitive means to determine the efficacy of involving principals in renovations.

Despite this limitation, this study has much to offer educational theory and practice. First, standard cost-analyses of renovations take account of capital expenditures only. However, this study demonstrates that policymakers should consider the cost of personnel resources as well. Indeed, if one uses a dollar metric to express principals' time commitment to renovations, it becomes clear that the cost to renovate schools is underestimated.

Second, this type of study can inform current debates regarding education reform, particularly those aspects of reform that involve principals. For instance, many states have implemented new student assessments and begun the process of creating accountability systems that confer rewards and sanctions. While these reforms affect everyone associated with schools, the pressures are increasingly converging in one place—the principal's office. This study, however, offers the possibility that despite the many benefits, principals' involvement with renovations hinders their ability to be instructional leaders. Ultimately, school officials, not scholars, must decide whether to involve principals in renovations. They can make this decision better by considering the information reported here.

Finally, these results bear on important debates about the nature and quality of principal preparation. Perhaps, the real work of learning how to manage renovations does happen on the job. However, successful leadership preparation programs are those that pay attention to the array of issues that principals need to address if they are to make meaningful improvements in their schools. The incidence of school renovations will grow in the coming years, and graduate preparation programs and professional development centers would be well-advised to provide thoughtful treatments of this topic.

While this study provides greater understanding of the effects of renovation on principals and schools, there are numerous opportunities for researchers to extend these analyses. A logical extension of this work is to trace the effects of renovations to even deeper points within the educational system. For example, how do renovations affect teachers and students? Questions about educational productivity can only be resolved with a more thorough understanding of how renovations affect student learning. Another important extension of this work involves looking more closely at the kinds of training that principals need to manage renovations effectively. Indeed, before policymakers seriously consider requiring principals to undertake extensive training in school renovations, they should first ascertain the likely efficacy of these efforts. Fortunately, these research programs are complementary.

NOTES

1. See, for example, William S. Bradley, "Working with an Architect to Design Your School," *Media & Methods* 35 (November-December 1998): 10; Karen K. Futral, "The Principal's Role in School Renovation," *Principal* (January

1993): 30–33; Patty Shafer, "Opening A New School: What Else Can Go Wrong?" *Principal* 79 (November 1999): 28–30; and Ashley Halliday, "Easing the Disruption of Construction," *Thrust For Educational Leadership* 29 (November-December 1999): 12–14.

2. See, for example, Basil Castaldi, *Educational Facilities: Planning, Modernizing, and Management* (Boston, Massachusetts: Allyn and Bacon, 1994); Glenn I. Earthman, *School Renovation Handbook: Investing in Education,* (Lancaster, Pennsylvania: Technomic Publishing Company, Inc., 1994); and Theodore J. Kowalski, *Planning and Managing School Facilities* (New York: Praeger, 1989).

3. See, for example, Christopher T. Cross and Robert C. Rice, "The Role of the Principal as Instructional Leader in a Standards-Driven System," *NASSP Bulletin* 84 (2000): 61–65; Jonathan A. Supovitz, "Manage Less, Lead More," *Principal Leadership* 1 (November 2000): 14–19; and Michael A. Zigarelli, "An Empirical Test of Conclusions from Effective Schools Research," *The Journal of Educational Research* 90 (November-December 1996): 103–110.

4. See, for example, Brian O. Brent, "Should Graduate Training in Educational Administration Be Required for Principal Certification? Existing Evidence Suggests that the Answer Is No," *Teaching in Educational Administration* 5 (1998): 1–8; and Joseph Murphy and Patrick B. Forsyth, *Educational Administration: A Decade of Reform* (Thousand Oaks, California: Corwin Press, Inc., 1999).

5. Faith E. Crampton, David C. Thompson, and Janis M. Hagey, "Creating and Sustaining School Capacity in the Twenty-First Century: Funding a Physical Environment Conducive to Student Learning," *Journal of Education Finance* 27 (Fall 2001):633–652; and Earthman, *School Renovation Handbook.*

6. Daniel Gursky, "Class Size Does Matter," *The Education Digest* 64 (October 1998): 15–18.

7. Kowalski, *Planning and Managing School Facilities.*

8. Ibid.; and U.S. Department of Education, *Condition of America's Public School Facilities: 1999* (Washington, DC: National Center for Education Statistics, 2000).

9. Kowalski, *Planning and Managing School Facilities.*

10. Sherry P. Carter and Stanley L. Carter, "Planning Safer Schools," *American School and University* 73 (August 2001): 168–70.

11. Cheri Loure, "Keeping Students Safe," *Catalyst for Change* 30 (Spring 2001): 16–20.

12. For a fuller discussion of issues related to building design and disabled persons, see Chapter 7 of this volume, "Infrastructure Funding Considerations and Students with Disabilities," by William T. Hartman.

13. Kowalski, *Planning and Managing School Facilities.*

14. Henry Sanoff, *School Design* (New York: Van Nostrand Reinhold, 1994).

15. National Center for Education Statistics, *Advanced Telecommunications in U.S. Public Schools, K–12* (Washington, D.C.: U. S. Department of Education, 1995).

16. This section draws significantly from Brian O. Brent and Marie Cianca, "Involving Principals in School Renovations: Benefit or Burden? *Journal of Education Finance* 27 (Fall 2001): 729–740.

17. Crampton et al., "Creating and Sustaining School Capacity."

18. Paul Ambramson, *School Planning and Management Construction Report* (Dayton, Ohio: Peter Li Education Group, 1999).

19. Large city districts have populations greater than 50,000, and small city districts have populations less than 50,000. Large central school districts enroll over 2,500 pupils, and small central school districts enroll fewer than 2,500 students.

20. Patricia A. Wohlstetter and Susan Albers Mohrman, *Assessment of School-Based Management* (Washington, D.C.: U.S. Department of Education, Office of Educational Research and Improvement, 1996).

21. For a thoughtful and comprehensive discussion of the needs assessment process and the use of school facility surveys, see Castaldi, *Educational Facilities.*

22. For a comprehensive discussion of how districts monitor the bidding and contracting phases of school renovation projects, see Earthman, *School Renovation Handbook.*

23. Ibid.

24. Kowalski, *Planning and Managing School Facilities.*

25. Earthman, *School Renovation Handbook.*

26. Such amendments are commonly referred to as change orders.

27. See, for example, Vonda M. Albertson and Sandra M. Kate, " Modernizing an Old School," *Principal* 79 (November 1999): 5–6, 8, 10–13.

28. Earthman, *School Renovation Handbook.*

29. U.S. General Accounting Office, *School Facilities: Construction Expenditures Have Grown Significantly in Recent Years* (Washington, DC: General Accounting Office, 2000).

Part III

THE FUTURE OF SCHOOL INFRASTRUCTURE FUNDING

CHAPTER 11

STRIKING A BALANCE IN SCHOOL INFRASTRUCTURE FUNDING

David C. Thompson
Kansas State University

ABSTRACT

A sound school finance system therefore is fair in distributing resources to all children, provides adequate money to carry out the full range of services assigned, does so at a high level of efficiency without engaging in counterproductive suspicion or begrudging of resources while expecting and receiving measurable assurances of accountability and productivity, and relies on stable and predictable revenue sources—all in the context of meeting the full slate of modern educational needs. To reach this end, school infrastructure funding must be included at full parity if children are to be equally advantaged and none left to the miserable physical conditions that exist in some schools in the United States at the start of the new millennium—i.e., a funding system that is truly unitary in form and effect.

Saving America's School Infrastructure, pages 235–253

235

INTRODUCTION

The preceding chapters in this book cannot be left to stand alone, as collectively they set the tone for a summary understanding of the past, along with powerful implications for forward-looking action. Clearly, the issues evidenced throughout this journey demand a new and brutally honest look to the future—a future that both invites and requires serious action on meaningful solutions. A balance, sadly lacking in the past, is needed in virtually every way: in recognizing the contribution of physical infrastructure to the aims of public schools, in solutions to the perplexing social and economic aggravations that have prevented reasonable solutions to infrastructure funding shortfalls, and in assigning primary responsibility for solutions to schools' infrastructure deficits to the various units of government.

This final chapter goes to all these issues in both a summary and forward-looking way. The chapter begins with a review of what has been learned throughout this book, in that much of the fragmentation of the past can be avoided in the future by recognizing the interconnected and overlapping pieces that make up the school funding picture. The chapter then moves to the critical aspect of what is wrong and how it can be fixed: i.e., we know far more about how public schools *should* be funded than is evidenced in the current actual practice of providing fiscal aid to schools. In other words, the principles of a sound system of funding public schools, including physical infrastructure, need to be squarely confronted and genuinely embraced because a significant part of the complexity in meeting today's enormous school infrastructure deficits rests in a longstanding failure by Americans to attend to the fundamentals of a sound and fully comprehensive school finance system. The chapter therefore focuses on taking lessons from the past and blending these pieces into a fuller understanding of what faces the nation by considering the infrastructure funding system of the future—a system necessarily predicated on a delicate and complex balancing of responsibility that relies on federal, state, and local units of government. Although not easy, public schools of the future will be forced to integrate all the concepts in this chapter into their strategic planning activities, an act that forces responsibility (at times painfully) upon policymakers at all levels.

LESSONS FROM THE MACRO-PERSPECTIVE

The overriding lesson that has emerged from this book's indepth examination of school infrastructure funding at the start of a new millennium is the staggering complexity of the problem and the costs of good (or even acceptable) solutions. No longer is it sufficient to merely provide schoolchildren with shelter from the elements: the modern educational environment has become inextricably interwoven with issues of instructional effectiveness, a vast array of safety and design standards,[1] and highly complicated by deeply divisive political issues. The issue of instructional effectiveness has proved weighty, with far-reaching implications for the future, as research has repeatedly demonstrated the prevalence of unsafe classrooms plagued by dangerous health conditions,[2] and as school improvement efforts such as class size reduction legislation has taken its toll by dramatically increasing space and quality requirements on local schools. The effect has been a backlog of unfunded physical infrastructure needs, growing in size and consequence each day in ways that ultimately increase costs far beyond what would have been required had the issue been more appropriately resolved at an earlier time—a cost that recently was estimated by Crampton, Thompson and Hagey to have increased more than 200% just between the years 1995–2001, in part due to expanded understanding of the importance and reach of what infrastructure really comprises.[3] And the enormity of the price tag is truly astounding, as latest estimates recite a deficit of approximately $260 billion—an unmet spending need of nearly $1,000 for every man, woman, and child living in the United States today and outstripping current spending levels by as much as 300% just to bring the nation's school buildings into passable condition for 21st century teaching and learning.[4]

Although calls for solutions to these issues have accelerated over the last decade as a result of heightened awareness of deepening infrastructure deficits, the literature of school finance indicates mostly marginal progress.[5] Gains thus far largely have been spurred in two ways, with some progress emerging as a consequence of the growing sophistication of states in recognizing that many educational innovations and mandates such as technology infusion depend heavily, if not entirely, on physical infrastructure readiness and capacity for both realistic implementation and effectiveness. Under these conditions, the most frequent vehicle for change has been legislation, but progress has been slow and painful in that just capturing usable spending and physical inventory data related to school infrastructure can be very difficult.[6] And when the data are known or reasonably estimated, the results are often disappointing: i.e., whereas no state fails to spend significant energy and money funding direct instruction, by 1998 there were still 11 states (22%) which reported no funding of any kind for school infrastructure, and an another six states that reported spending proportionately *less* than they did five years earlier—all in the face of growing awareness that physical infrastructure has a significant and growing relationship to instructional effectiveness. Apart from legislation, the other impetus has resulted from litigation,[7] which has forced some progress where otherwise none likely would have been observed.[8] In all, however, progress has been both overdue and welcomed, although it has not kept sufficient pace with how school revenues and expenditures have progressed in other more familiar areas, such as direct instruction and certain support services.

If support for school infrastructure in terms of raw dollars has lagged behind other more progressive areas of school funding, methods for funding physical capacity have trailed at an even greater pace. While no state any longer relies primarily on flat grants for general operating expenses, fully ten states in 2002 still depend on unequalized flat grants to fund school infrastructure. And while 27 states can legitimately claim that school infrastructure is funded under a state-sponsored equalization plan, very often those plans are limited in some fashion so as to thwart full equalization or are so underfunded as to waste much effort at equalizing only relatively small amounts of money. Even in states which claim to substantially aid or even fully support school infrastructure, the level of control exercised by the state often results in high levels of dissatisfaction at the local school district level or may result in local determination of needs that is starkly different from what the state's allocation of either dollars or approved building plans will permit. As a result of fundamentally arcane capital funding methods not keeping pace with progress in general fund financing systems, almost all states end up relying either entirely or overwhelmingly on local bond referenda to satisfy local infrastructure needs—a scenario that no doubt contributed to only 54% of bond referenda passing in 1998 in the fifty states.[9]

If public schools were only required to compete among themselves for an earmarked pool of dollars for general and restricted uses such as infrastructure, the situation would be difficult enough due to the size of backlog in unmet needs. But in the high-stakes volatility of a public policy arena, particularly in which highly politicized tax dollars are the coveted prize, public schools face an even more difficult task in that they compete directly with other governmental units for the same overall resources. While many units of government vie for the same prize, education's many levels often compete internally as well, as exemplified by the struggle for adequate resources between P–12 and higher education where public universities also have identified a price tag of $26 billion in deferred maintenance costs.[10] The scenario of internal competition is likely worsened by the realization that higher education, unlike public elementary and secondary schools, has no taxing authority of any kind and is solely dependent on its ability to generate external funding and the individual institution's ability to compete for limited state resources. That resources at this level are inadequate is clear from the data, in that the $5 billion invested in higher education in Fiscal Year 2001 amounted to only about 20% of accumulated deferred maintenance, a situation that is unlikely to improve in the near future given the sudden evaporation of the budget surpluses enjoyed by states in the last decade of the 20th century. Given such a context, the competition for limited state resources for infrastructure will likely heighten among competing types of educational organizations, with the result being an inevitable further erosion of infrastructure capacity.

From the macro-perspective, the net sum of progress relating to infrastructure funding systems at the start of a new millennium is that little has changed over the last decade; if any change has occurred, it is likely negatively cast as economic conditions have become more unfavorable. Public school facility needs are still largely regarded as a local responsibility, and state dollars (when available) are often marginal in amount and lacking the same equalization features that typically characterize other aspects of school funding. Options (when present) have generally not changed much over the past several decades, fundamentally relying on loans that must be repaid from inadequate local tax bases, local bond referenda at significant risk of defeat, lease-purchase options that avoid the basic intent of a voter referendum, and cash basis which has always been unfeasible in all but the very wealthiest school districts. In rare instances, federal support for facility needs has been available, but only on a limited and restricted basis such as asbestos abatement or through the Qualified Zone Academy Bond (QZAB) program, where qualifying districts only have to repay the loan principal. But in the face of data showing that the existing level of debt service is the single best predictor of success in funding new infrastructure needs at the local level (where an increase of one mill debt service increases the likelihood of failure at voter referendum by 39.8%), little seems to have changed in the long view.

LESSONS FROM THE MICRO-PERSPECTIVE

If the broader macro-perspective of school infrastructure funding is disheartening, the tone is not greatly improved by examining the individual circumstances challenging school districts at their own grassroots level of existence. Urban and rural schools, while differently impacted, face formidable challenges—challenges made worse by issues relating to equal educational opportunity for special populations and by the high costs of technological progress and the inevitable costs of litigating what might be regarded as the fundamental aims of schooling.

As a highly polarized society on many fronts, it is no surprise to single out the plight of urban schools in the context of unfunded infrastructure deficits. The data vividly point to the wildly fluctuating revenue and expenditure patterns in urban school systems, where politics rule supreme as bond referenda, school closings, decisions about siting new schools, efforts to obtain legislative authorizations, and legal demands for equity and access—to name only some examples—are all intensely political components of the struggle for adequate capital budgets.[11] The model presented by Cibulka and Cooper for understanding these pressures posits demand-side drivers (e.g., rapidly changing demographics, reactionary educational privatization, oppressive municipal overburden, burgeoning state regulation) and supply side drivers (e.g., rising construction costs, inadequate state support, intense citizen opposition, gross mismanagement, and unwieldy political and legal controls on spending). Even when help aimed at urban districts is well-intended, it may go awry as a result of the bureaucracy that follows closely after a major governmental act, as evidenced in the wake of New Jersey's supreme court ruling for plaintiffs in *Abbott v. Burke*[12] so that no less than seven major agencies became immediately entangled in directing and controlling behavior relating to educational programming, fundraising, wage and price controls, contracts, affirmative action, and loss control—an irony in that the very system meant to redress a broken educational system actually made it easier for non-plaintiff districts to raise capital funds because *Abbott* had had the effect of making bond referenda unnecessary and thereby best advantaging smaller districts which did not suffer from the depth of infrastructure deficits present in New Jersey's urban systems.

Not surprisingly a different, but perhaps equally deleterious, set of school infrastructure problems face rural schools at the start of the new millennium. The analysis in this book illustrates a unique set of issues in rural America, outlining a litany of ills related to high incidences of rural poverty, inability to support school infrastructure in the form of local tax capacity, and the relationship of these issues to the difficulty and impracticality of attempting to provide equal and adequate school facilities under such conditions.[13] Data provided in this book on rural schools show high levels of inadequate school facilities, inability to pass local bond referenda, and generally lower rural performance relating to ability to fund infrastructure needs when compared to more urban districts with larger tax bases. While rural schools' infrastructure dilemma may lack the enormity and severely entangled political complexity faced in urban areas, rural schools' needs weigh heavily against their limited economic capacity and are exacerbated by their own style of political disadvantage when attempting to show increasing needs in the face of explosive issues such as static or declining enrollments.

At the same time that infrastructure needs are generally increasing due to a multitude of external forces, those needs are heightened by an ever-increasing population of special needs children who struggle to overcome many barriers. The data are powerful in describing how students with physical and other disabilities are more vulnerable to their educational environment, so much so that the design and layout of the physical environment, which includes the building, interior finishes, outdoor spaces, room arrangement, and selection of equipment, is believed to have a profound effect on children's behavior.[14] To deepen the dilemma is the strong force of federal law that exists to protect special needs children under the Individuals with Disabilities Education Act, Section 504 of Rehabilitation Act of 1973, the Americans with Disabilities Act of 1990, and other federal regulations on access to facilities such as the Uniform Federal Accessibility Standards and the Americans with Disabilities Accessibility Guidelines. As pointed out by Hartman, these laws and regulations cover not only students, but parents, guardians, and all members of the public in ways stretching far beyond the school day to fundamentally make all activities occurring within a school equally accessible to the general public. The implications of this analysis are profound, as advocates propose that the only way to meet the letter and spirit of federal law is through universal design which takes into account such factors as equitable use, flexibility in use, low physical effort, size and space for approach and use, and so forth. By inference, these standards apply retroactively to current facilities as well as new construction, increasing costs exponentially if undertaken with a spirit of full compliance. With no federal financial assistance available and with the best available data stemming from a 1995 U.S. General Accounting Office report[15] estimating needs at $5.2 billion for accessibility modifications to existing structures, the demands on public funds for school infrastructure are enormous and likely still underestimated.

If history has generally taught modern civilization one immutable lesson, it is that human needs expand continuously and almost never go away. Clearly, the explosion of technology in education has driven infrastructure costs in a direction no one could have anticipated just a few decades ago, as the fundamental nature of schooling is in an extreme and unprecedented evolution that foresees no end. Insidious to the dilemma is that technology cannot be viewed as a stand-alone cost, as it profoundly affects every other aspect of school funding: i.e., the initial acquisition and maintenance costs of technology itself, the initial and permanent costs of integration and application of technology into teaching and learning, and the enormous costs of building technology capacity into new construction and the even greater costs of retrofitting technology into existing facilities in order to better ensure equal educational opportunity to all children in all places. The costs extend beyond school borders in most instances and is unevenly applicable when it is understood that technology does not already exist just outside every schoolhouse door, as there are costs associated with simply bringing the wiring to every child's school.[16] Widely underestimated in terms of eventual costs, an entire new industry has sprung up around rethinking how infrastructure is perceived, as it must now be understood to include all the attendant costs associated with making technology fully functional. The data are staggering in the enormity of unmet technology funding needs, estimated at $53.7 in 1999. Of even greater eventual impact, however, is the assessment by Crampton et al. of states' minimal understanding of their own educational technology plans and their lack of readiness to incorporate technology into accepted and permanent funding schemes. Lack of conceptual understanding by states of the scope of technology and their apparent failure to conceive of technology as something that can no longer be tagged on to existing funding programs or funded by external one-time infusions suggest that public schools may face hard times in the foreseeable future, particularly as states deal with the high cost of technology in the simultaneous context of cycles of state revenue shortfalls and soft economies—conditions which may cast technology and infrastructure as allies and enemies at times, as they alternately join forces to fight against funding reductions and at other times compete head-on for the same finite dollars.

At the most elemental level, all these issues are ripe for bitter dispute at both macro- and micro-levels. Education is in direct competition with other governmental social services for tax resources, while simultaneously the broader education community is at war within itself as public schools compete with higher education for a larger share of available funds. At the same time, public elementary and secondary education frequently finds itself at angrily contentious odds with its "owners," as states and school districts sometimes pursue litigation as a way to resolve starkly different views on equitable and adequate resource distribution. While school funding litigation has historically focused on general fund financing, the courtroom has increasingly been viewed by unhappy plaintiffs as a valuable tool to force greater funding for school infrastructure.

Although capital funding litigation has historically stayed in the background compared to general fund or special education funding litigation, the potential for vast and far-reaching costs to taxpayers and government is enormous.[17] Earlier discussions in this book on the relationship between educational opportunity in the form of equal access and student outcomes point up the ripeness of this issue, particularly as research becomes more sophisticated in identifying causal relationships between physical environment and educational productivity. Early litigation held the promise of a likely future, as in *Pauley v. Kelly*[18] in 1982 when the West Virginia court took an intense interest that extended to specifying standards for equal educational opportunity in the context of facilities. While *Pauley* has not yet lived up to reformers' early expectations, other rumblings of similar sentiments by courts have been heard around the nation, as in *Roosevelt v. Bishop*[19] in Arizona in 1994 where the court expressed shock at school facility conditions and reached beyond the infrastructure dispute, on which suit was originally brought, to order the state to revise its entire P–12 education system to provide equal access to educational opportunity. Other instances of litigation-driven facility reform exist as well, as in some instances state legislatures have watched their sister states' experience and have acted in advance to engage infrastructure funding as a consequence of litigation trends or as a result of a more general trend toward greater legislative support based in copycat behavior. Litigation on the basis of school facilities, while still relatively small in number of actual case filings, indicates that infrastructure is still in the early stages of recognition as an integral part of equal educational opportunity—a sleeping giant with vast linkages that cut across rural and urban schools to touch every district in the nation with deep fiscal implications. For states, the scope and expense of these implications are sobering: if general education is believed to be costly, infrastructure far outstrips it by representing the single-most expensive aspect of school district operation—i.e., bricks and mortar. If this trend matures to its potential, the present-day school district will look far different in the foreseeable future.

PRINCIPLES OF A SOUND SCHOOL INFRASTRUCTURE FUNDING SYSTEM[20]

The chapters in this book, taken collectively, identify continued significant problems for both states and school districts alike. While much credit should be given to various individual states for their willingness to move toward a greater state role in capital funding, much remains to be done to move school infrastructure funding issues toward a full and productive solution in the total scheme of school fiscal support mechanisms. At the heart of any such solution are certain principles upon which a sound funding system must be built: namely, the principles of *equity, adequacy, efficiency, accountability, stability,* and *parity* must apply to all aspects of financing schools. These concepts are familiar to everyone knowledgeable about broader school finance, and it is therefore no surprise to demand in this book that a sound infrastructure funding system must reflect these principles in the same manner and extent that they are included, evaluated, and tested in general fund financing.

Equity

A longstanding fundamental cornerstone of school finance theory, equity means that a school funding system must exhibit the utmost concern for resource accessibility. Accessibility is generally evaluated in light of whether equally situated children can access equal amounts of resources, and whether unequally situated children can access resources in ways appropriately inverse to their fundamental inequalities. Operationally, these are often referred to as horizontal and vertical equity, respectively. Horizontal equity is best conceptualized as the basis for state equalization formulas in general fund financing, wherein the inherent tax base inequalities of local school districts are offset by the presence of a state general aid formula so that all children in all school districts in a given state have access to roughly equal financial support for educational programs. Vertical equity is best conceptualized as providing resources to children based on differing educational needs such as language differences, learning disabilities, and so forth. Vertical equity is often applied to also adjust for other dimensions, such as price differentials found in high cost markets or sparsity issues related to ruralness—i.e., a market basket approach or similar terminology to better ultimately equalize resource accessibility. In sum, equity seeks to level the educational playing field for children when the realities of geographic residence creates natural (but illegitimate) inequalities that would affect the quality of educational services. To this end, state general aid formulas are designed to adjust for these differences, albeit within the constraints of the various economic and political realities of each individual state.

Educational infrastructure, however, has largely been ignored when considering the state's obligation to fund public schools. Largely a function of historical tradition, capital expenditures have been left to depend on the highly unequal wealth bases of each individual school district across virtually every state in the Union. Until recently, only a very few states provided any aid for capital projects, and the amounts of funding and formula distribution methods have seldom kept pace with needs and have not been highly responsive to issues of equity. The reality of a new millennium and a future where individuals' economic and social success will be driven by educational achievement, however, argue strongly that paying for school infrastructure as defined in this book is a fundamental responsibility of the states, as the evidence clearly indicates that capital costs place an unconscionable and highly unequal burden on local districts absent state intervention and that the linkages between student achievement and infrastructure are sufficiently valid so as to require aggressive state intervention to eradicate the inherent inequities in total local financing.

Current data on state methods of funding infrastructure suggest that states have far to go to substantially satisfy the demands of equity. Sielke's work earlier in this book reported a fundamentally modest response by many states in aiding school infrastructure, with some states still failing to recognize the relationship of infrastructure to states' constitutional responsibility for education. The data reported in tables in Chapter 2 showed generally low percentages of state aid to infrastructure when compared to general fund financing, as well as consistently heavy dependence on bonding mechanisms and other restrictions tied to local tax bases—a condition typically *not* present in general finance schemes in any state. Almost no state provides aid to infrastructure with the same proportional enthusiasm demonstrated in other school aid. Yet it is fundamental to all logical propositions that areas unsupported by states are eventually supported by state dollars in the form of draining away monies from areas such as direct instruction in order to pay for those unfunded areas—the alternative proposition is that deferred construction and maintenance grows largely unchecked due to districts' unwillingness to rob direct instruction to pay for bricks and mortar. Either way, states' failure to provide equitable and equal support for school infrastructure is unacceptable under principles of equity—a failure that must be corrected without further delay.

Adequacy

A second concept gaining new popularity calls for an adequate level of school funding, equitably distributed via a state aid formula. Adequacy is variously defined, depending on whether it is the state or local school districts offering their understanding of the concept, but in all cases adequacy takes into account that enough money to meet needs must be available. In fact, it is often argued that equity might easily be satisfied with equality of poverty: i.e., distributing small amounts of money with meticulous care for equity still results in a highly unacceptable situation by starving districts of badly needed money.[21] Adequacy presumes equal access as a fundamental prerequisite, but it focuses on demanding resources in sufficient supply to meet the needs of children in schools.

Adequacy applied to school infrastructure funding is particularly sensible, as capital costs generally represent the largest combined outlays of cash and debt that school districts ever face. The underlying logic supporting an argument for adequate infrastructure funding is sensible, in that the vast sums of money spent on direct instruction and support services are at jeopardy for waste and underutilization if the physical infrastructure is undervalued or dysfunctional. Adequacy in funding capital costs relates to a spectrum of considerations, ranging from aid for debt service to more easily missed needs such as sensitivity to regional cost adjustments, sparsity factors, municipal overburden, and small school adjustments. The fundamental principle of adequate funding for infrastructure is identical to arguments made for adequate funding for direct instruction–.i.e., enough money for good instruction includes enough money to provide a good physical environment for learning.

Current data on state methods of funding school infrastructure again suggest that states have far to go to substantially satisfy the demands of adequate funding levels, and in fact the data on school infrastructure deficits strongly suggest that adequacy is a more pressing problem than equitable aid distribution methods. The data reported in tables in Chapter 2 and other areas of this book were unable to identify any state that has completely, or even substantially, overcome its infrastructure shortfall, despite the occasionally sharp prodding of the judicial system. Most authors in the field tend to characterize state aid to infrastructure in terms of tokenism—a salute to a concept focusing more on equitable formula construction than on adequate revenue streams in proportion to identified needs. As a result, creating a sound infrastructure funding system that meets the needs of all children everywhere will require incredible resolve and financial commitment by states if there is to be any hope of solution to a deepening backlog of unmet school infrastructure needs.

Efficiency

A third principle of a sound school finance system invokes the concept of efficiency. The image of efficiency is alternatively viewed as a demand for cost-effectiveness, in which the grantor of funds (usually in the form of the state or local taxpayers) expects that money spent on schools will be used wisely for the best opportunity for return on investment. Underlying concepts to efficiency are multiple, focusing on minimization of unnecessary costs, ease of administration, effective compliance without excessive or expensive monitoring, and incentives for continual improvement in services rendered. In combination with earlier principles outlined here, an efficient school funding system necessarily provides an equitable distribution of adequate funds, with great care to obtain the greatest return.

Efficiency applied to school infrastructure funding is ultimately practicable, although in practice it can easily result in penury, waste, and overstandardization when misunderstood and misapplied. The enormous cost of capital projects literally begs for intense scrutiny to avoid waste and duplication, and examples of neglect, deceit, fraud, and other kinds of malfeasance are often recounted as ample justification for tight controls.[22] Such a scenario can therefore actually backfire by launching such an intense search for inefficiency that considerable money is wasted in an unreasonable witch hunt for compliance problems. Efficiency can also be used to sourly dissect even the most worthy problems, frustrating otherwise good outcomes by creating a form of inefficiency in an avid search of efficiency itself. Overstandardization is yet another unintended dysfunction of efficiency, as a truism in school finance is that increased funding results in increased control, and the logic applies when seeking state support for the extremely high cost involved in capital projects: i.e., states may be tempted to seek to control of funding in ways that lead to decisions too far removed from the local level, resulting in failure to understand local needs, political favoritism, or leading to capital projects that seem to come out of a box.[23]

In actual practice, general and capital school aid formulas pay more attention to courting equity, while performing poorly on the dimensions of adequacy and efficiency. Current data on state school infrastructure funding practices provide sizable evidence that states which have assumed a hand in infrastructure funding try to do so by incorporating at least some aspects of equalization principles and with some effort at exercising the kind of significant control that results in greater uniformity. There is, however, little concrete evidence on acceptable measurement of efficiency, and much data point to nearly nonexistent infrastructure inventories and long-range capital improvement plans in many states which are prerequisite to efficiency concepts. Such measurement is essential, however, not only to gauge the return on investment but also to prevent a different inefficiency that is likely to arise as states try to juggle limited resources: i.e., given the substantial increase in funding that will be required of states to avoid simply shifting resources from another governmental function in order to pay for school capital projects, development of a sound school infrastructure funding system will have to include objective measures by which to judge the efficiency of the larger system of governmental expenditures.

Accountability

A fourth principle of a sound school finance formula provides accountability at the state and local levels through generally accepted budgeting, accounting, and auditing procedures. An underlying concept central to the whole notion of accountability is building community trust regarding performance-based budgeting that links fiscal accountability to student outcomes. In sum, accountability to the state and local community for wise resource utilization is an essential element of a good school finance formula, and inherent is a promise that management of fiscal resources will be above reproach and will help in achieving the fundamental aims of schooling.

Accountability applied to infrastructure funding is at once difficult and mandatory. The linkage between student outcomes and the physical environment is both intuitively accurate and difficult to demonstrate with preciseness, a difficulty that plagues much of the production-function debate in schooling. Historically, there have been sufficient cases of mismanagement of school funds, particularly in the capital funding arena, to invoke the strict laws that characterize use of bond proceeds, application of bid laws, awarding of construction contracts, and so forth. At the most fundamental level, though, accountability applies to all areas of a good school aid formula, and infrastructure funding requires the same rigid standards and openness, if for no other reason than the vast sums of money required to engage such projects and in order to convince the public that its long-term investment in capital planning and spending is likely to provide both safety and a reasonable return for taxpayers' sacrifice. In actual practice, states and local school districts have made good progress on the bookkeeping side of the accountability equation, but much remains to be done to make clear connections between investment in school infrastructure and student outcomes—an important area for development in the context of an increasingly critical public.

Stability

A fifth principle of a sound school finance system is clear evidence of stability and predictability in revenues and expenditures. All organizations have a need for these same traits, but the public sector in the form of schools has an especially critical justification for stability, particularly when preparing children with life skills and work skills that will form the basis for repaying society's investment in education. Evidence from many studies of educational productivity point to the need for uninterrupted services (e.g., special education; early childhood; and primary grades) in order not to seriously impede, or even irreparably damage, educational development. As such, school funding schemes should be predicated on stable revenue sources, and patterns of expenditures should be projected on the basis of long-term strategic plans that help predict and smooth expenditures over time in consonance with revenue streams.

In the context of school infrastructure funding, stability is a critical issue for many good reasons. Capital acquisition, construction, improvement, and maintenance are tied to multi-year schedules that repeat cyclically, resulting in the need for continuous revenue streams that do not vary much with changes in external economic and social environments. The high cost of infrastructure needs demand large amounts of money, at times in lump sums and at other times in regularized payments, as well as unexpected contingency issues. Earlier discussion in this book, particularly in the context of urbanized school systems, pointed to the difficulty in smoothing such issues to reach the desired level of predictability, and in other school systems there are continual problems related to inability to raise sufficient funds timely or at all due to tax base deficiencies. A sound infrastructure funding system, then, requires recognition of the inability of local units of government to shoulder the entire burden, thereby introducing the need for wise and genuine participation in capital needs funding by the state and even federal governments. While some recognition of these issues is present in current infrastructure funding plans in the various states, much remains to be done because systems are overly dependent on local property wealth, too tied to the variability in voter referendum whims, and too dependent on changes in economic conditions that either result in failed referenda or having to rob an already under-funded general fund to satisfy debt repayment schedules.

Parity

The principles of equity, adequacy, efficiency, accountability, and stability make up the elements of a sound school finance system in the context of how experts and consumers of research generally think about funding public education. Balanced properly, these traits offer the greatest likelihood of success in ensuring all students in all school districts with equal opportunities to obtain high quality instruction that will allow them to compete in life on a level playing field. As these characteristics apply to school infrastructure funding, however, there is a missing element: i.e., these principles have been incorporated into the financing of general fund operations, special education, grant programs, and even auxiliary services such as transportation and food services, but the area of infrastructure has received only marginal attention. In sum, a sound school finance system must take into account the critical contribution of infrastructure to creating the environment in which equal learning can occur—in essence, a sound school finance system must provide *parity* for infrastructure funding at the same level provided to other operating expenses.

The argument favoring parity in school infrastructure funding has formidable barriers. The tradition of local control and responsibility for facilities is powerful and must be overcome with difficulty—a tradition with proponents at both local and state levels. Likewise, the enormity of the price tag for full parity must be recognized and accepted at all levels of government and public discourse without yielding to the temptation to simply move the same money around in ways that merely result in changed priorities. At the same time, the most difficult barrier rests in recognizing that even states have practical limits to their financial ability to support education, a recognition that inevitably requires establishing a federal role in support of school infrastructure funding. Although federal involvement is likely an instantly unpopular recommendation in many venues, it should be considered that a federal role is less of an intrusion into local affairs than it is an unbiased recognition that a sizable portion of the school infrastructure deficit has its origins in unfunded federal mandates: e.g., accommodating special education students under IDEA and Section 504, general handicapped accessibility under ADA, and a plethora of construction science standards and codes for safety such as OSHA pronouncements on asbestos and so forth. The logic in arguing for a federal role in school infrastructure funding parity has little to do with ideological preferences and much to do with recognizing the fiscal limitations facing local and state units of government and equally as much to do with promoting the concept that the federal government should be held responsible for funding the mandates it forces on other units of government.

A sound school finance system therefore is fair in distributing resources to all children, provides adequate money to carry out the full range of services assigned, does so at a high level of efficiency without engaging in counterproductive suspicion or begrudging of resources while expecting and receiving measurable assurances of accountability and productivity, and relies on stable and predictable revenue sources—all in the context of meeting the full slate of modern educational needs. To reach this end, school infrastructure funding must be included at full parity if children are to be equally advantaged and none left to the miserable physical conditions that exist in some schools in the United States at the start of the new millennium—i.e., a funding system that is truly unitary in form and effect.

CONCLUSION

The complexity of a fair funding system for schools, with all its attendant levels and prohibitive costs, makes it an elusive goal. No local school district has ever provided a perfect education for all its children, and no state has managed to construct a perfect aid formula to fully offset the inequalities that occur naturally and by human oversight in school funding. Likewise, the federal government has been quick to exercise a heavy hand in mandating programs that largely work to children's benefit, but in many cases it has left its well-intended mandates badly underfunded or completely unfunded. If it is a virtue that the framers of the U.S. Constitution left education to the individual states, then that virtue itself suffers from a lack of funding because states have often been unwilling or unable to embrace school funding to the fullest extent of its potential to do good for children.

The consequence is that there is no extant school funding system to which policymakers can turn for a model to be unquestioningly adopted. In the case of embracing school infrastructure funding as a dimension of equal educational opportunity, all levels of government have far to go in trying to catch up with the more progressive thinking that presently supports general fund financing. It is unlikely that rapid closing of this conceptual gap, much less parity in school infrastructure funding, will occur without dramatic rethinking by local, state, and federal policymakers of the meaning of educational opportunity and the contribution of physical environment to student learning outcomes. Progress in other educational areas in the past has been strongly related to the ability of researchers to link student achievement outcomes to variables that make a difference. It is likely that backfilling and remedying the infrastructure deficit in education will depend jointly on hard research data on the effects of the physical environment on student learning and a dramatic reconceptualization of the role of all three levels of government in taking responsibility for investing in children as the best hope for the future. Short of that, the deficit, now already of unconscionable proportion, will only fall away to totally impossible depths.

NOTES

1. See, for example, David C. Thompson and R. Craig Wood, *Analysis for Plaintiffs: Roosevelt Elementary School District et. al v. C. Diane Bishop et al.* (Manhattan, Kansas: UCEA Center for Education Finance, 1992), an affidavit prepared on behalf of plaintiffs at the request of The Arizona Center for Law in the Public Interest. A partial listing of such organizations publishing standards includes the American Concrete Institute (ACI), American Institute of Architects (AIA), American Institute of Steel Construction (AISC), Architectural Woodwork Industry (AWI), American Welding Society Code (AWSC), National Building Code (NBC), National Electric Code (NEC), National Fire Protection Association (NFPA), National Illuminating Engineering Society (NIES), National Plumbing Code (NPC), Uniform Building Code (UBC), Underwriters Laboratories, Inc. (UL), American Association for Health, Physical Education, and Recreation (AAHPER), American Association of School Administrators (AASA), American Institute of Electrical Engineers (AIEE), Association of Physical Plant Administrators (APPA), Association of School Business Officials (ASBO), American Society of Mechanical Engineers (ASME), American Society for Testing and Materials (ASTM), Council of Educational Facility Planners, International (CEFPI), National Board of Fire Underwriters (NBFU), and the National Bureau of Standards (NBS).

2. See, for example, Jonathan Kozol, *Savage Inequalities: Children in America's Schools* (New York: Harper Perennial, 1992); and U.S. General Accounting Office, *School Facilities: The Condition of America's Schools* (Washington, D.C.: February 1995). See also, Zachary Ross and Betsy Walker, *Reading, Writing, and Risk: Air Pollution Inside California's Portable Classrooms* (Washington, D.C.: Environmental Working Group, 1999).

3. *Modernizing Our Schools: How Much Will It Cost?* (Washington, D.C.: National Education Association, 2000). See also, Faith E. Crampton, David C. Thompson, and Janice M. Hagey, "Creating and Sustaining School Capacity

in the Twenty-First Century: Funding a Physical Environment Conducive to Student Learning," *Journal of Education Finance* 27 (Fall 2001): 633–652. See also, *The Maintenance Gap: Deferred Repair and Renovation in the Nation's Elementary and Secondary Schools* (Arlington, Virginia: American Association of School Administrators, Council of Great City Schools, and National School Boards Association, January 1983); Ann Lewis, *Wolves at the Schoolhouse Door: An Investigation of the Condition of Public School Buildings* (Washington, D.C.: Education Writers Association, 1989); Sharon J. Hansen, *Schoolhouse in the Red: A Guidebook for Cutting Our Losses* (Arlington, Virginia: American Association of School Administrators, 1992). See also, two special issues of the *Journal of Education Finance* on the status of state and local funding of capital outlay, David S. Honeyman, R. Craig Wood, and David C. Thompson, eds., Winter 1988 and Spring 1988, Vol. 13 no. 3–4, with reports from 24 states and one Canadian province. Most recently, see also a special issue *Journal of Education Finance* 27 (Fall 2001) with guest editors Faith E. Crampton and David C. Thompson on the topic of school infrastructure funding. See also U.S. General Accounting Office, *School Facilities: The Condition of America's Schools.*

4. For a fuller discussion of unmet funding needs for school infrastructure, see Chapter 1 of this volume, "Unmet School Infrastructure Funding Need as a Critical Educational Capacity Issue: Setting the Context," by Faith E. Crampton.

5. David C. Thompson, "Methods in Financing Educational Facilities in the United States," Testimony to the Special Committee on School Finance (Topeka, Kansas: Kansas Statehouse, November 1990). See "Capital Outlay and Debt Service Programs," pp. 48–52, as well as individual state chapters and Table 11 in *Public School Finance Programs of the United States and Canada, 1993–1994*, Vol. I-II, eds. Steven D. Gold, David M. Smith, and Stephen B. Lawton, eds. (Albany, New York: American Education Finance Association and the Center for the Study of the States, Nelson Rockefeller Institute of Government, State University of New York, 1995); and U.S. General Accounting Office, *School Facilities: Construction Expenditures Have Grown Significantly in Recent Years* (Washington, D.C.: March 2000).

6. See Chapter 2 of this volume, "Overview of State Funding of School Infrastructure," by Catherine C. Sielke.

7. See Chapter 8 of this volume, "School Finance Litigation: A Strategy to Address Inequities in School Infrastructure Funding," by David C. Thompson and Faith E. Crampton.

8. For a history of school finance litigation and school infrastructure funding issues, dating back to 1973, see David C. Thompson, R. Craig Wood, and David S. Honeyman, *Fiscal Leadership for Schools: Concepts and Practices* (New York: Longman, 1994), 556–558. See also, Faith E. Crampton and Terry N. Whitney, "Equity and Funding of School Facilities: Are States at Risk?" *State Legislative Report* 20 (Denver, Colorado, and Washington, D.C.: National Conference of State Legislatures, February 1995), where particular attention is given to *Roosevelt v. Bishop*, 877 P.2d 806 (1994), a landmark state supreme court decision where the state school funding system was found unconstitutional based largely upon inequities in school facilities.

9. U.S. General Accounting Office, *School Facilities: Construction Expenditures Have Grown Significantly in Recent Years.*

10. For a fuller discussion of the funding needs for higher education facilities, see Chapter 4 of this volume, "Capital Costs and Higher Education Finance," by Mary McKeown-Moak.

11. See Chapter 5 of this volume, "Capital Needs and Spending in Urban Public School Systems: Policies, Problems, and Promises," by James G. Cibulka and Bruce S. Cooper.

12. *Abbott v. Burke* 153 N.J. 480, 710 A.2d 450 (1998).

13. See Chapter 6 of this volume, "Funding School Infrastructure in Rural America," by Jeffrey Maiden.

14. See Chapter 7 of this volume, "Infrastructure Funding Considerations and Students with Disabilities," by William T. Hartman.

15. U.S. General Accounting Office, *School Facilities: Construction Expenditures Have Grown Significantly in Recent Years.*

16. See Chapter 9 of this volume, "Funding Technology versus Bricks and Mortar: Can We Have It All?" by Faith E. Crampton, Janis M. Hagey, and Kathleen C. Westbrook.

17. See Chapter 8 of this volume, "School Finance Litigation: One Strategy to Address Inequities in School Infrastructure Funding," by David C. Thompson and Faith E. Crampton.

18. *Pauley v. Kelly,* 255 S.E.2d 859 (W. Va. 1979).

19. *Roosevelt v. Bishop,* 877 P.2d 806 (1994).

20. This section draws significantly from Faith E. Crampton and Terry N. Whitney, *Principles of a Sound School Finance System,* a monograph of the Education Partners Project and Foundation for State Legislatures (Denver, Colorado, and Washington, D.C.: National Conference of State Legislatures, July 1996). For indepth development of school finance theory, see also David C. Thompson and R. Craig Wood, *Money and Schools,* 2d ed. (New York: Eye on Education, 2001).

21. See, for example, David C. Thompson, R. Craig Wood, and David S. Honeyman. *Adequacy of Revenue in Financing Schools: Expert Witnesses' Analysis for Plaintiffs in Fair School Council v. Oklahoma* (Manhattan, Kansas: UCEA Center for Education Finance, 1992).

22. For example, see Chapter 5 of this volume, "Capital Needs and Spending in Urban Public School Systems: Policies, Problems, and Promises," by James G. Cilbulka and Bruce S. Cooper; see also, Susan Breslin and Eleanor Stier, *Promoting Poverty: The Shift of Resources Away from Low-Income New York City School Districts* (New York: Community Service Society of New York, 1987).

23. For example, see John A. Thompson, "Funding and Spending in Paradise: Notes on the Hawaii Model of Educational Finance," *Journal of Education Finance* 12 (Fall 1986): 282–294.

ABOUT THE EDITORS

Professor Faith E. Crampton's professional career has spanned public education, senior administrative positions in state government, senior research and policy positions in national education and legislative organizations, and graduate faculty positions in public and private research universities. Her current position is Associate Professor of education finance and economics of education in the Department of Administrative Leadership at the University of Wisconsin Milwaukee. Prior to joining the graduate faculty at UWM, she was a senior researcher with the National Education Association, Washington, D.C., where she specialized in education funding issues. She is past President and Program Chair of the Fiscal Issues, Policy, and Education Finance Special Interest Group of the American Educational Research Association (AERA) and a past member of the Board of Directors of the American Education Finance Association (AEFA) where she chaired the Outstanding Dissertation Award Committee and the Dissemination Committee. Currently, she is a member of the Board of Directors of the University Council for Educational Administration's (UCEA) Center for Education Finance. She has held graduate faculty appointments in education finance and the economics of education at the University of Oregon and the University of Rochester, New York. At the administrative and policy level, she served as Program Principal in Education Finance for the National Conference of State Legislatures in Denver, Colorado, and Deputy Director of the Ohio Student Loan Commission. She has served as an expert witness in state school finance litigation and as an expert consultant to state legislatures on the reform of state education funding systems.

Saving America's School Infrastructure, pages 255–258
Copyright © 2003 by Information Age Publishing
All rights of reproduction in any form reserved.

Her research focus rests primarily on the study of policy goals of state education funding systems. She has published widely in journals such as the *Journal of Education Finance, Journal of School Business Management, Journal of the Council of Education Facilities Planners International, Educational Considerations,* and *School Business Affairs,* in addition to authoring a number of monographs, reports, book chapters, and policy briefs on state education finance legislation and litigation. She is Executive Editor of the scholarly journal, *Educational Considerations,* and a member of the editorial staff of the *Journal of Education Finance.* She was principal investigator for the NEA-funded research project, the School Modernization Needs Assessment, which culminated in the NEA publication, *Modernizing Our Schools: How Much Will It Cost?,* a 50-state analysis of unmet funding needs for school infrastructure and education technology. The results of this study, the first of its kind, garnered national media attention and was followed by invited briefings for United States Congressional staff and White House Council of Economic Advisors. She was guest editor with David C. Thompson of the Fall 2001 special issue of the *Journal of Education Finance* on the crisis in school infrastructure funding.

Dr. Crampton has presented scholarly papers at the conferences of numerous major national and international research and policy associations, such as the American Education Finance Association (AEFA), American Educational Research Association (AERA), British Educational Management and Administration Society (BEMAS), International Intervisitation Programme (a conference convened by the University Council for Educational Administration and the Commonwealth Council on Educational Administration), National Conference of State Legislatures (NCSL), National Conference of Professors of Educational Administration (NCPEA), Organizations Concerned About Rural Education (OCRE), and the University Council for Educational Administration (UCEA). She received her Ph.D. in Educational Policy and Leadership from The Ohio State University; M.S.Ed. in Educational Administration from Western Illinois University; and A.B., magna cum laude, from Augustana College. Most recently, she was recognized in the Chancellor's Report of the University of Wisconsin Milwaukee as one of the university's "Exceptional New Faculty."

Professor David C. Thompson's professional career has spanned classroom teacher, elementary principal, high school principal, superintendent of schools, and currently the professoriate. A specialist in education finance litigation, his publication record contains nine books including multiple editions and exceeds more than 70 book chapters, monographs, and refereed articles. A frequently invited author in highly respected circles, he has published chapters in four consecutive American Education Finance Association Yearbooks, the *Journal of Education Finance,* the NOLPE

(National Organization on Legal Problems of Education) Handbook of School Law, West's *Education Law Reporter*, books by the Association of School Business Officials International (ASBO) and the National Organization on Legal Problems of Education (NOLPE), and many others. He is coauthor of the NOLPE book *Education Finance Law: Constitutional Challenges to State Aid Plans* (1993), with a second edition (1996). He has served on scholarly review boards including West's *Education Law Reporter* and *Journal of Education Finance*, has written an annual invited review of education finance litigation for *EdLaw Reporter*, has written a regular column for the journal of the Council of Educational Facility Planners International, and served as Editor of the scholarly journal *Educational Considerations*. His school finance text, *Fiscal Leadership for Schools: Concepts and Practices* (New York: Longman, 1994) appeared in August 1993. He is coauthor of *Principles of School Business Management*, 2nd edition (Reston, Virginia: ASBO, 1995). His current finance text, *Money and Schools*, 2nd edition (New York: Eye on Education, 2001) is used in nearly 100 universities and is slated for a third edition. He is currently under contract for a new text with Prentice-Hall (in press). He is also author of the National Education Association (NEA) study *School Finance Litigation: Does It Make A Difference? A Review of Literature and Analysis of Data in Four Selected States* (in press). Finally, he is coeditor of the text, *Saving America's School Infrastructure* (Information Age Publishers), with the foreword by The Honorable Senator Edward M. Kennedy.

Professor Thompson's extended reputation has led to service as consultant or expert witness for various state departments, state legislatures, attorneys general, and attorneys and litigants in school finance totaling thousands of school districts and several million children, including various types of consultation in the states of Alabama, Arizona, California, Delaware, Florida, Illinois, Indiana, Iowa, Kansas, Kentucky, Nebraska, Ohio, Oklahoma, Pennsylvania, South Dakota, Texas, Vermont, Washington, West Virginia, and Wyoming. He has additionally served as consultant to school finance committees, including legislatures and governors' task forces. His research in school finance and litigation has been presented to most major national organizations including the American Education Finance Association (AEFA), Education Law Association (ELA), American Educational Research Association (AERA), National Conference of State Legislatures (NCSL), National Center for Education Statistics (NCES), National Conference of Professors of Educational Administration (NCPEA), National Rural Education Association (NREA), University Council for Educational Administration (UCEA), and other keynote addresses to large legislative audiences. His work has also been presented by himself or by others on his behalf in seminars for groups such as the National Association of Attorneys General. He was footnoted in a decision of the United States Supreme

Court; see *BOE of Oklahoma City Public Schools, Independent School District No. 89, Oklahoma County,* v Dowell 111 S.C. 630 (1991) at 643, fn. 5. In 2000, he received the University Council for Educational Administration's *Award of Appreciation for Sustained and Meritorious Service* for his contributions to the profession through the UCEA Center for the Study of School Finance.

Dr. Thompson is Professor in the Graduate School and Chair, Department of Educational Administration and Leadership and founding Co-Director of the University Council for Educational Administration's (UCEA) Center for Education Finance at Kansas State University.

ABOUT THE CONTRIBUTORS

Brian O. Brent is Assistant Professor in the Warner Graduate School of Education, University of Rochester, New York, where he specializes in school finance. Dr. Brent's research interests include micro-level resource allocation practices, nontraditional revenues, and the cost-effective use of education dollars. He has published on these topics in many forums, including the *Journal of Education Finance, Educational Policy, Leadership and Policy in Schools, Economics of Education Review, Journal of School Business Management, Phi Delta Kappan,* and *School Business Affairs.* He is co-author of *Raising Money for Education* (Corwin, 1997) with David H. Monk. In addition, Dr. Brent serves on the boards of the American Education Finance Association (AEFA) and the New York State Education Finance Research Consortium. He is also on the editorial boards of *School Business Affairs* and *Leadership and Policy in Schools.* Dr. Brent received his Ph.D. from Cornell University and is also a certified public accountant who holds a Masters of Taxation degree.

Marie Cianca is a Lead Principal in the Rochester City School District in Rochester, New York, and serves as Managing Director for Special Education and Student Support Services. She has also held positions as a secondary school administrator and an elementary principal in the Rochester schools. She began her career as a classroom teacher and has taught secondary social studies, special education, and elementary education. In addition, she has served as a staff development specialist at the district level and as an associate in the New York State Department of Education, provid-

Saving America's School Infrastructure, pages 259–265

ing statewide training to administrators, teachers, and school board members in special education issues. Dr. Cianca co-authored, with Brian O. Brent, "Involving Principals in Schools Renovations: Benefit or Burden?" in the Fall 2001 special issue of the *Journal of Education Finance* on the crisis in school infrastructure funding, edited by Faith E. Crampton and David C. Thompson. She also authored a chapter titled, "Skeptical About Peer Review: A Principal Speaks," in *The Peer Assistance and Review Reader,* edited by Gary Bloom and Jennifer Goldstein and published by the New Teacher Center at the University of California, Santa Cruz. Currently, Dr. Cianca serves as a member of the New York State Education Department Commissioner's Advisory Panel on Special Education. She received her Ed.D. in Educational Administration from the University of Rochester, and she holds an M.S. in Curriculum and Instruction and a B.S. in History with a concentration in Secondary Education from the State University College at Brockport, New York.

James G. Cibulka is Dean of the College of Education at the University of Kentucky, where he also is Professor of Administration and Supervision and Education Policy and Evaluation. He received his Ph.D. from the University of Chicago in Educational Administration and his A.B., magna cum laude, from Harvard College in Government. Dr. Cibulka has worked as a teacher and administrator in the public school systems of Chicago and Duluth, Minnesota. He was on the faculty at the University of Wisconsin Milwaukee between 1972 and 1995, where he established a new Department of Community Education and directed the Ph.D. Program in Urban Education. From 1995 through 2002, he was Chair of the Department of Education Policy and Leadership at the University of Maryland, where he also was Associate Dean for Graduate Education, Research, K-16 Relationships, and Outreach. He is a past editor of *Educational Administration Quarterly* and is a past recipient of the William Davis Award for the best article published in that journal. Dr. Cibulka is past president of the Politics of Education Association, an international group of scholars active in research on this topic. Dr. Cibulka has published widely on issues of education policy and politics, including urban education governance, education accountability systems, and education finance. He has appeared as an expert witness in lawsuits concerning urban education finance and metropolitan segregation in schooling. Currently, he is Secretary of Division A, Administration, of the American Educational Research Association, and has been Program Chair for Division L, Education Policy.

Bruce S. Cooper is Professor and Vice Chair, Division of Administration, Policy and Urban Education (APUE), in the Fordham University Graduate School of Education, New York City. His Ph.D. is from the University of

Chicago, and he has taught at University of Pennsylvania and Dartmouth College, where his research has included the financing, equity, and budgeting of schools, and recently the failed attempts of the National Education Association (NEA) and American Federation of Teachers (AFT) to merge into the United States' largest union. His research on school finance included work with Coopers & Lybrand on building a model that tracks resources to children in the classroom and a new software product, In$ite for Schools. His books include *Advocacy or Accuracy: The Politics of Research in Education*, the 1999 Yearbook of the Politics of Education Association published by Sage; and *Optimizing Education Resources* published by JAI Press in 1998. Recent publications include *Promises and Perils Facing Today's School Superintendents*, with Lance Fusarelli, jointly published by Scarecrow Press and the American Association of School Administrators; and entries in the 2003 *International Encyclopedia of Education* on auditing, accounting, and budgeting and the contributions of James S. Coleman to education. Recent articles include "Urban Teachers Unions Face their Future: The Dilemmas of Organizational Maturity," with Marie-Elena Liotta, in *Education and Urban Society*; and "Advanced Budgeting Technology in Education: The Future Is Now," with Sheree T. Speakman, in *School Business Affairs*.

Janis M. Hagey is Intergovernmental Affairs Coordinator for the External Partnerships and Advocacy Unit of the National Education Association (NEA) in Washington, D.C. In that capacity, she communicates NEA education policy positions to state legislators and other elected and appointed officials; monitors emerging legislative, socioeconomic, and political trends that affect public education; and provides resources, information, and training in these areas to NEA state affiliate staff and members who are state legislators or appointees to national education commissions. She served as joint project coordinator for the NEA project, Effecting State Legislative Change in the Critical Funding Area of School Modernization, with Faith E. Crampton, that culminated in the publication of *School Modernization: How Much Will It Cost?* (NEA, 2000). Prior to joining the NEA headquarters staff, she was a lobbyist for the Maryland State Teachers Association and served as UniServ Director for local NEA affiliates in Michigan, Colorado, Iowa, and Maryland. In these positions, she has addressed audiences at major policy organizations, such as the National Conference of State Legislatures, National Caucus of Black Legislators, and the Midwest Region of the NAACP. Most recently, she co-authored with Faith E. Crampton and David C. Thompson, "Creating and Sustaining School Capacity in the Twenty-First Century: Funding a Physical Environment Conducive to Student Learning," in a special issue of the *Journal of Education Finance* (Fall 2001) on the crisis in school infrastructure funding, edited by Faith E. Crampton and David C. Thompson. Also, she has published articles in *Edu-

cational Leadership in the areas of accountability, volunteerism, and cost of teacher layoffs. Ms. Hagey was recently recognized by U.S. Congresswoman Connie Morella for her community work as a member of the Prince Georges County Redistricting Commission (Maryland). In addition, she was appointed by former Maryland Governor Schaefer to serve on a state-wide citizens' advisory commission on the use of federal Title II funds. Ms. Hagey holds an M.S. in Curriculum Development and Instruction from Eastern Michigan University and a B.S. in Secondary Education from The Ohio State University.

Vivian J. Hajnal is Associate Dean of the College of Education and a faculty member in the Department of Educational Administration at the University of Saskatchewan, Saskatoon, Canada. She has extensive experience in industry as well as in public and private education. Her research focuses on teacher work life, teacher compensation, and education finance, and has been published in journals such as the *Journal of Educational Administration* and the *Alberta Journal of Research*. In addition, she authored the chapter on Saskatchewan school finance in the *Public School Finance Programs of the United States and Canada, 1998–1999* (American Education Finance Association and National Center for Education Statistics, 2001). Recent papers have examined education reform policies and provincial funding for special education. Her current research activities include studies of education finance equity, as well as restructuring and amalgamation of school divisions. At present, she also serves as a member of the Board of Directors of the American Education Finance Association. In her role as Associate Dean, she has come to appreciate the importance of equity considerations, raised so succinctly in the finance literature, to other policy issues.

William T. Hartman is Professor of Education in the College of Education at Pennsylvania State University and co-founder and the Executive Director of the Center for Total Quality Schools at Penn State. He was a recipient of the university's Graduate Faculty Teaching Award for 1999. Prior to coming to Penn State in 1986, he was on the faculty at the University of Oregon and Stanford University. He has served on the Board of Directors of the American Education Finance Association. He was a Visiting Fellow in Education at the University of Sussex (England) in 1994 and at the University of Melbourne and at Hughes Hall, Cambridge University in 2003. Dr. Hartman has a Bachelor of Mechanical Engineering with High Honors from the University of Florida, a Masters of Business Administration from Harvard University, and a Ph.D. in Educational Administration from Stanford University. His areas of research and scholarship include school budgeting, special education finance, school finance equity, resource allocation at the school and district levels, total quality management in education, and microcomputer models in educational administration. His latest books are *School District Budgeting* (Association of School Business Officials International, 1999) and *Resource Allocation and Productivity in Education* (Greenwood Press, 1998). He has served as a consultant to various government agencies at the federal, state, and local levels, to research organizations, to private industry, and to special interest groups in education.

Jeffrey Maiden is Associate Professor of Educational Leadership and Policy Studies at the University of Oklahoma where he teaches courses in education finance, school business administration, quantitative research methods, and administrative technology. He was recipient of the Jack A. Culbertson award in 2000, which is presented annually by the University Council for Educational Administration (UCEA) to an outstanding junior professor of educational administration in recognition of his or her contributions to the field. His research interests are focused on education finance, including intergovernmental fiscal relationships, the fiscal effects of educational reform, educational capital outlay and debt service, and education finance litigation. The results of his research have been published in the *Journal of Education Finance* and the Yearbook of the American Education Finance Association. Dr. Maiden has also published in the area of educational technology planning, implementation, and policy. In addition, he was principal investigator of a comprehensive study examining the weighting factors embedded in the Oklahoma state education funding formula and co-principal investigator of the Oklahoma Leadership and Technology Development Grant through the Bill and Melinda Gates Foundation. Dr. Maiden earned his Ph.D. in Educational Leadership at the University of Florida.

Mary P. McKeown-Moak is a partner in the Austin, Texas office of MGT of America, Inc., a national management research and consulting firm specializing in service to public sector clients. Since joining MGT, she has focused on projects related to strategic planning and marketing of colleges and universities; outsourcing or privatization; educational resource allocation; faculty productivity; peer selection; benchmarking and performance indicators; performance reviews; and development of funding and allocation formulas for higher education. In the past five years, she has assisted 21 states in development or revision of their funding mechanisms for higher education. Prior to joining MGT, she was the senior financial officer of the Arizona University System, where she was responsible for space management and capital construction; system financial, capital, and strategic planning; budgeting and resource allocation; accounting; auditing; enrollment management; human resources; and acted as liaison with the executive and legislative budget and planning offices. Dr. McKeown-Moak also served as Director of Strategic Planning for Arizona State University, Associate Director for Finance and Facilities at the Maryland State Board for Higher Education, and held various positions for the University of Illinois Foundation, Sangamon State University, the Illinois State Board of Education, and Eastern Michigan University. She has taught courses on accounting, educational management, higher education, and educational administration at five universities. Dr. McKeown-Moak is past president of the American Education Finance Association, former chair of the State Higher Education Finance Officers, and past president of the Fiscal Issues, Policy, and Education Finance and the Futures Research and Strategic Planning Special Interest Groups of the American Educational Research Association. She is the author or editor of four books and numerous articles on educational finance, intercollegiate athletics, and management, and has served as an expert witness on higher education funding. Dr. McKeown-Moak received her Ph.D. in Administration, Higher, and Continuing Education from the University of Illinois at Urbana-Champaign.

Catherine C. Sielke is Associate Professor in the School of Leadership and Lifelong Learning at the University of Georgia. Dr. Sielke received a B.A. from the University of Michigan, an M.A. and Sp.A. from Eastern Michigan University, and a Ph.D. from Michigan State University. She teaches graduate courses in school finance, the economics of education, and school business and resource management. Prior to joining the faculty at the University of Georgia, she was a high school English teacher and Assistant Superintendent of Finance in Michigan K–12 school districts. In addition, she was an Assistant Professor at Western Michigan University. Her research is published in the *Journal of Education Finance, Educational Considerations, School Business Affairs,* and *The American School Board Journal.* The subject matter of several of her articles is state funding of school infrastructure. Dr. Sielke was lead editor of the *Public School Finance Programs of the United States and Canada, 1998–1999,* and lead author of *Highlights of the American Education Finance Association's Public School Finance Programs of the United States and Canada.* She has presented papers at the conferences of the American Education Finance Association, the American Educational Research Association, the University Council for Educational Administration, the American Association of School Administrators, and the Association of School Business Officials International. Also, she is a member of the Board of Directors of the American Education Finance Association and is Chair of the Editorial Board of the Association of School Business Officials International. Dr. Sielke serves on several task forces and committees of the National Center for Education Statistics, including the revision of the federal accounting handbook.

Kathleen C. Westbrook is the author of over 50 articles, book chapters, research articles and reports on the financing of educational facilities and technology, and editor of *Financing Technology in the Global Educational Workplace*, the 1997 Annual Yearbook of the American Education Finance Association. She has authored articles in the *Journal of Education Finance, Educational Facilities Planner,* and *School Business Affairs,* and she is a member of the editorial advisory board of the *Journal of Education Finance.* She is past president of the Fiscal Issues, Policy, and Education Finance Special Interest Group of the American Educational Research Association, and editor of its 1992 annual monograph, *The State of the States '92: Bridging Troubled Finance Waters.* She has held graduate faculty positions, specializing in facilities and technology financing and implementation, in the Department of Educational Leadership at Loyola University of Chicago and the School of Education at Portland State University, Portland, Oregon. Dr. Westbrook is founder and principal of The deerStar Group, a consulting firm that works with public, private, and parochial schools and non-profit institutions regarding facility and technology infrastructure issues and conducts training in technology and infrastructure application, specification, and implementation. In 1998 and 1999, she served as a technical consultant for the technology portion of the National Education Association study, *Modernizing Our School: How Much Will It Cost?* (NEA, 2000). Currently she holds an adjunct appointment as Science and Technology Associate in Argonne National Laboratory's Division of Educational Programs where she trains elementary and secondary teacher in technology applications. In addition, she has held appointments as adjunct professor in technology at National-Lewis University, Aurora University, and College of DuPage, Illinois. Dr. Westbrook's career has included teaching positions at the middle school, high school, community college, and higher education levels in vocational and computer areas as well as private sector positions, such as Facilities Manager, Director of Technology, and Technology and Website Project Manager. Dr. Westbrook was awarded her Ph.D. from the University of Illinois at Champaign-Urbana.

INDEX